Hiking Huntsville

Volume 2

MARCUS WOOLF

MONTVIEW
COMMUNICATIONS
Huntsville, AL

Montview Communications
2606 Bonita Circle
Huntsville, AL 35801
Montviewcommunications@gmail.com
HuntsvilleTrails.com

Although the author and publisher have made every effort to ensure that the information in this book was correct at press time, the author and publisher do not assume and hereby disclaim any liability to any party for any loss, damage, or disruption caused by errors or omissions, whether such errors or omissions result from negligence, accident, or any other cause.

Project Management by Marla Markman, MarlaMarkman.com
Cover and Interior Design by Kelly Cleary, kellymaureencleary@gmail.com

Ordering Information:
Quantity sales. Special discounts are available on quantity purchases by corporations, associations, and others. For details, contact the publisher at the address above.

Publisher's Cataloging-in-Publication Data:
Names: Woolf, Marcus, author.
Title: Hiking Huntsville , volume 2 : a guide to more than 70 trails and greenways in the Huntsville Metro
Area / Marcus Woolf.
Series: Hiking Huntsville
Description: Includes index. | Huntsville, AL: Montview Communications, 2022.
Identifiers: LCCN: 2022909456 | ISBN: 979-8-9861788-2-0 (paperback) |
979-8-9861788-3-7 (ebook)
Subjects: LCSH LCSH Hiking--Huntsville (Ala.)--Guidebooks. | Huntsville (Ala.)--Guidebooks. | Hiking--Alabama--Guidebooks. | Natural history--Huntsville (Ala.). | Huntsville (Ala.)--History. | BISAC SPORTS & RECREATION / Hiking | TRAVEL / Special Interest / Hikes & Walks
Classification: LCC GV199.42.A2 .W66 v. 2 2022 | DDC 796.5109761--dc23

Printed in the United States of America

For Wendy, Mom and Dad

CONTENTS

Acknowledgments

I couldn't have made this book without the generosity of many people, especially my wife, Wendy. Her love and support carried me through often-difficult work that lasted more than two years. I would also like to thank my parents, who helped edit the text and provided constant encouragement. A big hug to my friend Andy Somers for advising me on mapmaking, and thanks to authors Karen Somers and James Dziezynski for sharing their wisdom on the process of creating guidebooks. A big shout-out to my longtime friend Brenda Constantino for volunteering to teach me the finer points of Adobe Illustrator. And this book would have never reached its full potential without the guidance and expertise of Marla Markman and the creative hand of Kelly Cleary.

I also received valuable assistance from people at key local organizations, including Melanie Manson of the Land Trust of North Alabama, Katheleen Theriault of the Hays Nature Preserve and Ben Hoksbergen of the University of Alabama in Huntsville. I also got excellent help from local experts on several subjects, including botanist Lynne Weninegar, ecologist Soos Weber, and local trail historian Bruce Martin. Also, thanks to Erin McMahon and Chad Edwards with Huntsville Area Mountain Bike Riders (HAMR) for offering background information on trails and their organization's important work.

I want to give kudos to the city of Huntsville and Mayor Tommy Battle for understanding and appreciating the value of greenways and outdoor recreation. Finally, a big round of applause for the volunteers who work with HAMR, the Land Trust of North Alabama and other local groups to build and maintain our local trails. Without their hard work, hikers wouldn't be able to enjoy fantastic trail systems throughout the Huntsville area.

Preface

If you lived in Huntsville 30 years ago, you probably could've named every restaurant in town, and there was a good chance you had eaten at most of them. Now, with the population booming, it seems a new place to eat opens every week. And that can be a good thing. With growth comes more choices, greater variety, and opportunities to experience something new.

It's a similar situation with our trail systems. When I was young, local hikers had few places to go other than the trails on Monte Sano Mountain—and even the options on Monte Sano were limited until the 1990s, when the Land Trust of North Alabama began building trails on the western slope. Today, that is no longer the case. The Huntsville metro area boasts more than 150 trails and greenway paths. From the Keel Mountain Preserve in Gurley to the Mill Creek Greenway in Madison, the area's diverse trails explore a range of environments, including rugged mountains, rivers and streams, rural fields, and ancient wetlands.

When I wrote *Hiking Huntsville* Volume 1, I began with familiar ground and included the trails on Monte Sano, as well as Huntsville Mountain and Green Mountain. For this second book, I ventured farther and covered places I had rarely visited or never explored, like Wade Mountain and Rainbow Mountain. Their ridges and high bluffs offered me a fresh perspective, with panoramic views of vast ravines and the surrounding Tennessee Valley. In the wild woods of Chapman Mountain, I found stands of massive trees and a secluded spring once used by moonshiners. At the Bethel Spring Nature Preserve, a trail climbed high into the hills to reveal one of the largest waterfalls in Madison County. Down in the lowlands of the Hays Nature Preserve, a path explored an exotic swamp with tupelo trees that date back hundreds of years.

I also walked all of the local greenways for this book, from the Aldridge Creek Greenway near Hobbs Island to the Bradford Creek Greenway in Madison. These paved paths run through corridors of woods bordered by rivers, streams and farm fields. I found the greenways to be peaceful, quiet places to exercise, decompress after a stressful day, or enjoy some fresh air. Plus, they're great spots to take kids for some outdoor fun.

With all of these encounters, I was struck by the abundance and diversity of our local trails. While I've lived in Huntsville most of my life, I had visited just a fraction of our hiking areas before working on this book. I've always appreciated my hometown, but I value it even more after venturing out to experience all that it has to offer. I hope this book will serve as a helpful companion as you launch your own adventures to see new places and learn more about the mountains, valleys, fields and streams that make this place unique.

Introducing the Huntsville Metro Area

Over the past decade, the population of the Huntsville metro area has boomed, and it now includes nearly half a million people. According to the United States Census Bureau, the Huntsville metro area comprises Madison County and Limestone County and covers more than 1,300 square miles. It includes the major cities of Huntsville, Madison, Athens and Decatur, as well as several smaller neighboring communities. This book focuses on Huntsville and Madison, plus Hazel Green to the north and Gurley and Owens Cross Roads to the east.

The two fastest-growing cities in the metro area are Huntsville and Madison. According to the 2020 census, Huntsville is home to a little more than 215,000 people, making it the most populous city in the state. Between 2010 and 2020, the city population exploded, gaining nearly 35,000 people. In the latest count, the city of Madison also showed significant growth. It recorded a population of 56,933, up from 42,938 in 2010. The census reported that the greater Huntsville metro area has a population of 491,723, projected to rise to 528,141 by 2030.

Of course, these statistics only reflect the area's most recent history. Huntsville was settled in 1805 when John Hunt, the city's namesake, moved his family from Tennessee to Big Spring and began farming. The population grew gradually throughout the 1800s, and local trails trace that history. For example, the trails at Bethel Spring Nature Preserve lead to the ruins of a springhouse and a mill that operated in the 1800s. At Wade Mountain Preserve, you can investigate a curious rock wall that stretches across the forest. While its origin is uncertain, it's believed that early settlers constructed it to serve as a property boundary.

Until World War II, Huntsville remained a small Southern town. Then the U.S. Army established Redstone Arsenal, and the population grew significantly. In the 1960s, the city made further strides when NASA created the Marshall Space Flight Center and the U.S. Army Aviation and Missile Command. While strolling the Elgie's Walk Greenway in south Huntsville, you'll skirt the border of Redstone Arsenal and learn about the city's early involvement in the space and defense industries. Closer to the heart of town, the Gateway Greenway details the city's military history, from the American Revolution to more recent wars.

Whether you're new to this area or you were born here, you'll probably learn something new as you explore the local trails and greenways. While most of us hit the trails to simply enjoy the outdoors, a hike is also an opportunity to explore local history. While working on this book, I learned a great deal about the evolution of the Huntsville area. Actually, researching the history was one of my favorite aspects of the project. Somehow, when you know the stories behind the names on the map, hiking becomes much more fun and fulfilling.

LOCAL HIKING AREAS
Monte Sano State Park
(See Hiking Huntsville Volume 1)

As the defense and space industries have fueled growth in the metro area, it has resulted in a much larger population of people who want to hike, bike and run local trails. Fortunately, both governmental and private organizations have greatly expanded the quantity and quality of nearby recreation areas. On the eastern side of Huntsville, Monte Sano State Park has historically been a primary destination for all sorts of trail activities. Over the past decade, the Alabama State Parks Division has improved and expanded the park's facilities, while local groups, such as the Huntsville Area Mountain Bike Riders (HAMR), have constructed and overhauled many trails on the mountain. There are now 35 miles of trails in the state park. Compared to the 1980s, when I was growing up on the mountain, these paths are more diverse, easier to navigate and better maintained.

Land Trust of North Alabama Nature Preserves

In the 1980s, local builders broached the idea of developing the western slopes of Monte Sano. This led to the formation of the Huntsville Land Trust, which raised enough money to purchase 547 acres on the mountain and prevent the development. Now known as the Land Trust of North Alabama, the organization has protected some 9,000 acres of land in six counties. It has also greatly expanded the number of trails in the Huntsville metro area, from Monte Sano to Madison. Its nine preserves and greenways include more than 70 miles of trails that are maintained regularly by Land Trust volunteers. All of these multiuse trails are open to hikers and mountain bikers, while a couple of preserves also serve horseback riders. While the Land Trust does take donations, it does not require users to pay a fee to enjoy the trails.

Greenways

While Monte Sano State Park and the Land Trust have expanded and improved local trails, city governments have also added areas to walk and ride bikes in a peaceful, natural setting. The cities of Huntsville and Madison operate at least a dozen greenways, which are basically corridors of undeveloped land in urban areas. There are more than 27 miles of local greenways where you can stroll through shaded forests and watch horses grazing in sunny fields. You might see great blue herons soaring above a rushing river or see a hawk perched in a towering oak tree.

While the greenways explore natural landscapes, the trails themselves are paved and mostly level, allowing people of all abilities to access the outdoors. In most cases, there is a buffer zone between the trails and nearby roads, so people can walk, run or ride without worrying about vehicle traffic. Because the greenways are safe and cross easy terrain, they are great places to walk or ride with children.

CLIMATE

The Huntsville metro area climate is classified as "humid, subtropical." It rains frequently in winter, spring and summer, while fall is typically drier. Madison County and Limestone County each receive about 55 inches of rain per year, while the national average is about 30 inches.

Winter is cool in the day and cold at night, with highs in the 50s and lows in the 30s. Occasionally, daytime and nighttime temperatures drop below freezing. During spring, the weather is pleasant, with highs in the 70s and low 80s, and lows in the 50s. When summer arrives, it becomes progressively hotter and more humid, with highs in the 80s and 90s and lows in the upper 60s and 70s. It's still very warm in early September, so the cool, crisp weather of fall shows up later that month or in October. From October through the end of November, highs range from the mid-60s to the mid-70s, and lows range from the low 40s to the low 50s.

Winter

During winter, cold air masses move into the area frequently. Occasionally, mild air from the Gulf of Mexico arrives in the Huntsville area and lingers for several days. When the cold air meets the Gulf air, northern Alabama can experience periods of low clouds and rain. As a result, the region gets about 43 percent of its normal annual precipitation from December through March. Occasionally its snows, though accumulations are typically just a few inches. Over the past 30 to 40 years, there have also been a few significant ice storms. Keep in mind that weather can be erratic in winter, and you might also see days where it's sunny and 65 to 70 degrees. During a three-day stretch in January of 2022, high temperatures went from the 70s to the 30s, and at least three inches of snow blanketed the Tennessee Valley.

Spring

As spring arrives, warm, moist air moves in and clashes with the cold air, causing the greatest variety of weather during this time of year. You can expect plenty of thunderstorms and other severe weather, including an occasional tornado.

Summer

Day-to-day changes in the summer season are rather small, other than the thunderstorms that provide relief from the heat on about one-third of the days. Temperatures frequently rise to 90 degrees or higher but rarely reach 100 degrees.

Fall

During the fall, the weather is usually dry and pleasant. The air masses are cooler in the lower levels, and the thunderstorm activity of summer decreases sharply. The dry air is very favorable for harvesting cotton and hay crops, important to the economy of the area. A major departure from the relatively dry weather of fall is an occasional rainy spell of one or more days associated with a decaying hurricane drifting northward from the Gulf of Mexico.

GEOGRAPHY AND GEOLOGY

The Huntsville metro area lies within two major physiographic regions: the Highland Rim and the Cumberland Plateau. Portions of Limestone County and western Madison County lie in the Highland Rim, which includes some mountainous terrain but is primarily rolling hills and fertile valleys. Eastern Madison County lies within the Cumberland Plateau, which features more hills and mountains.

The western and eastern sections of the Huntsville area have different landscapes due to different degrees of erosion, says Ben Hoksbergen, a lecturer in the department of history at the University of Alabama in Huntsville. In the western and eastern sections, the underlying bedrock layers are basically the same. But the upper layers that make up the rugged mountains of eastern Madison County have eroded away in western Madison County and beyond.

So why was there more erosion in the west? It's the result of increased fracturing of the bedrock within the radius of the Nashville Dome, an area of tectonic uplift centered on Nashville. As Hoksbergen explains, tectonic plates pushed together along the axis of the Appalachian Mountains, and the bedrock to the west of the mountains buckled. This formed a broad area of structural uplift known as the Cincinnati Arch. The southernmost part of the Cincinnati Arch was the Nashville Dome. As this area was uplifted, the bedrock fractured near the center of the dome, accelerating erosion.

The portion of north Alabama from Huntsville west to The Shoals lies on the outer edge of the Nashville Dome. This area has heavily eroded into rolling hills. But east of Huntsville, the upper layers of the Cumberland Plateau remain and form the more rugged terrain we are familiar with.

Another major feature of the local landscape is the wide and deep

Tennessee River, which flows in a northwesterly direction for about 200 miles across north Alabama. The river plays an important role in the region, providing electric power for people throughout the Tennessee Valley and serving as a transportation corridor for a wide range of goods. Plus, it's a hub for recreation, especially boating and fishing. But it also serves the hiking community. You can walk the Tennessee River Greenway to get a close look at this major waterway, and several other trails, such as the Flint River Greenway, follow rivers and creeks that feed into the Tennessee River.

LANDSCAPE HIGHLIGHTS
Mountainous Terrain

Madison and Huntsville sit at the southern end of the Appalachian Mountains. From the craggy ridgetops of Rainbow Mountain to the lush springs on Chapman Mountain, the hiking trails in the Huntsville area explore diverse terrain with impressive natural features. Rising as high as 1,600 feet, these peaks are topped with ridges and rocky outcrops that provide hikers with inspiring views of the Tennessee Valley. As you're traversing the tops of mountains in the area, you won't see a lot of standing water. That's because rainwater typically flows into sinkholes and other fissures in the rock. The water then flows undergound and emerges from springs at lower elevations. At places like Keel Mountain and Chapman Mountain, trails lead you to natural springs where the water seems to magically emerge from hillsides and rock formations.

Waterfalls

Many creeks in the area are much more impressive after seasonal rains. After a good downpour, some of these streams feed waterfalls that plunge from high bluffs and roll down rocky drainages. If you're willing to walk a bit, you can reach hidden falls tucked away in deep pockets of woods. On Monte Sano, the remote Flat Rock Trail leads to a cascade that flows into an isolated draw. But you don't have to walk several miles to see such waterfalls. At the Bethel Spring Nature Preserve southeast of Huntsville, a one-mile path climbs to one of the largest and most spectacular falls in Madison County.

Rivers and Streams

Alabama is blessed with an abundance of freshwater resources. About one-sixth of the state's surface area is composed of rivers, streams, lakes, reservoirs, ponds, wetlands and estuaries. In the Huntsville area, hiking trails and greenways follow a number of creeks, rivers and streams. Of course, the most prominent waterway is the Tennessee River, which courses across north Alabama and passes through Limestone and Madison Counties. Near Ditto Landing in south Huntsville, the Tennessee River Greenway offers an excellent view of this important river, which has long fueled the economy and energy production for the northern part of the state. Several rivers and creeks in the Huntsville area are tributaries of the Tennessee River, including the Flint River, which originates in Tennessee. From the Hays Nature Preserve in Owens Cross Roads, you can access the Flint River Greenway, which follows the broad, slow-flowing Flint as it winds among remote woods and farm fields. Other greenways, such as Aldridge Creek and Indian Creek, will take you along other streams that cut through Huntsville and Madison.

FLORA
Forests

Most of the trails in the Huntsville area explore forests dominated by hardwoods, such as oak and hickory. North Alabama is home to dozens of oak species, with white oaks, black oaks and southern red oaks being some of the most prevalent. Other common hardwoods include southern shagbark hickory trees, yellow poplars and sweet gum trees. During fall, the leaves of hardwood trees transform and display striking colors. The maples and hickories glow gold and orange, while the oaks form a canopy of rich reddish-brown. As the poplars beam with bright yellows, the sweet gums boast brilliant shades of red. As fall fades, the hardwoods lose their leaves, giving winter hikers clear views of distant mountains and valleys.

Mixed in with the hardwoods are softwoods such as eastern red cedars and a variety of pines, including loblolly, shortleaf and Virginia pines. Throughout the year, these conifers add splashes of deep green to the fields and forests of north Alabama.

You'll find forests with a very different feel while hiking the area's river bottoms and wetlands. For example, the Hays Nature Preserve occupies a bottomland forest that borders the Flint River. A tangle of brush covers the forest floor, which is flooded with marshes and ponds, including a large, shallow pool formed by a beaver dam. Deep in the preserve, a path skirts a tupelo tree swamp that resembles a Louisiana bayou. Along the banks of the Flint River, wet, rich soil supports its own blend of plant life, including willow oaks, water oaks, elms, sycamores and birches.

Whether you're strolling beside a river or hiking in the hills, you'll notice that some sections of the forest are especially dense and choked with brush and smaller, younger trees. These are areas of "succession forest," where the original oaks and hickory trees were cut and cleared for farming and timber. In older forests, where the trees were never cleared or the land has more fully recovered, the trees are taller, stouter, and widely spaced, with little or no brush between them.

Wildflowers

With its plentiful water sources, ample rain and diverse geography, Alabama is one of the most biodiverse states in the country, boasting a wide array of native plants and wildflowers. You'll find some of the most impressive collections of flowers by exploring the banks of mountain streams and nearby slopes. During the first burst of blooms in March, you'll find trilliums, Virginia bluebells, anemones, spring beauties and violets. Mid-May brings beautiful Indian pink, fire pink, spiderwort and orchids.

Local greenways also offer impressive displays of wildflowers. When spring arrives, large fields of brilliant yellow marigolds border the Flint River Greenway path in Owens Cross Roads and the Bradford Creek Greenway in Madison.

For more excellent wildflower hikes, see Hiking Huntsville Volume 1, which contains one of the most popular destinations, the Wildflower Trail, which skirts Fagan Creek at the base of Monte Sano Mountain. While the creek bottoms are flush with flowers, the higher elevations also have something to offer. The Sinks Trail, which is included in Volume 1, begins high on Monte Sano and leads to a large colony of Virginia bluebells, which bloom in April.

***Some less appealing plants, such as poison ivy, poison oak and poison sumac, are included in the "Other Potential Trail Hazards" section on page xxiv.*

FAUNA
Mammals

Of all the animal encounters I've had while hiking, one of the strangest took place on Huntsville's Monte Sano Mountain. At the age of 13, I was still new to the mountain and new to hiking, and I often walked alone. On one foggy winter morning, I was traveling solo on the mountain's plateau when a group of ghostly figures emerged from the mist. I stopped in my tracks when I recognized a collection of horns, narrow faces and snouts, and realized a herd of goats was wandering the trail like some sort of Billy Goats Gruff fairy tale. (Were there also some trolls around somewhere?!) While goats aren't especially dangerous, they carry serious expressions . . . and horns. But there was no cause for concern, as the goats simply wheeled right and ambled away, disappearing into the white veil. To this day, it sometimes seems like a dream.

Today, the goats of Monte Sano are gone, and their fate remains a mystery. But I share the story because animal encounters can make lifelong memories. And there are still plenty of opportunities to see wild animals while exploring local trails. Alabama is home to 62 native mammals, and you have a good chance of seeing several species. With regard to larger mammals, you're most likely to encounter white-tailed deer, especially if you're walking in the early morning or early evening. It's common to see a doe and fawns or a single buck dashing through the woods or scampering across mountain roads. In recent years, coyotes have made more appearances, but you're more likely to see one lurking in a residential area than trotting near a hiking trail. In mountainous areas, people have also caught glimpses of bobcats, but sightings are very rare. Not quite as elusive are gray foxes and red foxes. As far as the ultimate North American carnivore—bears—you won't see any in this part of Alabama.

While the larger carnivores are absent or rarely seen, rodents are everywhere. (There are 22 rodent species in Alabama, and most have several litters each year.) If you hear something rustling in the forest, it's most likely a gray squirrel or eastern chipmunk. If the rustling is really loud, it might be an armadillo barreling its way through the woods. In Alabama, eastern cottontail rabbits are abundant, but I honestly see more of them in neighborhood yards than I do in hiking areas. While exploring the woods, you might also see woodchucks, moles and the occasional opossum. Beavers are present in wetland areas, but they use underwater entrances to access their burrows, so it's difficult to spot them.

When it comes to omnivores—creatures that eat both plants and animals—one of the more common species in the area is the raccoon. You might see one in the forest, but they're mostly known for frequenting residential areas, where they forage amongst garbage—thus the nickname "trash pandas."

If you hike at dusk during the spring or summer, you might also see bats darting around as they come out to feed. There are 15 species of these winged creatures in Alabama, and in the Huntsville area you'll primarily see little brown bats and big brown bats.

Birds

With its many mountains, forests, fields and wetlands, the Huntsville area is an excellent place to view birds while hiking. Several species of North American birds migrate to the tropics during winter. Then, during spring, they pass through Alabama as they return to their breeding grounds. These neotropical migrants flock to the hardwood forests of Monte Sano and other area mountains. While walking mountain trails, you might hear the calls of indigo buntings and warblers, or spy some flycatchers and vireos.

Local forests are also home to some impressive permanent avian residents, including red-shouldered hawks and red-tailed hawks. During a hike, it's a real thrill to see one of these beauties soaring overhead. As you visit mountain overlooks and walk along bluffs, you may also see turkey vultures circling as they ride the air currents.

As you explore remote stretches of trail in the mountains and bottomland forests, listen for the call of the barred owl, which resembles a person saying, "Who cooks for you, who cooks for you all." Measuring up to 24 inches long, with a wingspan up to 50 inches, this impressive bird is quite a sight when you see one take flight. While owls mostly feed at night, it's not unusual to see this species out during the daytime.

In the lowlands, while walking near farm fields and forest openings, keep an eye out for barn owls, which are a little smaller than barred owls and measure 13 to 15 inches long with a wingspan of 31 to 37 inches. Bottomlands, wetlands and riverbanks are also good places to see great blue herons, green herons and belted kingfishers.

Reptiles

There are 50 species of snakes in Alabama. In the Huntsville area, hikers frequently see several species of nonvenomous snakes, like the garter snake, eastern milk snake, black kingsnake, black rat snake, black racer, and the eastern hognose snake, which is often mistaken for the copperhead. Hikers should be aware that three venomous and potentially dangerous species are sometimes seen along local trails. These include the eastern diamondback rattlesnake, the copperhead and the cottonmouth, which mostly inhabits riverbanks, swamps, streams, springs and ponds.

Much less threatening are the several turtle species that inhabit local streams and woodlands. While there are 30 species of turtles in Alabama, hikers will mostly encounter the eastern box turtle, which is primarily a land animal.

Alabama also has at least 30 species of frogs and toads. On summer nights, you'll hear the croaking drone of American bullfrogs rising from swamps, ponds and lakes. In these areas, you might also see green frogs or hear the chirping call of the cricket frog. In marshes and woodlands, listen for the spring peeper, which, like the American toad, spends most of its time on land. As you're exploring forests, you might spy a gray treefrog, but you'll need a sharp eye—this chameleon can change to shades of gray, brown and green to camouflage itself.

Amphibians

For great entertainment in spring or summer, visit one of the local creeks or streams to hunt for salamanders. There are more than 40 salamander species in Alabama, and Huntsville-area hikers have observed several, including the marbled salamander, northern slimy salamander, southern zigzag salamander and green salamander. To find these fascinating creatures, head to the Wildflower Trail at the base of Monte Sano. It leads to Fagan Creek, where you can explore the shallow waters and small pools.

***Some wildlife, such as spiders, mosquitoes, and other creatures that can sting or bite, are included in the "Other Potential Trail Hazards" section on page xxiv.*

COMFORT, SAFETY AND ETIQUETTE

From short strolls to daylong treks, the trails in the Huntsville area afford a wide range of hiking experiences. You can take a brief walk on a flat, paved greenway path or travel for hours in rugged mountainous terrain. The trips in this book are all day hikes, as overnight camping is not allowed at local nature preserves, greenways and U.S. Space & Rocket Center trails.. But even a day trip requires some planning. A hike of any type and duration will be more enjoyable if you take the time to consider the route you will take, the environment you will explore and the things you need to carry. Some knowledge and planning can go a long way toward making you safer and more comfortable in the outdoors.

It's important to remember that trail conditions can change, and you might experience or encounter things that differ from what I describe in the book. There has been a tremendous amount of trail building in recent years, so it's possible that trail routes or trail names have changed. You might find that trail signs and blazes (trail markers on trees) have been altered. Also, you might hike a trail during summer, while I have described what you might encounter in winter. For all of these reasons, it's important to prepare properly for your hike, carry a map and other navigational tools, and stay aware of your surroundings as you walk.

WEATHER AND THE ENVIRONMENT

Before you hit the trail, consider the weather you will face and dress appropriately for the full spectrum of weather you might experience. Fall and winter daytime temperatures in the Huntsville area can reach the 60s and 70s, while afternoons can be cooler. Dress in layers so that you can shed or add clothing to regulate your body temperature. Because weather is not totally predictable, it's also a good idea to pack a waterproof shell when traveling in fall or winter to not only keep you dry in rain but also shield you from chilly winds.

Spring is a great time to enjoy blooming wildflowers along the trail, but it's also the season for severe thunderstorms and tornadoes. If you're exploring the mountains, avoid hiking on exposed ridges when lightning is present. Also avoid bodies of water if there's a chance that lightning might strike.

Summers in Alabama are hot and humid, and it's critical to drink plenty of water while hiking. Dehydration can lead to serious illness, including heat cramps, heat exhaustion and heat stroke. Even if you don't become seriously ill, dehydration can make people confused and disoriented and cause them to make poor decisions. This is one way that people get lost in the outdoors. Dehydrated people can also lose their balance and fall, possibly injuring themselves. Be sure to take all the water you'll need on a hike (about one liter or more per hour), and don't plan on taking water from streams. Many of the creeks and streams in the area are seasonal and don't run consistently, and drought conditions can leave a creek bone-dry. Even more important, rivers and streams can carry bacteria that will make you seriously sick. If you get into an emergency situation and have to take water from a stream, filter it or boil it to kill bacteria.

Insects such as mosquitoes can be heavy along the trails in summer, so be sure to pack whatever repellent you prefer. An insect repellent with at least 30% DEET or 20% picaridin will also ward off ticks, which are a concern during the spring. It's recommended that you wear long pants during tick season, and you can ward off ticks by treating clothing with permethrin, which is available at sporting goods stores. You should also check your body from time to time to see if ticks have hitched a ride. They tend to latch on to warm, moist areas and frequently hide out where the seams of your clothing meet your skin. At the end of your hike, do a full-body check to make sure you're tick-free.

One thing a lot of people don't think about is sun exposure. Many Huntsville-area trails are shaded by forest, but you can still catch quite a few rays during a day of hiking. Also keep in mind that many greenway paths are more exposed to sun. Before you leave the house, or immediately before you start walking, apply a high-SPF sunscreen. These products are more effective when applied to cool, dry skin. Try to choose a water-resistant sunscreen that will hold up during heavy sweating. If you plan to be out for more than a couple of hours, take the sunscreen with you, because you will probably need to reapply it.

OTHER POTENTIAL TRAIL HAZARDS
Snakes

In all my years of hiking Huntsville trails, I've had very few encounters with venomous snakes, but it has happened. While trail running one summer morning, I rounded a bend and had to suddenly leap over a coiled rattlesnake sunning itself smack dab in the middle of the path. In addition to the eastern diamondback rattlesnake, two other venomous snakes inhabit the area: the copperhead and the cottonmouth. Take some time to browse the internet and learn how to identify these snakes. It's rare to encounter a venomous snake on a trail, as I did. In general, day hikers can avoid them by staying on established paths. If you wander off the trail and enter tall brush or rocky areas with lots of crevices, you're more likely to encounter a snake. If you do leave the trail for a snack break, examine rocks and the surrounding terrain before sitting down. (If you're geocaching, examine hiding spots carefully before reaching in to retrieve a cache.)

If you do come across a venomous snake, slowly back away to a safe distance of at least 6 feet and either wait for the snake to leave or go back the way you came. Just don't approach the snake or try to make it go away.

Spiders

Honestly, my only bad spider experience on a trail happened while mountain biking on Monte Sano in the summer. I took a huge web straight to the face, flinched, and flew over the handlebars. Ooof, that hurt. But people rarely get bitten by spiders while day hiking. Still, it's possible to encounter a black widow or brown recluse, two venomous species that inhabit the area. Before you hike, learn to identify these two types of spiders. As with snakes, you're more likely to encounter a spider when you leave the trail to take a break or go exploring. Before you sit on the ground or a rock to have a snack or water break, examine the area to make sure it's free of anything that will sting or bite. When you're ready to hike again, examine anything you've set down—your pack, a jacket, a food bag, etc.—to make sure it's spider-free. If you do get bitten by a venomous spider, exit the trail immediately and go straight to the hospital.

Poisonous Plants

In spring and summer, hikers should be on the lookout for three troublesome plants—poison ivy, poison oak and poison sumac. These plants are covered in an oil that causes rashes and blisters. If you're not familiar with these plants, take a few minutes to research them online and learn to recognize them. In this case, a little knowledge can prevent a whole lot of discomfort.

Poison Ivy: This plant has three leaflets, thus the old saying, "Leaves of three, let it be." It grows as a vine that runs close to the ground or climbs up the sides of trees or other vertical objects. Its three leaflets have jagged teeth on the edges, and there is usually a red spot where the bottom two leaflets join. Also, the stems of the plant appear to be hairy. Poison ivy grows in a wide variety of forested environments and greenways, and it often grows along the edge of trails. In spring and summer, consider wearing long pants if you're heading to areas where poison ivy might be present.

Poison Oak: Like poison ivy, a poison oak plant has three leaflets, but the plant looks more like a shrub. Its leaflets sit at the end of upright stems that can be up to three feet tall. Also, the teeth on the edges of the leaflets are more rounded than those on poison ivy.

Poison Sumac: This plant looks very different from poison ivy or poison oak. It has seven to 15 leaflets that grow in pairs along a stem that is often bright red. Its oblong leaflets have a wavy pattern and smooth edges. The plant grows as a shrub or tree and can be up to 20 feet tall. It typically grows in a swampy area, and during summer it produces a white fruit that can remain on the plant into the fall and winter.

If you're exposed to these plants . . .
If you have a mild rash, wash the affected areas with cold water (and soap, if you have it) as soon as possible. Don't use hot water, as it can open your pores and make things worse. Then head to the drugstore and pick up an anti-itch cream (Extra Strength Benadryl Itch Stopping Cream works well) or hydrocortisone cream. You might even find products made specifically for relief from poison ivy and poison oak. I've also used calamine lotion, and some people say it helps to take antihistamine medicine. Usually, a mild rash will go away in a few weeks. If you get a severe rash, see a physician, who might prescribe a low-dose steroid.

Steep and Slippery Terrain

When it comes to trail hazards, hikers are more likely to suffer a twisted ankle or painful fall than a snakebite. Be especially careful when descending steep, rocky terrain, where a misstep can easily lead to a rolled ankle or even a fall. Consider using trekking poles on a steep path like Monte Sano's McKay Hollow Trail. The poles will improve your balance and reduce impact on your legs, knees and ankles.

Trekking poles can also keep you upright while crossing bodies of water and streambeds. You'll be less likely to fall when you encounter swift water. When creeks and streams aren't flowing, they can still pose problems, however. Sometimes a thin layer of moss or other plant material can cover the rocks at the base of the creek or stream, creating a surface that's as slick as ice.

Preparing for Your Hike

Many people, especially those new to hiking, have a difficult time determining just how far they can walk in a day without wearing themselves out—especially when dealing with summer heat, winter chills and steep trails. Be honest about your physical abilities, particularly when you are considering a long hike over difficult terrain. Most people can do two to three miles in an hour. And remember that heat, cold, rain and the terrain can limit the number of miles you can hike.

Before you set out, try to examine a topographic map of the area to see just how much climbing and descending will be involved. This book includes an estimate of the total elevation gain and loss for each trip— the higher the numbers, the more difficult the hike. Examine maps to become familiar with the area you wish to visit. A little studying will come in handy should you get confused and take a trail that is not part of your planned route.

If you're new to hiking, one thing to consider is time—the time needed to choose a destination and plan your trip, as well as the time needed to gather your gear, reach the trail, and do the hike. Typically, this process takes people longer than they expect. As a result, people arrive at the trailhead later than they planned. In their rush to reach the trail, they might also leave behind essential items. This isn't such a big deal if you're doing a safe, short hike in nice weather when you have sunlight late into the afternoon. But let's say you want to hike several miles during the winter, when darkness falls relatively early. In this situation, you need to ensure that you have adequate time to complete your trip safely.

Footwear and Clothing

Another important step in the planning process is determining the clothing and gear you need. There may be no more important piece of equipment than your footwear. An ill-fitting pair of shoes or boots can quickly ruin a day in the woods. Whether you choose to wear a lightweight pair of low-cut hiking shoes, a midweight pair of boots, or heavy leather boots, get your footwear well in advance of your hike and test it before hitting the trail. You don't want to find out halfway through a long day hike that your shoes don't fit.

For warm-weather day hikes when you're carrying a lightweight pack, low-cut hiking shoes or supportive sandals are fine in most cases. Just be sure that your shoes have the traction, cushioning, support and protection needed for the terrain. For example, extremely rocky trails, like Green Mountain's Ranger Trail or Monte Sano's Toll Gate Trail, might require more ankle support and underfoot protection. In these cases, you might consider wearing hiking boots rather than low-cut shoes.

For cold, wet conditions, people often seek out shoes or boots with a waterproof membrane such as Gore-Tex. That's a good idea, especially if you're going to hike for long periods when it's cold and raining. But keep in mind that, in the South, high levels of humidity limit the ability of waterproof footwear to breathe. Some people prefer to buy a synthetic or leather shoe without a membrane and then add topical waterproofing agents. Also, if you wear shoes while crossing streams, water will flow in through the top and they'll get completely soaked. In this case, a shoe that is not waterproof will dry more quickly.

While they're not as thrilling as a new pair of shoes, socks are also a critical component of your outdoor wardrobe. If you hike in cotton socks, you're taking the expressway to Blister Town, which is not a pleasant place to visit. To prevent blisters, I typically wear merino wool socks, because they pull moisture away from my feet, whereas cotton socks just get soaked. You can also wear a synthetic hiking sock, as these will also wick moisture and help keep your feet dry. Once you become a hiker, you'll actually get excited when someone gets you socks as a gift.

Once you've chosen your socks and footwear, consider the rest of your clothing. For warm-weather hikes, you can wear a T-shirt and shorts made of synthetic materials that pull moisture away from your body and dry quickly. You can also choose clothes that combine synthetic fabrics with small amounts of cotton, which makes them a little softer but still allows them to keep you cool and dry. Just avoid all-cotton clothes, as these will soak up moisture like a sponge and hold onto it, making you feel like you're wearing wet rags. In recent years, companies have also introduced very lightweight wool garments, which could work for you if you don't tend to get hot easily.

In the fall, winter and early spring, the key to staying comfortable on the trail is to regulate your body temperature so that you're not too cold or too hot for long periods. The trick is to dress in layers so that you can add or subtract clothing as needed. In general, opt for synthetic fabrics or wool, or synthetics or wool blended with small amounts of cotton. Again, avoid items made only of cotton, since it doesn't dry easily, and in cold temperatures it can suck heat away from your body. Synthetic fabrics will dry quickest, and in cold weather synthetics and wool won't reduce your body temperature. In recent years, wool clothing has become more popular for cool and cold conditions because modern merino, a fine wool, is much softer and more comfortable than wool of the past.

Here are some thoughts on layering your clothing:

First Layer: Your first layer (aka "base layer") could be a thin top made of synthetic materials, a blend of synthetics and cotton, or wool. If you tend to get cold easily, wear long base layer bottoms made of similar materials.

Second Layer: When it gets cooler or downright cold, add a midweight top made of synthetics or wool. This could be a jacket or vest made of synthetic fleece, wool or "softshell" materials. (A softshell material is merely a waterproof or water-resistant fabric that is softer, and generally more breathable, than a traditional waterproof rain jacket.) On top of your base layer bottoms, wear shorts or long pants made of synthetic materials or wool. If you're going for a short walk on a day with no chance of rain, you can get away with wearing jeans.

Third Layer: If you're hiking in very cold temperatures, or you're walking for a long period of time where you'll take an extended break, consider carrying a down or synthetic "puffy" jacket. This will remain in your pack most of the time, but you'll slip it on for an added layer of warmth when needed.

Fourth Layer: The final piece is your waterproof shell. This can remain in your pack until you need it to protect you from rain or wind.

Accessories

We lose much of our heat from our extremities, such as our head and hands. One of the quickest ways to warm up is to put on gloves and a hat made of synthetic fleece or wool.

Equipment

For a quick day hike or trail run, you may not need to carry more than a bottle of water and a light snack. But if you plan to hike a few miles or explore rough or remote terrain, consider packing the following:

Water and Food

When day hiking, plan to carry all the water you will need for the entire day, which will typically be one liter or more per hour of hiking, depending on the weather (you may need more on a hot, humid summer day) and the difficulty of the trail. Do not count on drawing water from streams and springs, because they might not be flowing. If you do draw water from a river or stream, be sure to filter or boil it to kill bacteria.

When hiking for long periods in cold weather, you should bring a stove or other heat source to make a warm drink in case you get wet and chilled. It's also a good idea to carry energy bars that can deliver quick fuel to increase your energy level.

Map and Compass

Even experienced hikers can become disoriented in the outdoors, especially at the end of a long, tiring hike. Whenever possible, you should carry a map to aid in your navigation. I realize that more people are using smartphones to navigate, and there are great apps that allow you to navigate trails when you don't have a cell signal. But it's still good to have a nondigital compass and a paper map, because electronics can lose power. Before you set out on your trip, learn how to use a compass. This book includes compass directions with the trail descriptions to help you stay on course. Equally important, you should learn the basics of reading a map and matching contour lines and other map features to your surroundings. If you don't want to carry a guidebook on your hike, print the map you need on waterproof paper, or print it on regular paper and tuck it into a sealable plastic bag. You can give yourself some peace of mind by learning to use a compass and properly orient your map.

Global Positioning System (GPS) receivers are popular because they make land navigation easier. But, like any tool, a GPS receiver is helpful only if you take time to learn how to use it and understand its limitations. First, remember that batteries can fail, so you should not rely solely on a GPS receiver—always carry a map and compass as well.

First-Aid Kit

You can put together your own first-aid kit or purchase one from a gear store. Modern kits come in a wide range of sizes to accommodate different types of trips and various group sizes. No matter what type of kit you carry, be sure you know how to use its components, and always carry any manual provided with a kit.

For low-risk day hikes, a basic kit is fine. It should include:

- Manual
- Bandages, including gauze and medical tape. Moleskin is very handy for treating hot spots and even preventing blisters. Tincture of benzoin will help moleskin adhere to skin better. Leukotape is also great for preventing hot spots, and it sticks really well.
- Antiseptic to clean wounds
- Drugs, including something to reduce fever (like acetaminophen), something to reduce inflammation (like ibuprofen), electrolyte tablets to overcome dehydration, and antacid tablets
- Prescription medicines
- Cutting tools, like scissors or a razor
- Hydrocortisone cream for skin irritations
- Tweezers
- Duct tape

The number of bandages and the amount of drugs will depend on the size of the group. Many preassembled kits indicate the number of people the kit will serve over a certain period of time. Note that these numbers may be inflated, meaning the kits include twice as much stuff as you'd actually need. But some buffer is built in so you will have enough supplies to handle the unexpected.

Other important items to consider carrying:
- Insect repellent
- Stove/heat source: This allows you to make a hot drink to prevent hypothermia should you get lost or injured.
- Knife or multitool
- Flashlight or headlamp
- Whistle: If you're injured or separated from your hiking partners, use the whistle to signal others, because its sound will travel farther than the sound of your voice.
- Trekking poles: These can stabilize you on uneven or slippery ground and reduce pressure on your legs and knees.
- Gaiters: These keep moisture, mud, and trail debris from sneaking into your shoes or boots.
- Cell phone: You can get a cell signal on many Huntsville-area trails, so it's not a bad idea to carry a phone for emergencies. Plus, you can use navigation apps that work even when you don't have cell service. Just remember that batteries die, so consider packing a portable charger, and always carry a paper map for navigation.

Safety Measures

There are many precautions you can take to stay safe while hiking. One of the most important is to let someone know where you are going, particularly if you'll be hiking alone or plan to be gone for several hours. Provide a friend or relative with your itinerary, including the time you plan to return.

Avoid leaving valuables in your vehicle. Trailhead break-ins are not frequent, but they happen.

I love to hike solo, but if you're new to hiking, consider going with a partner or even a group. This not only adds security, but if you get lost, you will feel safer if you are not alone. Plus, in an emergency, it's best if someone can remain with an injured person while someone else goes for help.

The key to not getting lost is to be aware of your surroundings. It's easy to miss a trail junction or accidentally take the wrong path. If your map indicates you should be ascending, and you instead find yourself on a long descent, stop to examine your map and the terrain around you. If you get lost, find a comfortable spot and stay put. A rescue team can find you more easily if you are not wandering.

Trail Etiquette

With more and more people getting out and enjoying our many beautiful trails, it is more important than ever to treat the environment and fellow hikers with proper care and respect.

When you hike, be considerate of those who will follow you. They deserve the same high-quality experience you are seeking. To minimize your impact on the environment, follow these guidelines created by Leave No Trace, a nonprofit organization that educates people about these issues:

- Plan ahead and prepare. Know the regulations and special concerns for the area you'll visit. Schedule your trip to avoid high times of use, and visit in small groups when possible.
- Dispose of waste properly. If you pack it in, pack it out. This means carrying out all trash, leftover food and litter. Deposit solid human waste in catholes dug six to eight inches deep, at least 200 feet from water and trails. Cover and disguise the cathole when finished. Pack out toilet paper and other hygiene products.
- Leave what you find. Examine but do not touch cultural or historic artifacts. Leave rocks, plants and other natural objects as you find them.
- Respect wildlife. Observe wildlife from a distance, and do not follow or approach any animals. Never feed wildlife—feeding damages their health, alters natural behaviors, and exposes them to predators and other dangers. Protect wildlife and your food by storing rations and trash securely.
- Respect other visitors and protect the quality of their experience. Be courteous and yield to others on the trail. Take breaks away from trails and other hikers.

Using This Book

The book is arranged into 10 chapters. It includes individual chapters for nature preserves managed by the Land Trust of North Alabama and 13 greenways managed by the cities of Huntsville and Madison. It also includes chapters for the Hays Nature Preserve and the U.S. Space & Rocket Center. Each trail is numbered, from 1 to 73, so that you can quickly flip through the book to find a specific hike. Each trail description includes a one-way hike that goes in a specific direction. Some areas have numerous paths that can be walked in different sequences and directions, but I have tried to simplify things by making each trail description an exact journey. Each trip consists of capsulized summaries, distance, hiking time, elevation gain and loss, hiking difficulty, location, fees, facilities, driving directions, and highlights. For the actual hike directions, I include waypoints, the mileage mark for each waypoint and GPS waypoints.

Also, trail maps include the distance (in feet or miles) between trail junctions. These numbers will allow you to quickly get an idea of how far you'll travel on any section of a trail. At the end of many trail descriptions, I've included a Trail Facts section to share interesting notes, such as the origins of trail names and the history of areas that the trails explore.

GENERAL TRAIL DESCRIPTION

This brief summary indicates the type of terrain you'll encounter and highlights notable things you'll see along the way. It also calls out any special things you should consider before hiking the trail.

DISTANCE

The first figure listed in this section is an estimate of the one-way hiking distance for each trail. If you're planning to hike the entire length of a trail and then retrace your steps back to the trailhead, just double the hiking distance. The mileage for each trail was calculated using a measuring wheel, GPS unit and mapping software. But keep in mind that mileages in this book may differ from what you see on trail signs or certain maps. All these different sources can often conflict because they've been calculated by different people using different methods over time.

HIKING TIME

This is an estimate of the walking time for the average person for each trip. Estimates are based on my own experiences as well as hiking-time calculator formulas that factor in the terrain and elevation gain and loss. Hiking times do not include rest stops; your actual time on the trail will vary depending on how often and how long you stop. Your hiking time will also depend on other factors, such as your level of fitness, your stride, the weight you carry in a pack, and whether you're walking with kids. For these reasons, consider the hiking time a rough estimate.

ELEVATION GAIN/LOSS

The elevation gain and loss figures are a sum of all the uphill and downhill segments of a one-way hike on the trail. When the numbers are larger, there will be more changes in elevation, signaling that the trip is more challenging. One of the most strenuous paths, the McKay Hollow Trail, has an elevation gain and loss of +756 feet/-754 feet, meaning you climb a total of 756 feet of elevation and descend for a total of 754 feet of elevation. That's a real thigh-burner that will get your heart pumping. On the other hand, the paved and flat Aldridge Creek Greenway path has an elevation gain and loss of +7 feet/-0 feet, which is an easy stroll.

HIKING DIFFICULTY

Although it's somewhat subjective, the difficulty rating for each trip is based on distance, total elevation gain and type of terrain. The ratings are as follows:

Easy: A relatively short trip with little elevation gain and loss.

Moderate: A trip that requires a few hours of walking and/or includes a few climbs and descents but does not cover a great change in elevation.

Strenuous: This can be a hike of any length that includes very steep sections. Or it can be a long trip covering many miles and requiring several hours. This trip might include steep ascents and descents and great gains and losses in elevation.

LOCATION

This is a specific street address or a general location for the beginning of the trail. For the most part, you can put this information into a mapping app or software to find the parking area and trailhead.

FEES

This includes required fees to access or use the trails. While Monte Sano State Park has an entrance fee (see Hiking Huntsville Vol. 1), most other areas, including Land Trust of North Alabama trails, do not. At many Land Trust trailheads, you will see boxes where you can deposit a donation. I highly encourage visitors to contribute to the boxes or contribute to the Land Trust online (landtrustnal.org), because the organization does critical work to acquire, preserve and maintain recreation areas, and it often relies on volunteers to build and maintain trails.

FACILITIES

This includes restrooms, water sources, food sources or other structures (such as pavilions) located at a trailhead.

DRIVING DIRECTIONS

These directions begin at major road intersections and end at parking areas for trailheads. While it's probably easiest to use a navigation app, you might lose cell service near some trailheads, so you can carry a printout of these directions as a backup.

HIGHLIGHTS

These are some of the notable things you'll encounter during the hike, whether it's a natural feature such as a waterfall, a bluff view, or an area of historical significance. The highlights could also be things you will experience, such as solitude, easy terrain, or a physical challenge.

WAYPOINT/MILE

Each hike description begins with a waypoint, which is a point of interest along the route. This could be an important trail junction or an interesting feature such as a cave or waterfall. The first waypoint for each trail is the "Trailhead," which is the starting point for the trail. Subsequent waypoints are written as hyphenated numbers. These numbers begin with the number I have assigned to the trail (from 1 to 73), a hyphen, and then the number of that specific waypoint. For example, the Trough Springs Trail is the 50th trail in the book, and here is how the listing looks:

Waypoint/Mile

Trailhead (Waypoint 50) (34.7213, -86.5373) The Trough Springs Trail begins at the kiosk on the south side of the Trough Springs parking area.

50-1 (34.7206, -86.5370) (612 ft.) At the four-way junction, the Trough Springs Trail intersects the Natural Well Trail.

50-2 (34.7158, -86.5344) (0.5 mi.) The trail makes a hairpin turn to the north and descends.

GPS COORDINATES/DISTANCE

Each waypoint number is followed by GPS coordinates in parentheses. You can enter these coordinates into a GPS unit or mapping software or app to see the waypoint's exact position. There are several ways to express GPS coordinates, but I have used the Universal Transverse Mercator (UTM) coordinate system expressed in decimal degrees. With this format, the first number is the latitude, and the second number is the longitude. I've used this format because it's simple to plug these numbers into mapping systems like Google Maps and Apple Maps. There are several online sources that offer detailed explanations of the UTM system, but they can honestly get very detailed and down in the weeds. Rather than confuse anyone, I prefer to just recommend that you plug or paste in the numbers provided. For example, for the Trough Springs Trailhead listed above, plug in 34.7213, -86.5373 exactly as written. If you want to plug these numbers into a GPS unit, you might have to convert them to another format, such as degrees/ minutes/seconds. There are several websites where you can easily convert the format, such as www.fcc.gov/media/radio/dms-decimal.

Following the GPS coordinates is the mileage for that specific waypoint. For example, for the Trough Springs listing above, Waypoint 50-2 is 0.5 miles from the beginning of the trail.

TRAIL SECTION DISTANCES

On the maps in the book, you will see black circles at trail junctions. In between trail junctions, next to the trail route, you will see numbers, such as 0.1 mi., 0.2 mi., 0.3 mi., etc. These numbers indicate the distance between two trail junctions. You can use these numbers to quickly calculate how far you've traveled, or how far you need to travel.

TRAIL FACTS

At the end of many trail descriptions, I've included additional facts about the trail, such as background information on the names of trails and historical events related to the hiking area.

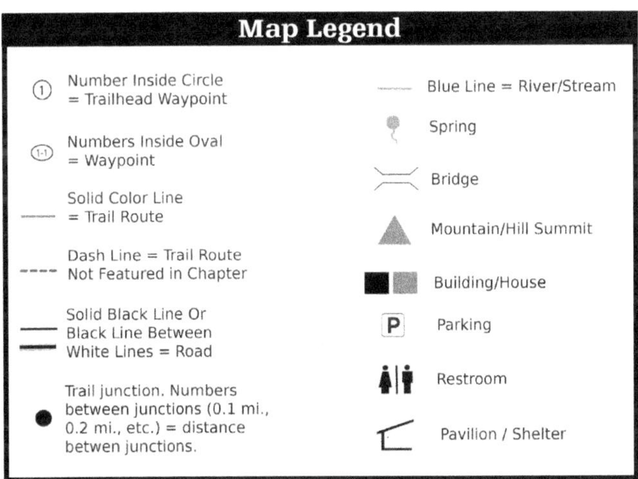

CHAPTER 1

Bethel Spring Nature Preserve

On a southern slope of Keel Mountain, towering curtains of water roll down a broad, rocky bluff and then plunge into a gaping sinkhole. This impressive set of waterfalls has quickly made the Bethel Spring Nature Preserve a favorite destination for local hikers.

The Land Trust of North Alabama opened the Bethel Spring Nature Preserve in March of 2020, making it one of the newest trail systems in the Huntsville area. Located in Gurley, Alabama, southeast of Huntsville, the preserve covers 360 acres and includes 1.6 miles of trails that explore Keel Mountain and the old farmland near its base.

Many people visit the preserve to see the waterfalls. While hikers tackle some steep terrain to reach it, the trail is only about half a mile each way, so a wide range of people manage to make the trip. But the falls aren't the only attraction at Bethel Spring. While this isn't one of the largest preserves in the Huntsville area, it has something to offer for just about everyone, whether you're an experienced hiker, a casual walker, a trail runner, or someone seeking a place to walk with kids. Those who prefer mellow terrain can walk two trails near the base of the mountain. One is the Bethel Creek Loop Trail, which has a gravel surface to accommodate people of all ability levels. The second level path is the Carpenter Trail, which is mostly dirt, but includes a boardwalk that allows people with mobility issues to visit the remains of a historic springhouse.

Hikers who want more of a challenge and a view of the waterfall can follow the rugged Falling Sink and Mill trails, which snake their way up and down Keel Mountain. In addition to offering a variety of hikes, Bethel Spring gives its visitors a glimpse of pioneer history, as the preserve is home to a spring and the remains of a mill dating to the 1800s.

General Information

Location: 2641 Cherry Tree Rd., Gurley, AL 35760

Hours: Open dawn to dusk.

Primary trail activities allowed: Hiking, biking

Pets: Leashed pets allowed on trails.

Fees: There are no required fees to use the trails, but donation boxes are located at some trailheads and parking areas.

Facilities: There are no facilities and no sources of potable water at the trailhead.

Information: (256) 534-5263; www.landtrustnal.org/properties/bethel-spring-preserve; questions@landtrustnal.org

Driving Directions: From the junction of U.S. 231/431 (Memorial Parkway) and U.S. 431 (Governors Drive), head east on U.S. 431. Travel 13.1 mi., and then turn left onto Cave Spring Road. Go 3.3 mi., and then turn left onto Old Gurley Pike. Follow Old Gurley Pike for 1.2 mi., and then turn right onto Cherry Tree Road. Take Cherry Tree Rd. 2.1 mi., and then turn left into the parking area for the Bethel Spring Nature Preserve.

Bethel Creek Loop Trail, Carpenter Trail, Mill Trail and Falling Sink Trail

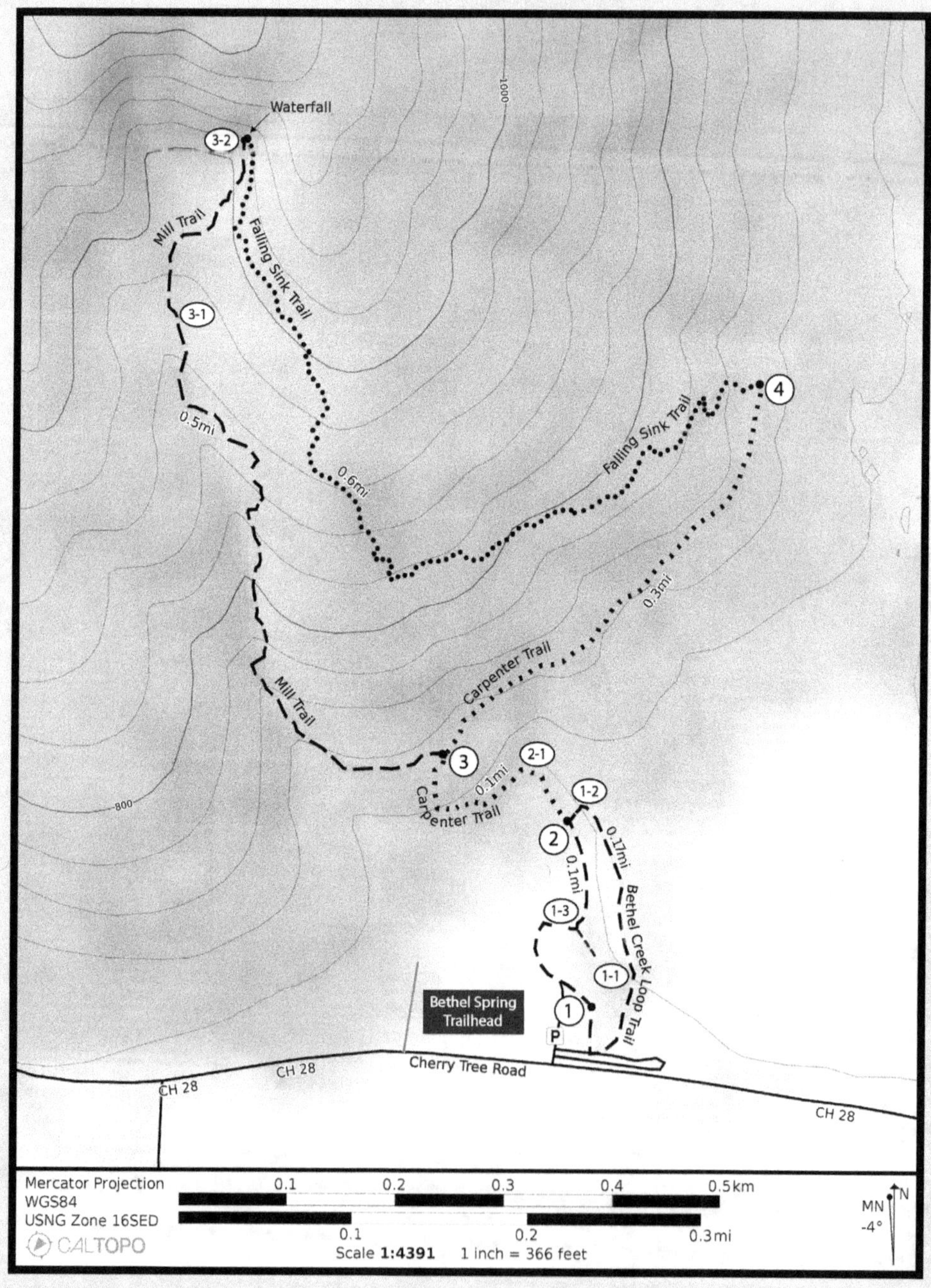

1. Bethel Creek Loop Trail

Looking for a place to stroll with the kids? Or maybe you'd like to run laps. This mostly level path is a great option for anyone seeking easy terrain. As the trail loops around Bethel Creek, it explores broad green fields and offers views of Keel Mountain to the north. Plus the trail is a loop, so you can walk or run it without ever straying far from the parking area. As a bonus, the gravel surface allows you to avoid dirt and mud, and it's stroller-friendly.

Distance: 0.3 mi.
Hiking Time: 5 to 10 minutes
Elevation Gain/Loss: +5 ft., -5 ft.
Hiking Difficulty: Easy
Location: Bethel Spring Nature Preserve, 2641 Cherry Tree Rd., Gurley, AL 35760
Fees, Facilities & Driving Directions: See page 2.

Highlights

Creekside Rest Spot: On the west side of the loop, a short path leads to benches that sit in the shade of trees beside the creek. This is a nice spot to duck out of the sun and cool off as you enjoy the peaceful sounds of the burbling creek.

Waypoint/Mile

Trailhead (Waypoint 1) (34.61122, -86.36257) On the east side of the parking area, begin at the trailhead kiosk and take the wide gravel path south toward Cherry Tree Road. At 83 ft., the trail turns left to descend toward a field. After a brief drop, you'll enjoy a picturesque scene where a wide, grassy field stretches toward a Keel Mountain ridge to the north.

1-1 (34.61125, -86.36210) (283 ft.) A 30-ft.-long wood and metal bridge carries you across Bethel Creek. The path then skirts the western edge of the field.

1-2 (34.61283, -86.36258) (0.17 mi.) A wood and metal footbridge crosses the creek and passes through a stand of cedars.

2 (34.61268, -86.36278) (0.18 mi.) The Carpenter Trail intersects on the right and runs north toward Bethel Spring at the base of the mountain. To continue on the Bethel Creek Loop Trail, turn left and go southeast.

1-3 (34.61186, -86.36264) (0.2 mi.) A gravel path measuring about 100 ft. leads to benches with a view of the creek. To continue on the Bethel Creek Loop, bear right and go west. After traveling about 425 ft., you'll return to the trailhead at Waypoint 1.

Trail Facts

A Generous Gift: The Bethel Spring Nature Preserve exists thanks to Doris McGee and Marcell Dean, two sisters who donated the land that their family had owned for more than 132 years. In 2014, when Marcell passed away, the Land Trust of North Alabama took over as stewards of the property. The trailhead and parking area lie next to the former site of the sisters' home. Unfortunately, the ground beneath the old family home sank into a cave, and the damaged structure was torn down. All that remains is a fireplace, which you can see near the parking area.

2. Carpenter Trail

The Carpenter Trail passes the spring that feeds Bethel Creek and then rises gradually to follow the base of boulder-strewn slopes. Near the beginning of the Carpenter Trail, a boardwalk leads to a bubbling spring and the remains of an old springhouse. From here, the path transitions back to a natural dirt surface. For the most part, it's packed earth with few seriously rocky sections, so it's good for hikers or trail runners seeking ankle-friendly terrain. The Carpenter Trail also provides access to the Mill Trail and Falling Sink Trail, which both lead to the major waterfall higher on the mountain. While the spring water appears at the base of the mountain, its origin is the waterfall located 400 ft. higher up. At the base of the falls, the water flows into a cave and exits at the spring.

Distance: 0.42 mi.

Hiking Time: 15 to 20 minutes

Elevation Gain/Loss: +116 ft., -35 ft.

Hiking Difficulty: Easy

Location: Bethel Spring Nature Preserve, 2641 Cherry Tree Rd., Gurley, AL 35760

Fees, Facilities & Driving Directions: See page 2.

Highlights

Bethel Spring: After walking about 170 ft., you'll reach Bethel Spring, where a narrow stream of water emerges from the remains of an old springhouse.

Waypoint/Mile

Trailhead (Waypoint 2) (34.61268, -86.36278) To reach the beginning of the Carpenter Trail, begin at the Bethel Spring Trailhead kiosk and go left to travel north on the Bethel Creek Loop Trail. Walk a little more than 0.1 mi. to the junction with the Carpenter Trail at Waypoint 2. At the junction, continue straight, heading north.

The trail moves toward a rocky slope, and at 149 ft. it transitions from a wide gravel surface to a narrow dirt path.

2-1 (34.61314, -86.36302) (172 ft.) To the right is Bethel Spring. Bend to the left and head southwest, following the white diamond blazes marked Carpenter Trail.

The trail rises gradually as it follows a bench of land that looks like it was an old road. Pines and hardwoods dominate the forest as the trail runs along the base of a boulder-covered slope. At 356 ft., the path turns right, and you begin a moderate climb heading straight up the slope.

3 (34.61326, -86.36394) (0.13 mi.) At a Y junction, the Mill Trail intersects on the left and goes west. To continue on the Carpenter Trail, bear right and head northeast.

The trail drops briefly to pass a gray, rocky bluff. At 0.15 mi., the trail climbs and then undulates as it traverses a dense forest of cedars and moss-covered hardwoods.

At 0.3 mi., the path levels out and soon widens. While there is rugged terrain to the left, the path itself has few rocky sections. On the right is denser forest of hardwoods, pines and cedars. In winter, you can see the top of a ridge to the northeast.

4 (34.61625, -86.36080) (0.42 mi.) The Falling Sink Trail intersects on the left and heads west. From this junction, you'll walk 0.6 mi. to reach the large waterfall.

Trail Facts

Bethel Spring: This spring, which feeds Bethel Creek, provided cold, pure water for family members who occupied the farm beginning in the 1800s. The spring water also flowed through the springhouse and kept the interior cool. Before refrigeration was invented, settlers used the springhouse to store perishable foods.

3. Mill Trail

Like the Falling Sink Trail, the Mill Trail climbs to the spectacular waterfall that is the highlight of the preserve. Some sections of this path are steep, though some people say that this route to the waterfall is a bit easier. Plus, it's 0.1 mi. shorter. Hikers interested in local history will also appreciate that this trail passes the remains of a mill that dates to the 1800s.

> **Distance:** 0.5 mi.
> **Hiking Time:** 30 minutes
> **Elevation Gain/Loss:** +372 ft., -9 ft.
> **Hiking Difficulty:** Strenuous
> **Location:** Bethel Spring Nature Preserve, 2641 Cherry Tree Rd., Gurley, AL 35760
> **Fees, Facilities & Driving Directions:** See page 2.

Highlights

Mill Ruins: When you've hiked 0.37 mi., you'll reach the stone foundation of a mill that operated in the 1800s. "This mill was the center of commerce of the Bethel Spring community," reports the Land Trust of North Alabama, noting that settlers used water from the falls to drive the mill wheel. "Past accounts suggest that a wooden trough funneled water from the falls to the location of the mill."

Waypoint/Mile

Trailhead (Waypoint 3) (34.61325, -86.36396) To reach the beginning of the Mill Trail, begin at the Bethel Spring Trailhead kiosk. Go left to travel north on the Bethel Creek Loop Trail for 0.1 mi. Then take the Carpenter Trail and walk 0.1 mi. to the junction with the Mill Trail.

The path is level for the first 300 ft. or so as it moves through the shade of cedars. Then the trail turns right to head north and climb alongside a dry drainage. For a little more than 0.1 mi., the trail alternates between moderate sections and short climbs that are steeper and more strenuous.

To the left, the dry drainage becomes steeper, and you get views of the nearby valley and mountain ridges on the horizon. This is a ruggedly beautiful part of the hike, where old, twisted cedars hug the trail, and you'll shimmy between rocks and trees as you scramble up the crooked path. Near 0.3 mi., the path mellows as it continues up the mountain.

3-1 (34.61677, -86.36665) (0.37 mi.) The trail passes the stone foundation for the old mill.

At 0.42 mi., the path hugs a rock wall as the sounds of the waterfall grow louder.

3-2 (34.61819, -86.36600) (0.5 mi.) The Mill Trail intersects with the Falling Sink Trail at the base of the falls. If you follow the Falling Sink Trail back to the parking area, you'll walk another 1.1 mi.

Trail Facts

Mill Products: Historians don't know for sure what the mill produced in the 1800s, but settlers likely used it to grind grain or mill lumber.

4. Falling Sink Trail

Rising nearly 400 ft. over a little more than 1 mi., this steep path leads to a massive waterfall. Many people who visit the falls do a loop that combines the Bethel Creek Loop, Carpenter, Falling Sink and Mill trails (1.8 mi.). Many people say that it's a little less strenuous if you go counterclockwise, but you'll get your exercise no matter which way you go. To see the falls in all their glory, you should go after a few days of rain. Chances are, portions of the trail will be wet and muddy, so wear sturdy boots or shoes, and consider hiking with trekking poles for added balance.

Distance: 0.6 mi.

Hiking Time: 30 minutes

Elevation Gain/Loss: +358 ft., -22 ft.

Hiking Difficulty: Moderate to strenuous

Location: Bethel Spring Nature Preserve, 2641 Cherry Tree Rd., Gurley, AL 35760

Fees, Facilities & Driving Directions: See page 2.

Highlights

One of Madison County's Largest Waterfalls: The Falling Sink and Mill trails lead to a massive waterfall, which is the main attraction in this nature preserve. This high, sprawling waterfall is really a combination of two wide cascades and a third, thinner stream on the far left. Together, they produce quite a spectacle, as an impressive amount of water drops dozens of feet as it pours down the rocky cliff. At the base of the cliff, the water continues its journey by dropping into a sinkhole that leads to a cave.

Waypoint/Mile

Trailhead (Waypoint 4) (34.61625, -86.36080) To reach the Falling Sink Trail, begin at the Bethel Spring Trailhead kiosk and go left to travel north on the Bethel Creek Loop Trail. Walk a little more than 0.1 mi. and turn right onto the Carpenter Trail. Travel 0.42 mi. on the Carpenter Trail to the junction with the Falling Sink Trail, which intersects on the left. Turn left onto the Falling Sink Trail and ascend, heading west and winding among cedars.

The hike begins with a gradual climb up a rocky slope, where the path is lined with boulders covered in moss and lichen. The path soon emerges from cedar groves to climb among hardwoods.

Bethel Spring Preserve waterfall

Over the next 0.5 mi., the path alternates between moderate climbs and short, steep sections. Occasionally, the path runs pretty level, giving you a chance to catch your breath as you traverse mountain slopes. As you move higher, green farmland and distant ridges become visible to the south.

After 0.5 mi., you reach a particularly steep part of the trail, but the climbing ends after about 80 ft. After a quick breather, you'll enjoy a relatively level section of the trail that traverses the slope.

At 0.55 mi., you'll cross a small drainage. After another 50 ft., you might begin to hear the waterfall, which comes into view after another 100 ft. or so.

3-2 (34.61819, -86.36600) (0.6 mi.) The Falling Sink Trail ends at the base of the waterfall. From this point, you can turn south to follow the Mill Trail back toward the parking area. If you connect the Mill, Carpenter and Bethel Creek Loop trails, your return trek will be about 0.7 mi.

Trail Facts

Paul's Cave: The sinkhole at the base of the large waterfall leads to Paul's Cave, which is 1,338 ft. long and 334 ft. deep.

***Warning: Do not enter this cave. It is not open to the public, and caving is extremely dangerous and requires expert skills and equipment.*

Hays Nature Preserve

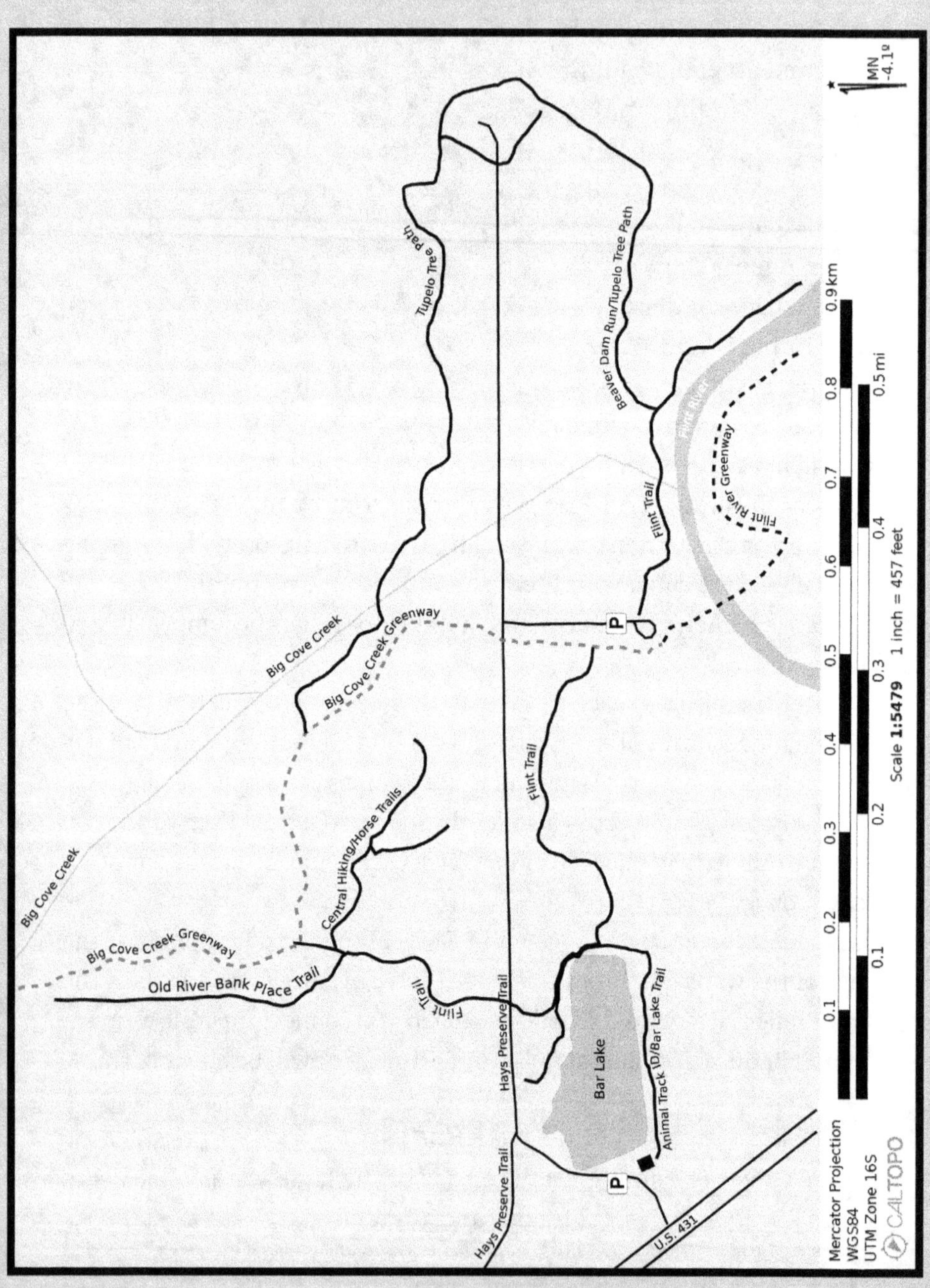

CHAPTER 2

Hays Nature Preserve

In 1999, Annie Hays and the Hays family donated 538 acres of land in Hampton Cove to the city of Huntsville to create a nature preserve. Since the Hays Nature Preserve was established, it has served as an environmental education center and a place for people to enjoy the outdoors.

While many natural trails in Huntsville and Madison explore mountainous terrain, the paths in the Hays Nature Preserve pass through bottomlands and wetland areas, including a tupelo swamp. Big Cove Creek and the Flint River also converge in the southern edge of the preserve. The abundance of water and lush forest makes this an excellent place for viewing wildlife, and it's an important part of the North Alabama Birding Trail.

Another interesting aspect of this preserve is that it neighbors two greenways, allowing visitors to access paved paths as well as natural trails. It's common for families to combine a greenway bike ride with a trip to the preserve, which is popular with kids. The top-notch playground in the preserve encourages open-ended play in a natural setting. Among its cool features are a wooden fort, a rock-climbing wall, a swinging bridge and a music station. Kids can also participate in environmental education programs hosted by the preserve.

For hikers, the preserve offers more than 10 miles of trails. If you're walking with kids, check out the western side of the preserve, where the Animal Track ID path runs along the south side of Bar Lake. Along the path, there are wooden boxes with etchings of animal prints. After kids try to guess what animal matches the prints, they can slide open the box to find the answer. If you'd like to take your kids fishing, Bar Lake is a great choice, as it's stocked with several species, and no license is required.

On the eastern side of the preserve, hikers will find several interesting natural features. On the Flint Trail, you can walk along the bank of the Flint River, where you might see great blue herons and green herons. The Flint Trail intersects with the Beaver Dam Run, a trail that visits massive trees and explores a wetland area created by beaver dams. The Beaver Dam Run also leads to one of the most fascinating spots in the preserve, a tupelo swamp that looks like something from a Louisiana bayou. In some parts of the preserve, you'll glimpse a neighboring golf course. But there will be other moments when you totally forget that you're anywhere near a bustling metro area.

General Information

Location: 7153 U.S. 431, Owens Cross Roads, AL 35763
Hours: Open 7 a.m. to 4 p.m.
Primary trail activities allowed: Hiking, biking, horseback riding
Pets: Leashed pets allowed.
Fees: There are no required fees to use the trails.
Information: (256) 427-5116; www.huntsvilleal.gov/environment/green-team/nature-preserves/hays-nature-preserve/

Driving Directions

Playground Area Parking

From the junction of U.S. 231 (Memorial Parkway) and U.S. 431 (Governors Drive), travel east on U.S. 431 for 9.7 mi. and turn left at the entrance to the Hays Nature Preserve. As you enter the preserve, you'll see roadside parking spaces on the left, beside the playground.

Central Parking Area

From the junction of U.S. 231/431 (Memorial Parkway) and U.S. 431 (Governors Drive), travel east on U.S. 431 for 9.7 mi. and turn left at the entrance to the Hays Nature Preserve. Travel 0.5 mi. on Hays Preserve Trail, and then turn right. Continue about another 400 ft. to the parking area. The trailhead lies immediately west of the parking area on a paved path.

SECTION 1:
Hays Nature Preserve (West Side)
Animal Track ID Trail/Bar Lake Trail, Flint Trail (West Side), Old River Bank Place Trail and Central Hiking/Horse Trails

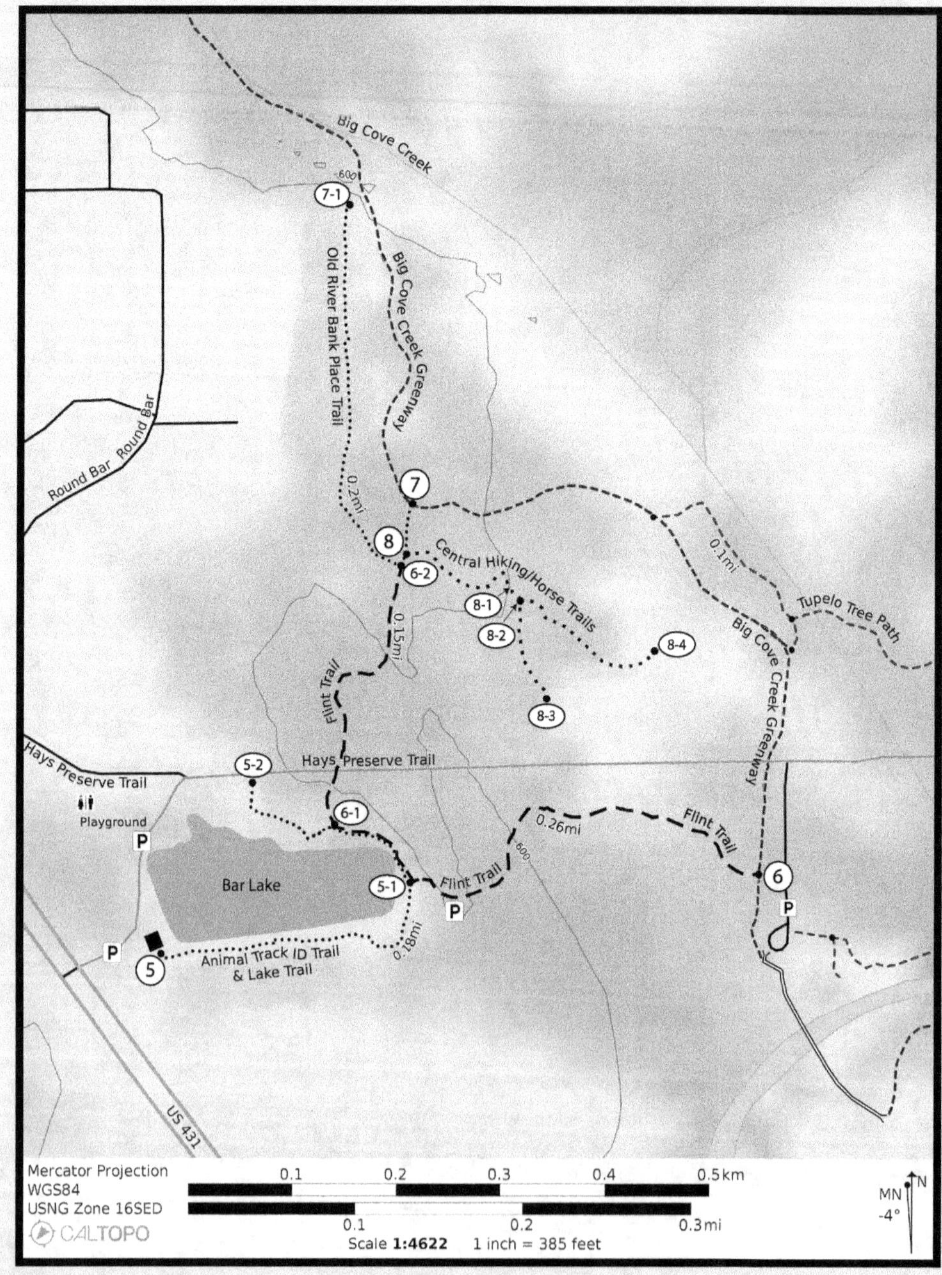

5. Animal Track ID Trail/Bar Lake Trail

This is a perfect trail for kids. As they walk the flat path in the shade of tall pines, they can identify tracks of animals that live in the preserve. The trail loops around Bar Lake, where kids can fish for catfish, bream, bass and trout.

Distance: 0.3 mi.
Hiking Time: 5 to 10 minutes walking time. Allow more time for kids to identify tracks.
Elevation Gain/Loss: +/-0 ft.
Hiking Difficulty: Easy
Location: Hays Nature Preserve, 7153 U.S. 431, Owens Cross Roads, AL 35763
Facilities: There is a restroom in the playground area.
Driving Directions: See page 14 and use the directions for the Playground Area Parking.

Highlights

Animal Tracks: Posted along the trail are wooden boxes with animal tracks carved into the front panels. After the kids have fun guessing which animal matches the tracks, they can lift the panel to discover the answer.

Waypoint/Mile

Trailhead (Waypoint 5) (34.64397, -86.47284) On the south side of the Education Center, take the path that enters the long stand of pines and heads east. You'll soon encounter the first of several animal track ID stations.

5-1 (34.64458, -86.47027) (0.18 mi.) At the east end of Bar Lake, the Lake Trail meets the Flint Trail. Continue straight to stay on the path that circles the lake.

6-1 (34.64505, -86.47107) (0.25 mi.) On the right, the Flint Trail heads north and leads to the Old River Bank Place area as well as the Big Cove Creek Greenway. To continue exploring the lake, bear left and head southwest.

5-2 (34.64537, -86.47190) (0.31 mi.) The Lake Trail ends at the Hays Preserve Trail, the road that passes through the preserve.

Trail Facts

Girl Scout Project: Local Girl Scout Troop 455 helped develop the trail and researched animals that inhabit the preserve (and their tracks).

6. Flint Trail (West Side)

This flat path provides a quick and easy way to move between the eastern and western sides of the preserve. If you begin your outing on the east side exploring the tupelo tree swamp and other attractions, you can take the Flint Trail to visit Bar Lake and the Animal Track ID Trail. Just be aware that this portion of the Flint Trail can be wet, so wear appropriate shoes or boots.

Distance: 0.48 mi.
Hiking Time: 15 minutes
Elevation Gain/Loss: +11 ft., -11 ft.
Hiking Difficulty: Easy
Location: Hays Nature Preserve, 7153 U.S. 431, Owens Cross Roads, AL 35763
Facilities: There are no facilities and no sources of potable water at the trailhead.
Driving Directions: From the junction of U.S. 231/431 (Memorial Parkway) and U.S. 431 (Governors Drive), travel east on U.S. 431 for 9.7 mi. and turn left at the entrance to the Hays Nature Preserve. Travel 0.5 mi. on Hays Preserve Trail, and then turn right. Continue about another 400 ft. to the parking area. The trailhead lies immediately west of the parking area, on a paved path.

Highlights

Bar Lake and the Animal Track ID Trail: Bar Lake lies at the western end of this portion of the Flint Trail. This small body of water is stocked with bream and other species, and it's a good place to take a kid fishing. For added entertainment, you can hike the Animal Track ID Trail and play a game trying to identify the tracks of various animals.

Waypoint/Mile

Trailhead (Waypoint 6) (34.64460, -86.46651) To reach the trailhead, begin at the parking area near the center of the preserve and Waypoint 6. At the northwest corner of the parking area, walk north on the Big Cove Creek Greenway path for a few feet to Waypoint 6, where the Flint Trail intersects on the left. Turn left onto the Flint Trail and head west into the forest.

Soon after you enter the shaded forest, you'll pass a sign for the Match Stick Forest, where a stand of sweet gum and other hardwoods include thin, straight trees resembling matchsticks sticking out of the wetland. From here, the trail moves through a hardwood forest and eventually widens. It then transitions to dirt and gravel as it moves beneath the boughs of sweet gum trees. Over the last 90 ft., the path rises to reach the eastern side of Bar Lake.

5-1 (34.64458, -86.47027) (0.26 mi.) The Flint Trail intersects with the Lake Trail, and both trails share a path as they head northwest to curl around the lake.

6-1 (34.64505, -86.47107) (0.33 mi.) The Flint Trail splits off from the Lake Trail and turns right to head north.

6-2 (34.64725, -86.47039) (0.48 mi.) The Flint Trail ends at a junction with the Old River Bank Place Trail. If you continue straight, you'll walk a little more than 200 ft. to reach the Big Cove Creek Greenway.

7. Old River Bank Place Trail

The Old River Bank Place Trail explores an ancient river levee. It doesn't offer the interesting natural features you'll find on the eastern side of the preserve, but it connects to the Flint Trail and Central Hiking Trails, allowing you to enjoy quiet solitude in less-traveled parts of the preserve.

Distance: 0.24 mi.
Hiking Time: 5 minutes
Elevation Gain/Loss: +/-0 ft.
Hiking Difficulty: Easy
Location: Hays Nature Preserve, 7153 U.S. 431, Owens Cross Roads, AL 35763
Facilities: At the trailhead in the center of the preserve near Waypoint 6, there are no facilities and no sources of potable water.
Driving Directions: From the junction of U.S. 231/431 (Memorial Parkway) and U.S. 431 (Governors Drive), travel east on U.S. 431 for 9.7 mi. and turn left at the entrance to the Hays Nature Preserve. Travel 0.5 mi. on Hays Preserve Trail, and then turn right. Continue about another 400 ft. to the parking area. The trailhead lies immediately west of the parking area on a paved path.

Waypoint/Mile

Trailhead (Waypoint 7) (34.64767, -86.47027) The path that explores the Old River Bank Place begins at a junction with the Big Cove Creek Greenway. To reach this junction, begin at the parking area near the center of the preserve and Waypoint 6. From the northwest corner of the parking area, walk north on the paved Big Cove Creek Greenway path. After walking 0.4 mi., you'll see to your left a sign marked Old River Bank Place. Turn left on the wide dirt and grass path that heads southwest into the forest.

8 (34.64735, -86.47029) (130 ft.) After walking 130 ft., you'll see on the left a path that heads east into the forest. Continue straight, traveling south.

6-3 (34.64725, -86.47039) (217 ft.) After walking another 87 ft., you'll reach a trail that intersects on the right and heads northwest. This 0.2-mi. path leads to a clearing and then turns north to pass through another wide clearing in the forest. The trail ends at a clearing beside the Big Cove Creek Greenway path at **Waypoint 7-1** (34.65026, -86.47090) (0.2 mi.).

Trail Facts

Ancient Levee: The trail crosses a levee that formed along the Flint River about 15,000 years ago. Back then, during the Ice Age, the Flint River system was significantly larger and spread from Keel Mountain (about 7 mi. east of Hays Preserve) to Drake Mountain, which is about 14 mi. northwest of Hays Preserve.

8. Central Hiking/Horse Trails

Hikers and horseback riders use these trails, which pass through dense stands of trees and cross land that is sometimes flooded. (Definitely wear shoes that you don't mind getting wet and muddy.)

Distance: 0.2 mi.

Hiking Time: 5 minutes

Elevation Gain/Loss: Little to no elevation gain

Hiking Difficulty: Easy

Location: Hays Nature Preserve, 7153 U.S. 431, Owens Cross Roads, AL 35763

Facilities: At the trailhead in the center of the preserve near Waypoint 6, there are no facilities and no sources of potable water.

Driving Directions: From the junction of U.S. 231/431 (Memorial Parkway) and U.S. 431 (Governors Drive), travel east on U.S. 431 for 9.7 mi. and turn left at the entrance to the Hays Nature Preserve. Travel 0.5 mi. on Hays Preserve Trail, and then turn right. Continue about another 400 ft. to the parking area. The trailhead lies immediately west of the parking area on a paved path.

Waypoint/Mile

Trailhead (Waypoint 8) (34.64735, -86.47029) To reach these trails, begin at Waypoint 7, where the Big Cove Creek Greenway meets the Old River Bank Place Trail. Travel south on the Old River Bank Place path for 130 ft. to Waypoint 8, where a nonblazed path intersects on the left. Turn left onto the path and travel east.

8-1 (34.64704, -86.46925) (354 ft.) A nonblazed path intersects on the left. Continue straight, traveling southeast.

8-2 (34.64692, -86.46909) (428 ft.) A nonblazed path intersects on the right. This trail heads south for about 290 ft. and ends at the edge of a large clearing at **Waypoint 8-3** (34.64613, -86.46885).

From Waypoint 8-2, you can also bear left and head southwest through the dense woods. After about 211 ft., the path exits the woods and continues to the southeast to angle across a wide field. After crossing the field, you'll reach a corridor that heads east and cuts through the forest for about 200 ft., ending at the edge of another field at **Waypoint 8-4** (34.64652, -86.46770). While this is the end of any identifiable trail, you can go straight and continue walking northeast to cross a wide field and meet the Big Cove Creek Greenway.

Trail Facts

Horseback Riding: The Hays Nature Preserve has miles of trails for horseback riding, and the Hampton Cove Equestrian Center offers programs that include rides in the preserve. For information, visit hamptoncoveequestrian.com.

SECTION 2:
Hays Nature Preserve (East Side)
Flint Trail (East Side) and Beaver Dam Run/Tupelo Tree Path

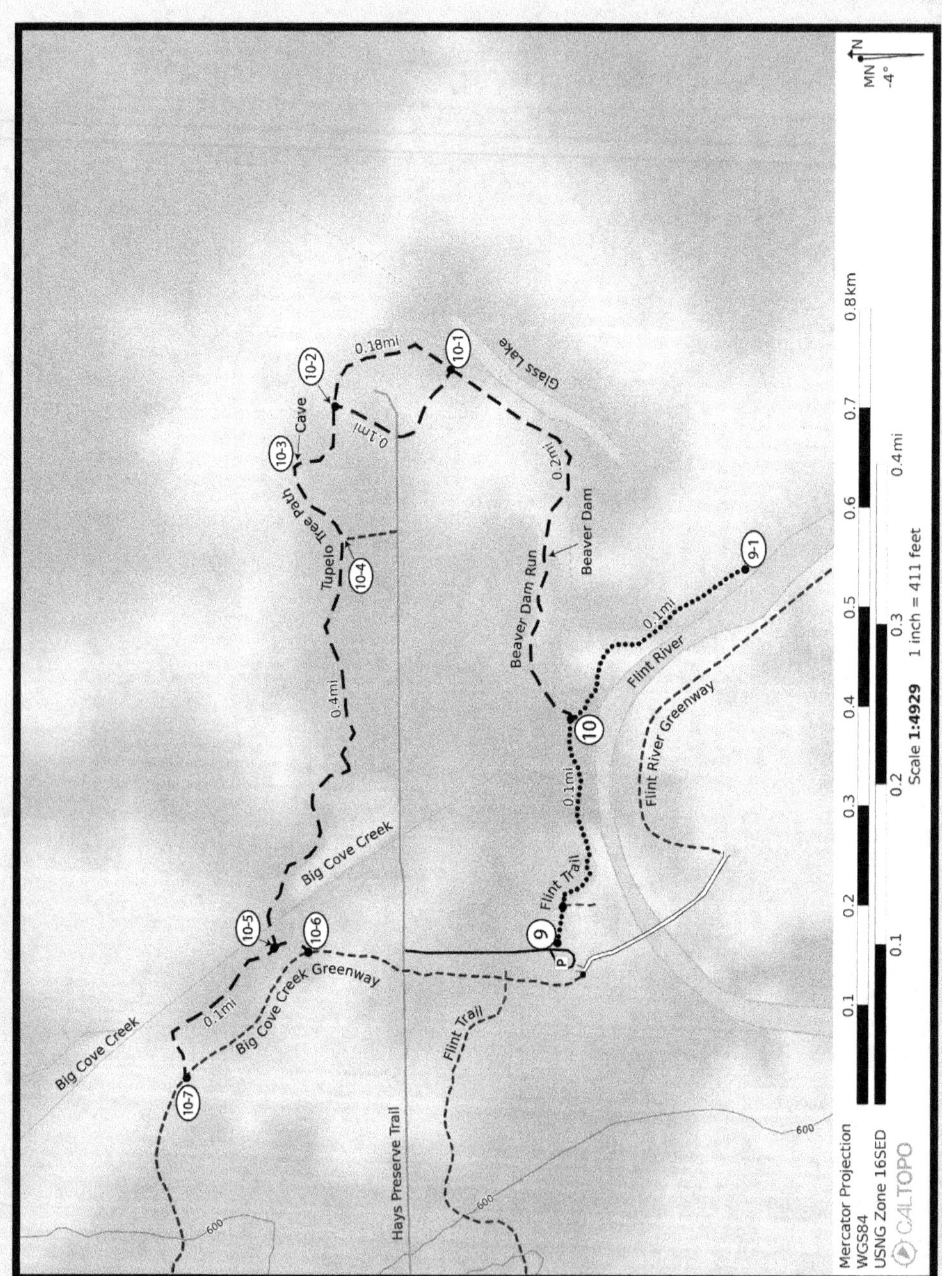

9. Flint Trail (East Side)

This short path passes through a popular picnic area beside the Flint River and continues for a short distance along the water. You can walk 0.1 mi. down the Flint Trail to reach the paths leading to an ancient beaver dam and tupelo tree swamp.

Distance: 0.3 mi.
Hiking Time: 10 minutes
Elevation Gain/Loss: +3 ft., -10 ft.
Hiking Difficulty: Easy
Location: Hays Nature Preserve, 7161 U.S. 431, Owens Cross Roads, AL 35763
Facilities: There are no facilities and no sources of potable water at the trailhead.
Driving Directions: From the junction of U.S. 231/431 (Memorial Parkway) and U.S. 431 (Governors Drive), travel east on U.S. 431 for 9.7 mi. and turn left at the entrance to the Hays Nature Preserve. Travel 0.5 mi. on Hays Preserve Trail, and then turn right. Continue about another 400 ft. to the parking area.

Highlights

Flint River: Near the beginning of the trail, hikers encounter one of the most attractive views in the preserve. The slow-motion Flint River has a commanding presence as it cuts a wide course through the forest. Look to the right to see a rust-colored bridge hovering over the green river. The curved metal rails of the bridge remind me of long tree limbs arching over water. For much of the way, the trail reveals more calming scenes as the river slides quietly through a pastoral landscape.

Waypoint/Mile

Trailhead (Waypoint 9) (34.64428, -86.46618) To reach the Flint Trail on the east side of the preserve, begin at the parking lot near the center of the preserve and Waypoint 9. At the southeast corner of the parking area, enter the concrete path at the information kiosk and head east.

At 183 ft., a wood bridge carries you across a stream that flows into the Flint River. After walking another 70 ft., you'll reach an area with several picnic tables that offer nice views of the river. A wide dirt path takes you through the shade of water oaks, while the wide river flows slowly on your immediate right.

10 (34.64398, -86.46369) (0.14 mi.) At the junction, the Beaver Dam Run Trail intersects on the left and heads northeast. To continue on the Flint Trail, bear right and head southeast to follow the river. For most of the way, the path moves through a wild corridor with thick woods to your left and the serene river to the right. But at 0.27 mi., you're reminded that civilization isn't too far away as the neighboring golf course comes clearly into view.

9-1 (34.64245, -86.46210) (0.3 mi.) The Flint Trail ends in tall grass beside the river.

Trail Facts

Flint River: Stretching 65.7 mi., the Flint River begins in Lincoln County, Tennessee, and flows south into Alabama's Madison County.

10. Beaver Dam Run/ Tupelo Tree Path

These trails visit some of the most interesting natural features in Hays Nature Preserve, including massive trees, an ancient beaver dam, a small cave and a tupelo tree swamp.

Distance: 0.9 mi.
Hiking Time: 20 to 30 minutes
Elevation Gain/Loss: +22 ft., -16 ft.
Hiking Difficulty: Easy
Location: Hays Nature Preserve, 7161 U.S. 431, Owens Cross Roads, AL 35763
Facilities: There are no facilities and no sources of potable water at the trailhead.
Driving Directions: From the junction of U.S. 231/431 (Memorial Parkway) and U.S. 431 (Governors Drive), travel east on U.S. 431

for 9.7 mi. and turn left at the entrance to the Hays Nature Preserve. Travel 0.5 mi. on Hays Preserve Trail, and then turn right. Continue about another 400 ft. to the parking area.

Highlights

Beaver Dam: When you've walked about 0.1 mi., you'll reach a pond formed by a beaver dam. This large pool of murky water formed when beavers ate and cut down trees in the area. It's impossible to know the exact age of the dam without carbon-dating the oldest piece of wood at its base. But it's believed that the dam is very old, and generations of beavers have migrated from the Flint River to this pond.

Cave: Over time, groundwater eroded the limestone layer in the forest to form this cave. Unlike the rest of the preserve, the cave and the hill it occupies do not sit in the floodplain of the Flint River and Big Cove Creek. This higher and drier land supports a different collection of tree species, like shagbark hickory and white ash.

Hays Nature Preserve tupelo tree swamp

Tupelo Trees: Less than a half-mile into the hike, you'll reach a striking collection of tupelo trees rising from a broad swath of murky water. It's an odd and mysterious scene—like something from a Louisiana bayou, not a north Alabama forest. According to local experts, these trees could be at least 300 years old.

Waypoint/Mile

Trailhead (Waypoint 10) (34.64398, -86.46369) To reach the Beaver Dam Run, begin at the parking lot near the center of the preserve and Waypoint 9. At the southeast corner of the parking area, enter the concrete path and follow the Flint Trail for 0.14 mi. to the junction with the Beaver Dam Run trail, which intersects on the left. Turn left and travel northeast on the Beaver Dam Run trail.

When you've walked about 450 ft., you'll encounter a massive oak that sits next to the trail. A little beyond 0.1 mi., you'll reach the "Ancient Beaver Dam" sign standing beside the pond. As you near 0.2 mi., the trail bends left to head north and skirt Glass Lake.

10-1 (34.64520, -86.45994) (0.2 mi.) A wide dirt and grass path intersects on the left and heads northwest. This path, measuring about 0.1 mi., curls to the northeast to pass a pump house and intersect with the Tupelo Tree Path at Waypoint 10-2. Instead of turning left at Waypoint 10-1, you can also continue straight. The path soon bends to the left and heads toward Waypoint 10-2.

10-2 (34.64623, -86.46033) (0.38 mi.) The trail that passes the pump house intersects on the left. At this junction, continue straight and begin ascending to the west. This is one of the few notable changes in elevation along the trail, and this moderate rise ends after only 100 ft.

10-3 (34.64662, -86.46103) (0.4 mi.) Look left to see the small, triangular cave opening at the base of a moss-covered rock.

As you continue down the wide dirt path, the sprawling tupelo swamp is on the right. At 0.45 mi., the state champion water tupelo tree (meaning it's the largest in the state) sits in the Yoo-hoo-colored water. You'll notice that the trees' trunks are flared at the base, similar to cypress trees. The broad base makes them more stable in muddy soil.

10-4 (34.64618, -86.46178) (0.49 mi.) A path intersects on the left. This is an unofficial trail that leads to Hays Preserve Trail, the road that runs through the preserve.

Beginning at 0.5 mi., a series of wood, stone and dirt walkways carries you across the murky water. The path soon leaves the flooded tupelo swamp to run through a mature forest.

10-5 (34.64686, -86.46625) (0.79 mi.) At the junction, you can go left or right. If you go left, you'll walk 90 ft. to meet the Big Cove Greenway path at **Waypoint 10-6** (34.64648, -86.46622). If you go right, you'll head northwest for 0.1 mi. and reach the trail terminus at the end of a wood bridge at **Waypoint 10-7** (34.64766, -86.46742).

Trail Facts

Tupelo Trees: A wide variety of animals live in the trunks of tupelo trees, including screech owls, wood ducks and fox squirrels. If you hear a knocking sound in the swamp, it could be a pileated woodpecker creating a cavity in a tupelo trunk.

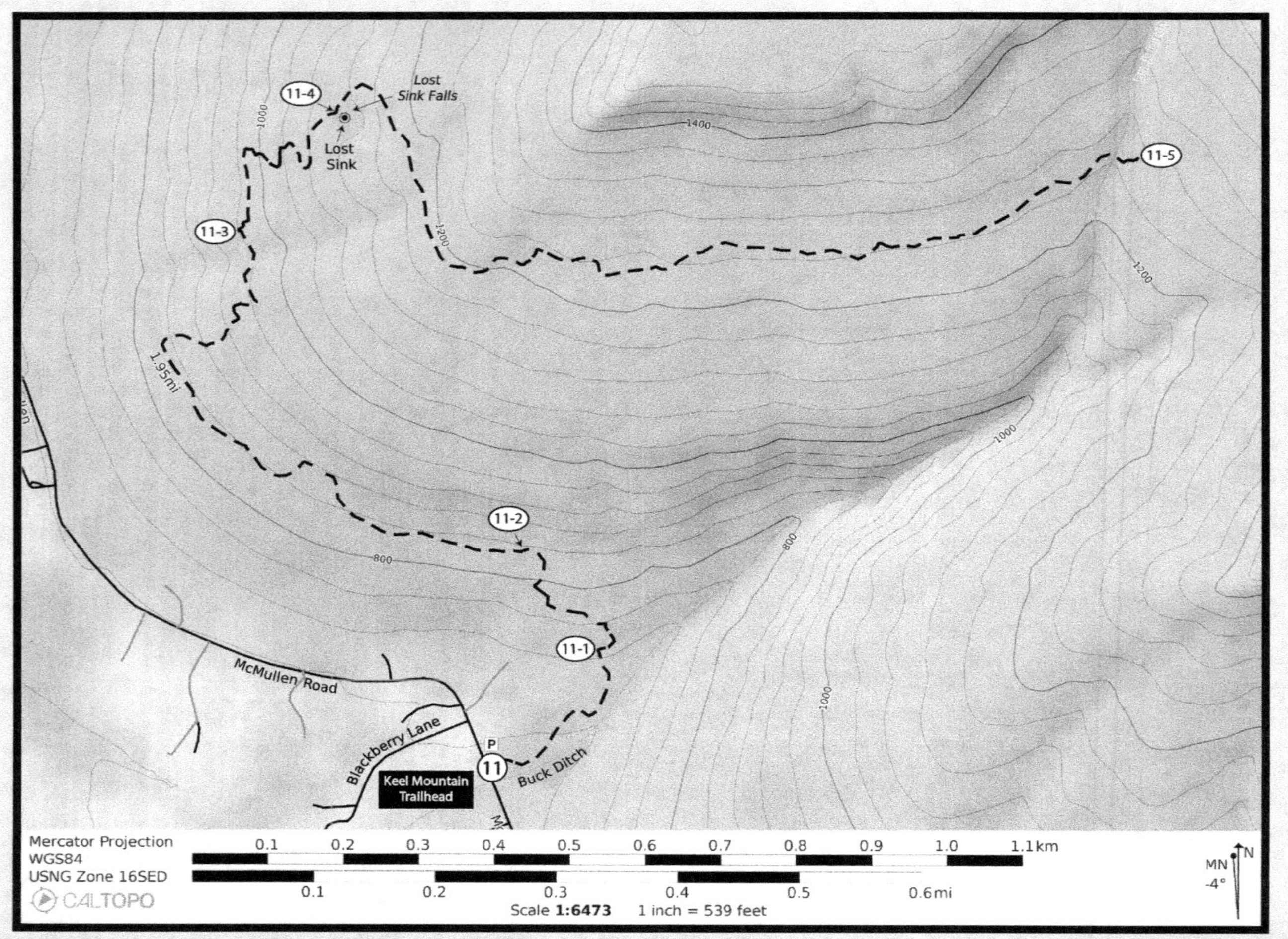

Keel Mountain
Preserve
11-4
Lost Sink Falls
Lost Sink
1000
1400
11-5
11-3
1200
1200
1.95mi
1000
11-2
800
800
1000
11-1
McMullen Road
Blackberry Lane
P
11
Keel Mountain Trailhead
Buck Ditch
Mercator Projection
WGS84
USNG Zone 16SED
CALTOPO
0.1 0.2 0.3 0.4 0.5 0.6 0.7 0.8 0.9 1.0 1.1km
0.1 0.2 0.3 0.4 0.5 0.6mi
Scale 1:6473   1 inch = 539 feet
MN
-4°
N

CHAPTER 3

Keel Mountain Preserve

In 1992, the U.S. Fish and Wildlife Service placed the Morefield's leather flower on the list of endangered species. The rare plant with purple, bell-shaped flowers grows on limestone outcrops of the Cumberland Plateau on south- and southwest-facing mountain slopes. In 2001, the U.S. Fish and Wildlife Service partnered with The Nature Conservancy and the Alabama Natural Heritage Program to preserve 310 acres on Keel Mountain to protect the endangered flower.

Located in Gurley, Alabama, east of Huntsville, the Keel Mountain Preserve was created to protect the plant, but this destination is also known for Lost Sink Falls. The 1.9-mi. Lost Sink Falls Trail takes you on a moderate climb to an intriguing cascade that slips over a bluff edge and plunges into a large sinkhole.

The waterfall is most impressive after a period of rain, so be prepared to tackle wet and sometimes muddy terrain as you trek through a dense forest of oak, hickory and pine.

General Information

Location: 1787 McMullen Rd., Gurley, AL 35748

Hours: Open 6 a.m. to 5 p.m.

Primary trail activities allowed: Hiking

Pets: Leashed pets allowed.

Fees: There are no required fees to use the trails.

Information: (205) 251-1155; www.nature.org/en-us/get-involved/how-to-help/places-we-protect/keel-mountain-preserve/

Driving Directions

From the junction of U.S. 231/431 (Memorial Parkway) and U.S. 431 (Governors Drive), travel east on U.S. 431 for 11.3 mi., and then turn right onto The Meadows Boulevard. Go 0.2 mi., and then take a sharp left turn onto Old Highway 431. Travel 1.6 mi. on Old Hwy. 431, and then turn right onto Cherry Tree Road. Go 0.4 mi. on Cherry Tree Rd., and then turn left onto Esslinger Drive. Travel 1.6 mi. on Esslinger Dr., and then take a sharp right onto McMullen Road. Go 0.8 mi. and turn right into the gravel parking area for the Keel Mountain Preserve.

11. Lost Sink Falls Trail

This trail leads to one of the most dramatic waterfalls in the Huntsville area. After you've hiked a little more than a mile, you suddenly reach the Lost Sink, which is a massive, rocky hole in the forest floor. On the far side of the sink, water tumbles down the bluff and then slips over the lip to form a curtain and plunge more than 100 ft. From the edge of the sink, you can see the full height of the falls and get excellent photographs. While the Lost Sink Falls Trail sports a few moderately steep sections, most reasonably fit hikers can make the trip to the falls. Just take your time and bring adequate water. **If you hike with kids, keep them close to you at the edge of the sink, because this is a dangerous area. Also keep in mind that this waterfall does not flow as powerfully during dry periods, so try to do this trip within a few days after a good rain.

Distance: 1.95 mi.
Hiking Time: 1.5 hours
Elevation Gain/Loss: +774 ft., -184 ft.
Hiking Difficulty: Moderate to strenuous

Highlights

Lost Sink Falls: A few minutes before you reach the falls you hear them, though it's just a whisper. The sound rises slightly as you wind up the slope. Then, topping a low rise, you get your first glimpse of Lost Sink Falls. Beyond a veil of trees, tucked in a dark alcove, a curtain of water slips over dark stone. Walk forward a few yards, and you'll see the massive hole in the floor of the forest and get a look at the full height of the falls. If it's rained lately, you'll get quite a show, as a column of water plunges at least 100 ft. into the sink and dashes against black, glistening stone. At the bottom of the sink, the water slips farther down and disappears into a dark hole.

Waypoint/Mile

Trailhead (Waypoint 11) (34.65500, -86.41308) At the southeast end of the parking lot, enter the level gravel path to the right of the information kiosk. Follow the yellow and green blazes with arrows showing which direction you should walk.

Lost Sink Falls

The trail quickly transitions to packed earth and skirts the stony Buck Ditch streambed. The path moves through the shade of tall pines and cedar trees surrounded by thick underbrush. An abundance of roots form thick ribs across the trail, and rocks fill the path after 0.1 mi.

11-1 (34.65635, -86.41176) (0.17 mi.) You reach a T junction, with trails running left and right. Ignore the path to the left and turn right. The trail begins to climb, heading east.

The path becomes very rocky and climbs gradually. At 0.28 mi., the trail might be difficult to discern as it winds among boulders, so keep an eye out for the white diamond blazes on trees.

11-2 (34.65761, -86.41281) (0.3 mi.) At a Y junction, ignore the path that goes right and climbs along the base of a fallen tree. The Lost Sink Falls Trail actually bears left here to cross the tree and then drops gradually.

The path soon runs level through cedars, shagbark hickory and other hardwoods. Then the trail alternates between level stretches and places where you climb briefly on rocky and rooted ground. At 0.7 mi., the trail approaches the Land Trust boundary and takes a sharp right turn to head northeast over steeper terrain.

11-3 (34.66147, -86.41693) (0.8 mi.) Ignore the path that continues straight. The Lost Sink Falls Trail takes a sharp right turn at this point, and the narrow, rocky path climbs the slope. (A blaze on a tree indicates the turn and the direction you should walk.)

Lost Sink Falls

Catch your breath on a brief level section of trail, and then wind your way up the rocky slope, covering more steep ground. Near the 1-mi. point, you'll hear the first faint noise from the waterfall.

11-4 (34.66291, -86.41553) (1.1 mi.) The trail nears the edge of the sink. On the right, a path follows the lip of the sink. If you head this direction, be careful! There's nothing between the path and a steep drop-off. It's also possible to walk down into the sink. Just be aware that there's no proper trail, and the slope is slippery, muddy and rocky.

Many people end their hike at the waterfall. The Lost Sink Falls Trail continues for another 0.8 mi., but there aren't any views or nice features. You basically walk through a moderately dense forest where the brush and grass hugging the path become wilder and thicker as you progress. However, this is a very remote area, so if you're looking to extend your walk and go where few others venture, turn left at Waypoint 11-4, and begin a moderate ascent.

At 1.2 mi., the trail becomes more level and crosses a drier slope. The narrow path is sandy, and a variety of grasses line the trail. The path alternates between level stretches and brief climbs. When you've gone about 1.5 mi., you'll enjoy a long, level stretch. Because this part of the trail sees less traffic, the grasses and other foliage lining the path will brush against your legs. You might consider wearing long pants if you plan to hike the entire trail.

11-5 (34.66236, -86.40396) (1.95 mi.) After you cross a rocky drainage and go another 100 ft., you'll begin to climb a slope and reach the end of the trail. A cairn (a stack of rocks) and orange ribbons in the trees mark the end of the trail. From here, retrace your steps to return to the trailhead.

Trail Facts

The Morefield's Leather Flower: This nature preserve protects the Morefield's leather flower, named for James D. Morefield, a botanist who was 21 years old when he first discovered it on Round Top Mountain in Madison County in 1982.

Lost Sink Falls

Wade Mountain Nature Preserve

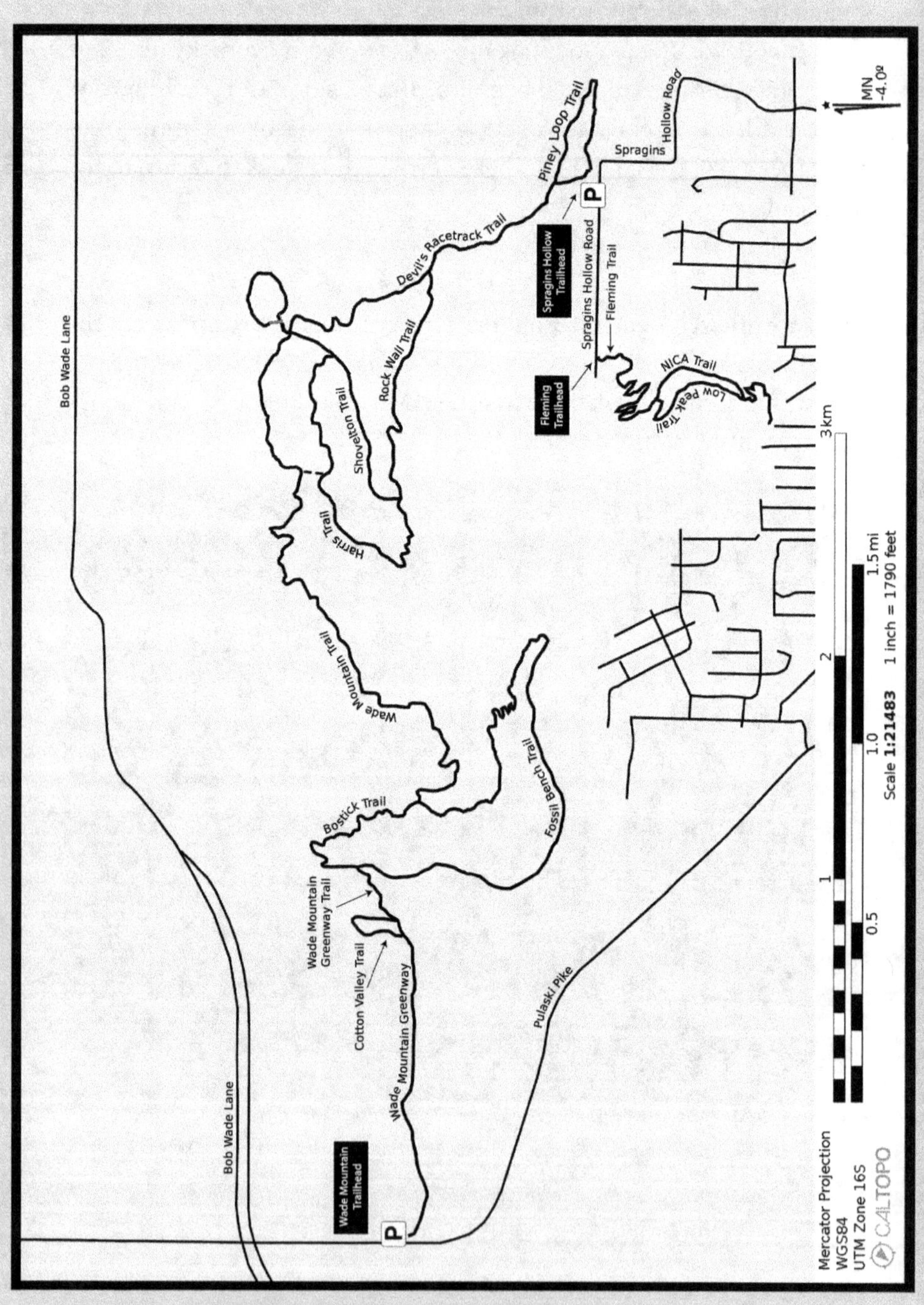

CHAPTER 4

Wade Mountain Nature Preserve

Compared to popular hiking areas like Monte Sano, the Wade Mountain Nature Preserve is much less familiar to many people in the Huntsville area. This is partly because Wade Mountain is located on the northern edge of Huntsville, well away from more densely populated parts of town. Also, the trail system has expanded over the years. When the preserve opened in 1997, it included only the Spragins Hollow Trailhead and the Devil's Racetrack Trail. But now the preserve covers 935 acres and includes more than a dozen trails measuring more than 12 miles in total. Slowly but steadily, people are discovering there's a lot more to explore in the preserve. While it might be a stretch to call Wade Mountain a "hidden gem," it's certainly an often-overlooked jewel in the collection of local trails.

While there are some easy walks within the preserve, many of the paths explore remote, rugged terrain, making this an ideal destination for adventurous hikers seeking more challenging treks.

One unique aspect of Wade Mountain is its microclimate, which some people describe as semiarid. The steep terrain is mostly composed of eroded limestone topped with a layer of sandy soil. As a result, water drains quickly from the mountain, leaving little moisture to serve local plants. This creates an unusually dry forest dominated by cedar, hickory and white ash. At the summit, you'll encounter glades with scrub grass and even cactus plants, creating a scene that resembles a mountain in the Western U.S. Adding to the Western feel is the fact that Wade Mountain is one of the only Land Trust properties where horseback riding is allowed, so you might share the trails with riders.

Several other features make Wade Mountain special. Because there's a trailhead west of the mountain and another to the southeast, you can leave cars at each end and walk the length of the mountain for a one-way trip exceeding five miles. As you're hiking, you'll also encounter places with a mysterious past. At the top of the list is the Devil's Racetrack, a grassy clearing that circles the summit, which supposedly served as a place for Cherokees to race their horses. For another strange bit of history, hike the Rock Wall Trail. No one is sure who constructed the long ribbon of stacked stones that stretches across the forest.

Perhaps Wade Mountain's most unusual feature is the trail designed specifically for mountain bikers. The Fleming Trailhead (a half-mile west of the Spragins Hollow Trailhead) provides access to the NICA Trail. This twisting path with banked turns was created so that local mountain bike teams could train for downhill competition.

General Information

Location: Wade Mountain Trailhead, 6946 Pulaski Pike NW, Huntsville, AL 35810; Spragins Hollow Trailhead, 10130 Spragins Hollow Rd. NW, Huntsville, AL 35810

Hours: Trails open dawn to dusk.

Primary trail activities allowed: Hiking, biking, horseback riding

Pets: Leashed pets allowed.

Fees: There are no required fees to use the trails.

Information: (256) 534-5263; www.landtrustnal.org/properties/wade-mountain-preserve/

Driving Directions

Wade Mountain Trailhead

From the junction of University Drive and U.S. 231/431 (Memorial Parkway), travel north on U.S. 231/431 for 7.8 mi. and then turn left onto Winchester Road. Travel 2.2 mi. on Winchester Rd. and then turn right onto Pulaski Pike. Travel 2.4 mi. on Pulaski Pike, and then turn right into the parking area for the Wade Mountain Greenway.

Spragins Hollow Trailhead

From the junction of I-565 and U.S. 231/431 (Memorial Parkway), travel north on U.S. 231/431 for 4.9 mi. and then turn left onto Hollow Road. Travel 0.7 mi. on Hollow Rd., and then turn right onto Spragins Hollow Road. Go 1.4 mi., and then turn right into the gravel parking area for the Spragins Hollow Trailhead.

SECTION 1:
Wade Mountain Greenway Trail, Cotton Valley Trail, Bostick Trail and Fossil Bench Trail

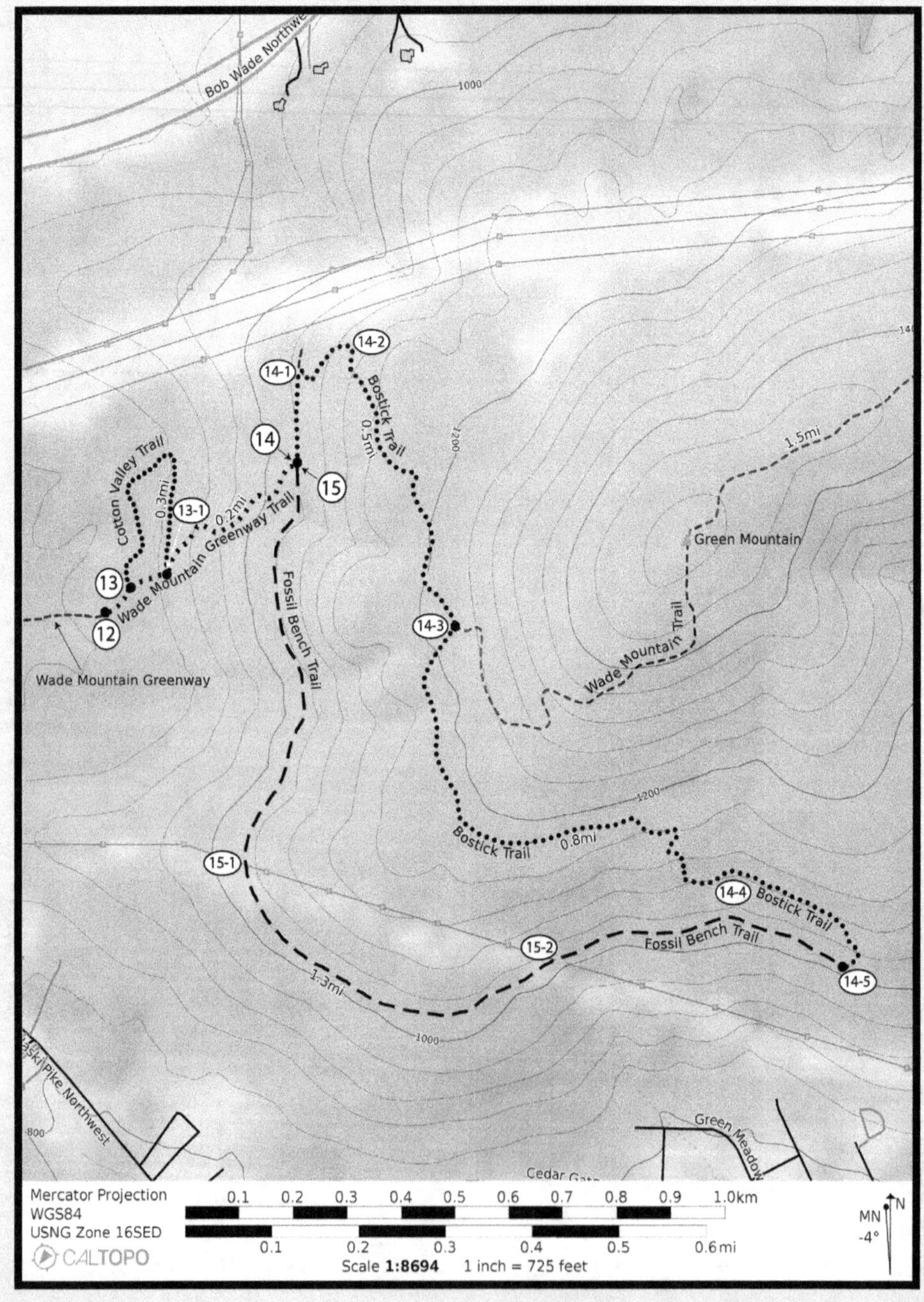

12. Wade Mountain Greenway Trail

While the Wade Mountain Greenway is paved, the Wade Mountain Greenway Trail is a natural path of packed earth and rock. It serves as the entryway to the trails that explore the western side of Wade Mountain. While this trail isn't especially steep, it does make a steady moderate ascent on a rocky slope to meet the Fossil Bench and Bostick trails.

Distance: 0.3 mi.

Hiking Time: 15 to 20 minutes

Elevation Gain/Loss: +181 ft., -0 ft.

Hiking Difficulty: Moderate

Location: Wade Mountain Nature Preserve, 6998 Pulaski Pike NW, #6946, Huntsville, AL 35810

Facilities: There are no restrooms and no sources of potable water at the trailhead, but there is a picnic table.

Driving Directions: See page 38 and use the directions for the Wade Mountain Trailhead.

Highlights

Escape the Crowds: The Wade Mountain Nature Preserve is not as well known as some other local hiking areas, so there are greater opportunities to escape the crowds. Granted, the paved greenway path sees heavy traffic at times, but the forest trails attract fewer folks. The Wade Mountain Greenway Trail will lead you to remote interior trails that offer plenty of solitude.

Waypoint/Mile

Trailhead (Waypoint 12) (34.81530, -86.62794) To reach the Wade Mountain Greenway Trail, begin at the Pulaski Pike Trailhead. Follow the paved Wade Mountain Greenway for 0.8 mi. to the spot where the paved path ends. Continue straight on the Wade Mountain Greenway Trail, a dirt path that heads northeast. The trail begins in a dense forest of pines and hardwoods with tangles of vines and scattered downed limbs.

13 (34.81571, -86.62762) (190 ft.) The Cotton Valley Trail intersects on the left and goes north. Continue straight, traveling northeast and rising gradually. Go another 250 ft. to reach Waypoint 13-1.

13-1 (34.81587, -86.62684) (440 ft.) The Cotton Valley Trail intersects on the left and runs north. Continue straight, ascending gradually to the north.

When you've walked about 0.1 mi., you'll wind through piles of boulders and continue a moderate climb in a more open hardwood forest.

14/15 (34.81755, -86.62410) (0.3 mi.) The Wade Mountain Greenway Trail ends at a T intersection with the Bostick Trail and Fossil Bench Trail. If you're up for an extended hike, you can take the Bostick and Fossil Bench trails, which form a 2.6-mi. loop.

13. Cotton Valley Trail

Add some distance to your day hike by taking this short, mostly level path that winds through tall pines and traverses an attractive slope of moss-covered boulders.

Distance: 0.35 mi.
Hiking Time: 10 minutes
Elevation Gain/Loss: +38 ft., -15 ft.
Hiking Difficulty: Easy
Location: Wade Mountain Nature Preserve, 6998 Pulaski Pike NW, #6946, Huntsville, AL 35810
Facilities: There are no restrooms and no sources of potable water at the trailhead, but there is a picnic table.
Driving Directions: See page 38 and use the directions for the Wade Mountain Trailhead.

Highlights

Diverse Landscape: Your hike begins in shaded woods with towering pines. Then the forest alternates between pines and hardwoods, and a wide drainage slices through the land. Finally, the route ends with a walk along an airy slope where tufts of moss cover the boulders scattered about.

Waypoint/Mile

Trailhead (Waypoint 13) (34.81571, -86.62762) To reach the Cotton Valley Trail, begin at the Pulaski Pike Trailhead. Follow the paved Wade Mountain Greenway for 0.8 mi. and then walk 440 ft. on the dirt Wade Mountain Greenway Trail. Turn left onto the Cotton Valley Trail and travel north on the path covered in pine needles.

Over the next 0.1 mi., the forest alternates between pine groves and areas with a mix of pines and mature hardwoods. At 0.25 mi., the trail skirts a deep drainage and then rises very gradually. Soon, the path turns away from drainage and runs south across a boulder-strewn slope.

13-1 (34.81587, -86.62684) (0.3 mi.) The Cotton Valley Trail ends at the intersection with the Wade Mountain Greenway Trail.

Trail Facts

Let's Go Places: The Cotton Valley Trail name is actually a nod to Toyota Motor Manufacturing of Alabama, which is a supporter of the Land Trust. Cottonvalley Drive is the road that leads to the Toyota manufacturing campus in northwest Huntsville.

14. Bostick Trail

The Bostick Trail provides access to expansive views to the north and explores remote woods on the lower flank of Wade Mountain. Those aiming to traverse the entire Wade Mountain Preserve can take the Bostick Trail to the Wade Mountain Trail, which crosses the mountain. The Bostick Trail also connects to the Fossil Bench Trail to create an easy to moderate 2.8-mi. loop.

Distance: 1.5 mi.
Hiking Time: 40 to 50 minutes
Elevation Gain/Loss: +181 ft., -205 ft.
Hiking Difficulty: Moderate
Location: Wade Mountain Nature Preserve, 6998 Pulaski Pike NW, #6946, Huntsville, AL 35810
Facilities: There are no restrooms and no sources of potable water at the trailhead, but there is a picnic table.

Driving Directions: See page TK and use the directions for the Wade Mountain Trailhead.

Highlights

Mountain Views: Once you've gone 0.1 mi. down the trail, a short spur trail continues straight to the north and leads to a powerline break. At the edge of this break there is a bench where you can sit and enjoy a panoramic view of the valley and low hills that lie north of Wade Mountain.

Rock Shelter: Plan to pause and take a break at 1.3 mi., where a small rock alcove occupies the top of a rocky drainage. Set deep in the forest, this is a peaceful place, and the rock shelter is one of the more visually interesting stops along the trail.

A small natural shelter lies near the Bostick Trail.

Waypoint/Mile

Trailhead (Waypoint 14) (34.81753, -86.62406) To reach the Bostick Trail, begin at the Pulaski Pike Trailhead. Follow the paved Wade Mountain Greenway to the Wade Mountain Greenway Trail. Follow the Wade Mountain Greenway Trail 0.3 mi. to its junction with the Bostick Trail and Fossil Bench Trail. Turn left and travel north on the Bostick Trail.

14-1 (34.81909, -86.62424) (0.1 mi.) Take a sharp turn to the right and ascend to the east to continue on the Bostick Trail. (If you continue straight at Waypoint 14-1, you can walk about 130 ft. to a powerline break. The path ends here and offers expansive views of the valley to the north.)

14-2 (34.81952, -86.62310) (0.2 mi.) The Bostick Trail turns right and climbs to the southeast. If you were to go straight here, you would hit the powerline break.

Near 0.2 mi., an old, faint trail inter-sects on the right. Ignore this and keep bearing left to stay on the Bostick Trail. At 0.3 mi., the significant climbing ends, and the path gently rolls along. Near 0.4 mi., the trail runs fairly level as the upper reaches of Wade Mountain tower over the forest.

14-3 (34.81500, -86.62094) (0.6 mi.) At the trail junction, the Bostick Trail goes right and descends to the southwest. If you go straight, you'll enter the Wade Mountain Trail, which ascends to the southeast.

The trail is mostly level as it tra-verses the lower slopes of Wade Moun-

Hiking the Bostick Trail on Wade Mountain

tain and crosses small, seasonal streams. At 0.9 mi., the path moves east to cross the southern side of the mountain. In this dry area, grass lines the single-track path surrounded by hardwoods and cedars. To the right, above the tops of the trees, you can see a hazy blue band of distant ridges. At 1.1 mi., the Bostick Trail begins to descend a rocky slope.

14-4 (34.81124, -86.61539) (1.3 mi.) The trail crosses a rocky drainage, and to the left, a few yards up the slope, is a rock shelter.

14-5 (34.80964, -86.61310) (1.5 mi.) After a short, steep drop, the Bostick Trail ends at the junction with the Fossil Bench Trail, which intersects on the right and heads northwest. The path to the left is an unmarked trail that heads east and soon goes beyond the Land Trust boundary.

Trail Facts

Marie Bostick: The trail is named in recognition of the Land Trust's executive director, Marie Bostick, who played a key role in preserving large portions of Wade Mountain.

15. Fossil Bench Trail

Compared with other Wade Mountain trails, Fossil Bench is wider and more consistently level, allowing hikers to add some easy extra miles to their hike. Plus, you can link this path and Bostick Trail for a moderately challenging loop that explores quiet and remote sections of Wade Mountain. As its name implies, this trail is rich in fossils, so scan rocks along the way to see impressions of ancient marine organisms.

Distance: 1.3 mi.

Hiking Time: 30 to 40 minutes

Elevation Gain/Loss: +87 ft., -108 ft.

Hiking Difficulty: Easy

Location: Wade Mountain Nature Preserve, 6998 Pulaski Pike NW, #6946, Huntsville, AL 35810

Facilities: There are no restrooms and no sources of potable water at the trailhead, but there is a picnic table.

Driving Directions: See page 38 and use the directions for the Wade Mountain Trailhead.

Highlights

Full of Fossils: The Fossil Bench Trail traverses a limestone foundation that was laid down 330 to 340 million years ago as marine deposits in a shallow sea. It's full of fossils of marine organisms, including crinoids, brachiopods, bryozoa and coral. This limestone bed is especially erosion-resistant because it's composed of calcareous shale, which does not dissolve as easily as the surrounding limestone, says Ben Hoksbergen, a lecturer in the department of history at the University of Alabama in Huntsville. "Grassy glades are a typical habitat in these types of environments, and fossils are easily exposed in the crumbly shale on trails and in open areas where the vegetation is sparse," he says.

Waypoint/Mile

Trailhead (Waypoint 15) (34.81761, -86.62425) To reach the Fossil Bench Trail, begin at the Pulaski Pike Trailhead. Follow the paved Wade Mountain Greenway to the Wade Mountain Greenway Trail.

Follow the Wade Mountain Greenway Trail 0.3 mi. to its junction with the Bostick Trail and Fossil Bench Trail. Turn right and travel south on the Fossil Bench Trail.

Gradually descend on the wide path, which is surrounded by cedars and mature hardwoods. You'll occasionally cross slabs of rock, though the trail is generally a mix of packed earth and grass.

The Fossil Bench Trail offers views of distant hills.

15-1 (34.81119, -86.62524) (0.48 mi.) The trail crosses a powerline break. Continue across the break, traveling southeast. At the middle of the clearing, look to your left (northwest) to see the distant folds of gray and blue ridges stretching to the horizon.

15-2 (34.80985, -86.61870) (0.9 mi.) Cross the powerline corridor again. Continue across, traveling northeast, and look to your right (east) down the corridor for more mountain views.

As you continue, the trail remains wide and generally level. While the path runs along the rim of a steep slope, curtains of trees obscure views of the valley below. Still, it's a nice walk, as the wide trail corridor allows ample sunlight to brighten the way.

14-5 (34.80961, -86.61315) (1.3 mi.) The Fossil Bench Trail ends at the junction with the Bostick Trail, which intersects on the left and climbs to the northeast.

Trail Facts

A Geology "Bench": In geography and geology, a bench is a long, narrow strip of land that's fairly level and has steeper slopes above and below it.

SECTION 2:
Wade Mountain Trail and Harris Trail

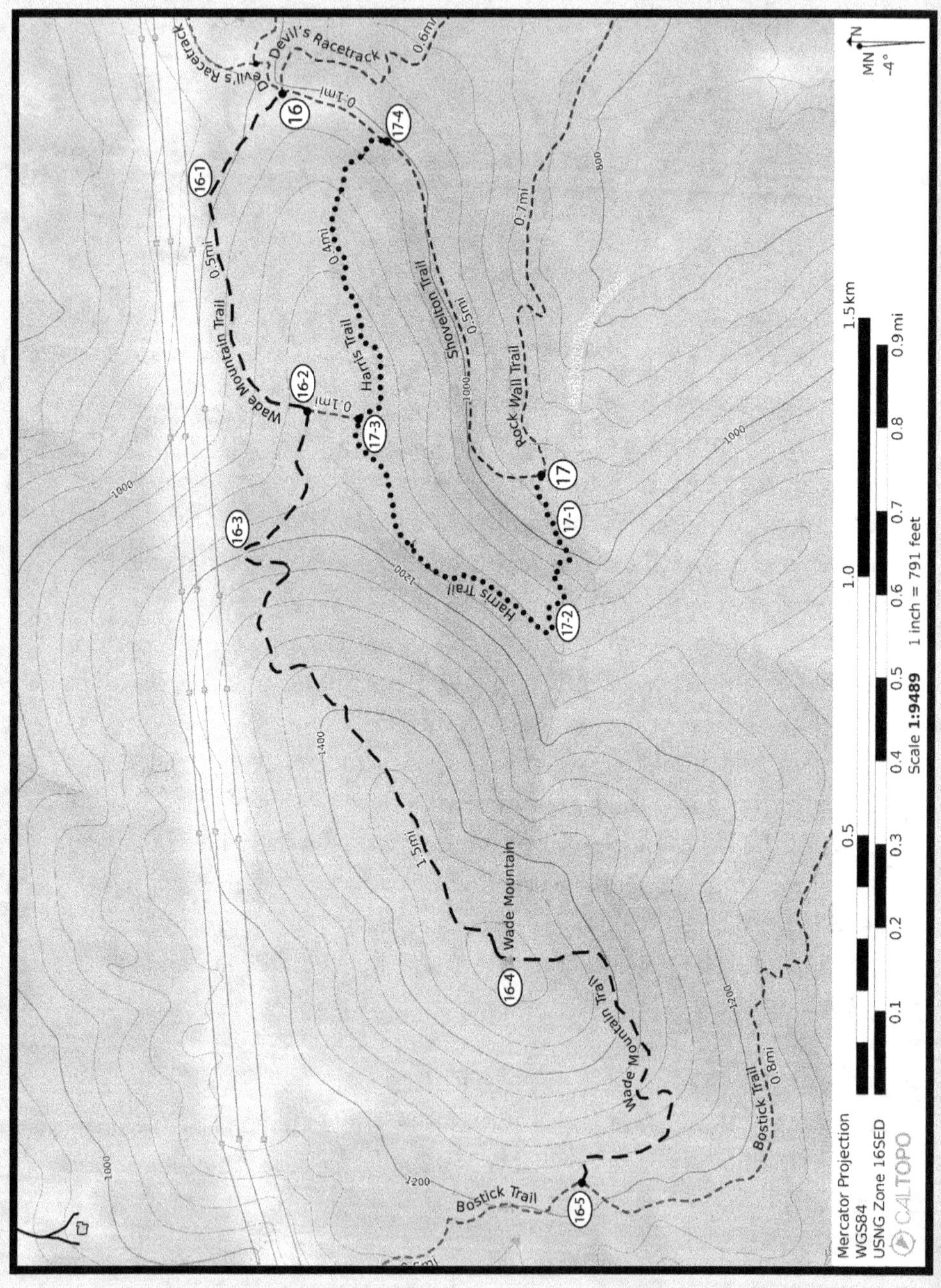

16. Wade Mountain Trail

The Wade Mountain Trail offers hikers the opportunity to do an extended day hike in mostly wild and remote forest. Linking the eastern and western sides of the Wade Mountain Nature Preserve, the trail stretches more than 2 mi. and climbs to the Wade Mountain summit at 1,493 ft.

Distance: 2.1 mi.

Hiking Time: 1 to 1.5 hours

Elevation Gain/Loss: +536 ft., -334 ft.

Hiking Difficulty: Moderate

Location: Wade Mountain Nature Preserve, 10130 Spragins Hollow Rd. NW, Huntsville, AL 35810

Facilities: There are no facilities and no sources of potable water at the trailhead, but there is a picnic table.

Driving Directions: See page 38 and use the directions for the Spragins Hollow Trailhead.

Highlights

Wade Mountain Summit: From the summit of Wade Mountain, you won't get any dramatic views. However, there's satisfaction in reaching the top of any mountain. Plus, this is not some heavily trafficked mountaintop with roads and houses. Sitting miles away from civilization, it's almost completely wild.

A Long Walk in Remote Woods: If you spot cars at the Spragins Hollow Trailhead (on the east side of the mountain) and the Wade Mountain Trailhead on the western side, you can link trails (including the Wade Mountain Trail) for a one-way hike that's at least 5 mi. Of course, your trek can be even longer if you take a less direct route. In a couple of places, the Wade Mountain Trail runs near powerline breaks, which interrupt the wilderness experience. But for much of the route, civilization will be out of sight and out of mind.

Waypoint/Mile

Trailhead (Waypoint 16) (34.82060, -86.59769) You can access the Wade Mountain Trail from the Pulaski Pike Trailhead on the western side of the preserve or the Spragins Hollow Trailhead on the eastern side of the preserve. This trail description begins at the Spragins Hollow Trailhead. At the north side of the parking lot, go left of the trailhead kiosk and follow the Devil's Racetrack Trail. At 1.3 mi., near the top of the mountain, you'll reach a four-way junction. Bear right to take the Wade Mountain Trail, which ascends gradually to the northwest.

16-1 (34.82173, -86.60018) (0.16 mi.) The Wade Mountain Trail reaches the powerline break and turns left to head west. You soon begin a moderate ascent in dense forest.

16-2 (34.81989, -86.60465) (0.5 mi.) At the junction, the Wade Mountain Trail turns right to head west. If you continue straight, you'll follow a connector trail that goes 353 ft. and ends at a junction with the Harris Trail.

16-3 (34.82121, -86.60768) (0.76 mi.) The trail reaches the powerline corridor and offers excellent views of the valley to the north. You'll soon make a left turn to go south and begin moving away from the powerline.

At 0.8 mi. you begin walking through a pretty section of the trail with stands of cedars and many trees wearing coats of moss. After another 0.1 mi., the path approaches the powerline again. On the north side of the mountain, you can see the green valley below. Another excellent section of the trail begins just beyond the 1-mi. mark. You'll pass through a boulder field and soon encounter massive oaks, including a tree so stout you can't get your arms around it.

16-4 (34.81640, -86.61630) (1.5 mi.) The path reaches the summit of Wade Mountain at 1,493 ft.

At 1.7 mi. the descent from the summit is slightly steeper, though it's still just a moderate drop. The trail passes a garden of pale stones brightened by layers of emerald moss. The forest is largely clear, allowing you to see distant ridges that look like blue haze above the trees. At 2 mi., the views disappear as the trail moves through dense stands of small cedars and younger hardwoods. The single-track path descends a boulder-strewn slope.

16-5 (34.81499, -86.62096) (2.1 mi.) The Wade Mountain Trail ends at the junction with the Bostick Trail.

17. Harris Trail

This interior trail takes you on a comfortable walk and includes nice spots to linger in the sun or relax in the shade. The Harris Trail also links to the Mountain, Shovelton and Rockwall trails, giving you several options for loop hikes on the east side of Wade Mountain.

Distance: 1.1 mi.
Hiking Time: 30 to 40 minutes
Elevation Gain/Loss: +242 ft., -180 ft.
Hiking Difficulty: Easy
Location: Wade Mountain Nature Preserve, 10130 Spragins Hollow Rd. NW, Huntsville, AL 35810
Facilities: There are no facilities and no sources of potable water at the trailhead, but there is a picnic table.
Driving Directions: See page 38 and use the directions for the Spragins Hollow Trailhead.

Highlights

Pleasant Rest Stops: This is the perfect trail for anyone who wants to decompress, move at an easy pace, and pause for a while to soak in what nature has to offer. At 0.2 mi., a wide and rocky streambed provides an attractive, sunny spot to rest awhile. At the end of the trail, a bench sits in a shaded cedar grove, making it the perfect place to sit and enjoy lunch.

Waypoint/Mile

Trailhead (Waypoint 17) (34.81548, -86.60605) To reach the Harris Trail, begin at the Spragins Hollow Trailhead. Take the Devil's Race-track Trail 0.6 mi. to the junction with the Rock Wall Trail. Then walk 0.7 mi. to the junction with the Shovelton Trail and Harris Trail. Follow the Harris Trail, which is a wide path that climbs to the northwest.

The trail soon narrows and crosses rocky drainages. Ahead, moss lines the slightly rutted path, which makes a gradual to moderate ascent through an open hardwood forest dotted with cedars.

17-1 (34.81552, -86.60724) (421 ft.) The Harris Trail turns right and ascends the hill going northwest. At this junction, an old path blocked with logs goes straight to the southwest.

After you've walked a little more than 0.1 mi., you'll turn right to head north and skirt a low band of rocks. At 0.16 mi., hook left to pass through the shade of cedars and wind your way through boulders. Near 0.2 mi., the trail gets a bit steeper, but only for about 40 ft.

17-2 (34.81542, -86.60885) (0.2 mi.) The trail approaches a sunny streambed with stepped rocks. This is a peaceful place to pause for a while. Continuing on, the Harris Trail hooks right to run north.

The path widens briefly and runs level across flat stone. But before you know it, the trail narrows again and rises gradually. The grade steepens slightly at 0.45 mi., and at 0.5 mi. you'll cross a stream that's about 8 ft. wide and fed by a spring. At 0.62 mi., the trail climbs gradually through woods that are more open, and the crown of a hill is visible on the left.

17-3 (34.81904, -86.60485) (0.7 mi.) At the T junction, a connector trail intersects on the left and runs north for about 350 ft. to meet the Wade Mountain Trail. Continue straight and travel southeast to stay on the Harris Trail.

At 0.9 mi., the trail eases into thicker forest and soon dives down a rocky slope in the shade of cedars.

17-4 (34.81865, -86.59895) (1.1 mi.) You reach the bottom of the rocky descent, and the Harris Trail ends at the junction with the Shovelton Trail, in a stand of cedars. A bench sitting in the shade makes a good place to take a break.

Trail Facts

Former Family Farm: For many years, most of Wade Mountain was part of the Harris family farm. The city of Huntsville purchased the center portion of the mountain from James Harris, a retired colonel, who still owns land near the mountain. So the Harris Trail crosses land that's actually owned by the city rather than the Land Trust of North Alabama.

SECTION 3:
Devil's Racetrack, Piney Loop Trail, Rock Wall Trail and Shovelton Trail

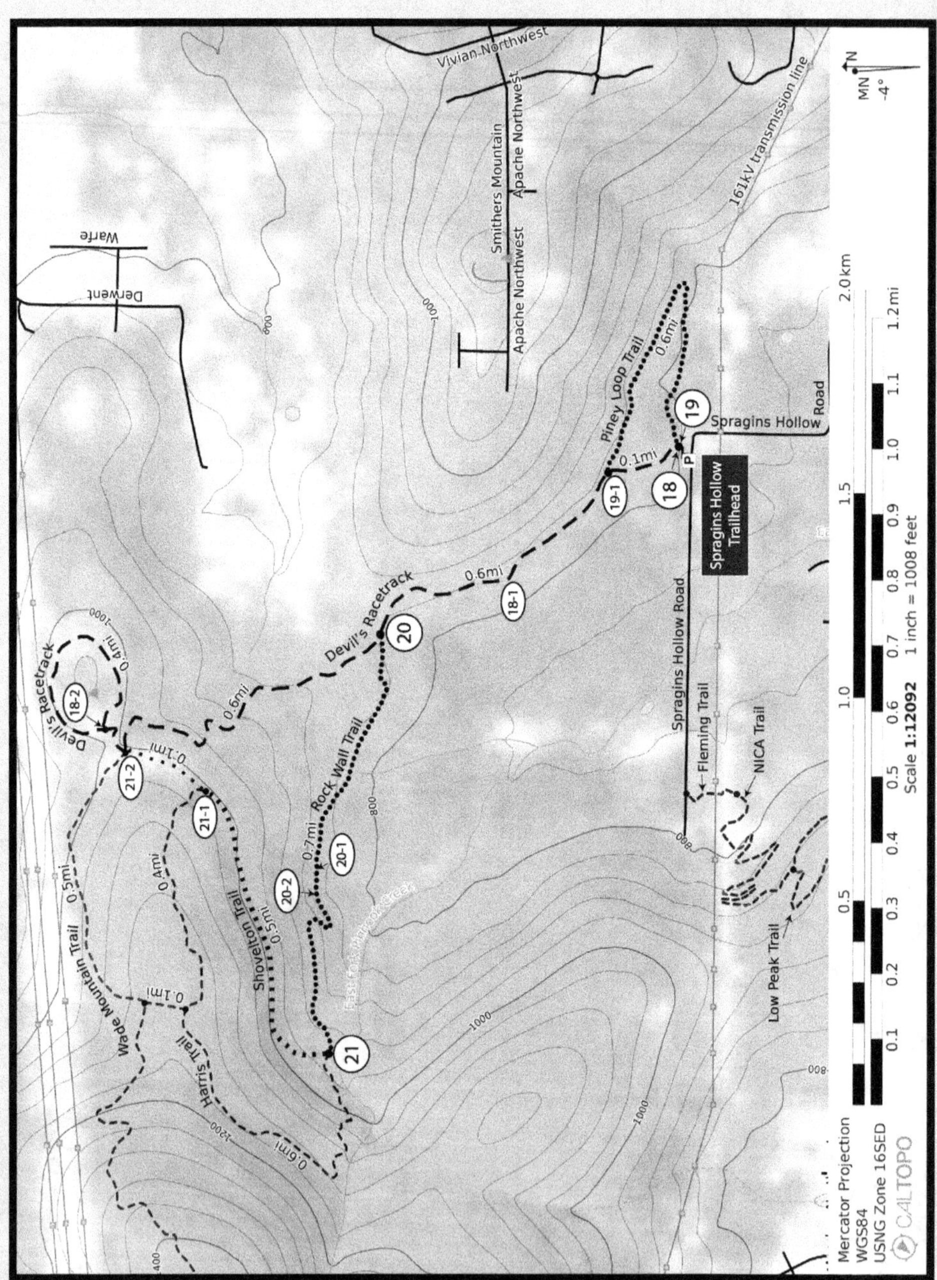

18. Devil's Racetrack

The Devil's Racetrack is one of the most popular trails on Wade Mountain, and it's an ideal day hike for a wide variety of hikers. The path climbs steadily for a little more than a mile, though it's never steep. Along the way, hikers ascend through an attractive hardwood forest, wind among fields of boulders, and cruise though shaded groves of cedars. At the top, they're rewarded with a walk along the "racetrack," a narrow path that encircles a scenic knoll topped with boulders, tall pines and cedars. If you do the entire trail and follow it back to the parking lot, the round trip is about 3 mi., which is perfect if you have a couple of hours to hike.

Distance: 1.8 mi.
Hiking Time: 45 minutes to 1 hour
Elevation Gain/Loss: +305 ft., -106 ft.
Hiking Difficulty: Easy to moderate
Location: Wade Mountain Nature Preserve, 10130 Spragins Hollow Rd. NW, Huntsville, AL 35810
Facilities: There are no facilities and no sources of potable water at the trailhead, but there is a picnic table.
Driving Directions: See page 38 and use the directions for the Spragins Hollow Trailhead.

Highlights

Devil's Racetrack Summit: If I had to pick a favorite trail on Wade Mountain, this would be it, mostly for the scenery and terrain at the summit. The trail climbs to a knoll at the top of the mountain. Here, a wide, grassy clearing surrounds a rock pile and stand of tall cedars and pines that are elevated on a bump of land. Compared with other nearby mountains, the soil here is drier and thinner, so Wade Mountain's peak looks unique. People have found prickly pear cactus growing at the summit, and to me it resembles a high-desert Western wilderness. Plus, there's the "racetrack," a narrow path that encircles the summit. According to folklore, local Cherokees raced horses around this path, and it's easy to imagine the rumble of pounding hooves and dust flying from the track. The scenery and the strange history make this a special place.

Waypoint/Mile

Trailhead (Waypoint 18) (34.80788, -86.58979) The Devil's Racetrack begins at the Spragins Hollow Trailhead. At the north side of the parking lot, go to the trailhead kiosk and head left. (The beginning of the Piney Loop Trail is to the right.) The Devil's Racetrack follows the log-lined path to the left of the picnic table and then goes north, shaded by tall pines and cedars.

19-1 (34.80950, -86.59043) (0.1 mi.) The Piney Loop Trail intersects on the right and heads east. To continue on the Devil's Racetrack, bear left and go to the northwest.

The trail quickly narrows and winds among boulders. At 0.15 mi., forested land on the left stretches to the west and meets a prominent hill.

18-1 (34.81171, -86.59346) (0.3 mi.) On the left is a set of three benches. To the west, you can see above the pines the top of a peak on Wade Mountain.

From the benches, the trail bends to the right and heads north, climbing gradually. Near the 0.5-mi. point, the path becomes rockier and rises moderately as small boulders line the trail. As you hike, you'll encounter a few more benches, such as the one at 0.6 mi.

20 (34.81466, -86.59503) (0.6 mi.) The Rock Wall Trail intersects on the left and is mostly level as it bends to the west. To continue on the Devil's Racetrack Trail, go straight and head northwest.

The Devil's Racetrack Trail climbs gradually into a section that's much more open. At 0.84 mi., you reach another bench and then begin winding among moss-covered boulders. At 1.2 mi., the character of the forest changes as the light dims and the path squeezes between cedars covered in moss.

21-2 (34.82040, -86.59798) (1.3 mi.) At the four-way junction, the Wade Mountain Trail intersects on the right and ascends gradually to the northwest. Also, the Shovelton Trail intersects on the left and goes south. To continue on the Devil's Racetrack, take a hard right turn and go to the northeast on the level path.

18-2 (34.82093, -86.59736) (1.39 mi.) At the Y junction, the Devil's Racetrack loop begins. Go to the right and head east.

At 1.6 mi., the trail skirts the powerline break and goes west, offering wide views of the valley to the north. Go another 978 ft. to complete the loop and return to Waypoint 18-2. From 18-2, continue straight to retrace your steps back to the trailhead.

Hiking the Devil's Racetrack Trail atop Wade Mountain

Trail Facts

Unusual Microclimate: Wade Mountain is steep, made mostly of limestone, and topped with a layer of sandy soil. As a result, water drains quickly from the mountain, creating an almost-arid climate that's rare for northern Alabama. As you hike Wade Mountain, you'll encounter a mix of trees that thrive in drier environments, including cedar, white ash and hickory. At the summit, the Devil's Racetrack Trail passes through a scrub glade, which is another feature found in arid mountain environments.

19. Piney Loop Trail

The Piney Loop Trail rises and falls gently as it winds through tall pines and sections of open hardwood forest. There are few if any attractions on this trail, so I recommend it simply as a way to add some distance to your hike or run.

Distance: 0.6 mi.
Hiking Time: 15 minutes
Elevation Gain/Loss: +66 ft., -37 ft.
Hiking Difficulty: Easy
Location: Wade Mountain Nature Preserve, 10130 Spragins Hollow Rd. NW, Huntsville, AL 35810

Facilities: There are no facilities and no sources of potable water at the trailhead, but there is a picnic table.

Driving Directions: See page 38 and use the directions for the Spragins Hollow Trailhead.

Waypoint/Mile

Trailhead (Waypoint 19) (34.80788, -86.58979) The Piney Loop Trail begins at the Spragins Hollow Trailhead. At the northeast end of the parking lot, proceed to the back of the trailhead kiosk and go right. As you head east, you'll cross a small wooden footbridge.

As the path begins, dense stands of honeysuckle line the path and hug the trunks of sweetgum trees. After walking nearly 300 ft., you walk through the first bed of pine needles, while cedars and oaks add to the forest mix.

As you continue on, the trail rises and falls easily, and the forest alternates between areas dominated by tall pines and sections where hardwoods reign. There aren't really any interesting views along the way, and there are few distinguishing features, save for a couple of depressions in the land.

At 0.3 mi., the trail makes a hairpin turn back to the northwest and cuts across a slope. The path alternates between packed earth and stretches of dirt and rocks. As you continue, you'll encounter more areas where honeysuckle has invaded the woods. At 0.6 mi., the forest once more transitions to hardwoods as you climb over a short rise.

19-1 (34.80950, -86.59043) (0.6 mi.) The Piney Loop Trail ends at the junction with the Devil's Racetrack Trail.

20. Rock Wall Trail

This trail visits one of the more interesting features on Wade Mountain. Near the 0.4-mi. point, a long wall of stacked stones stretches across the forest. No one really knows who built the wall, so you can speculate on its origin as you climb gradually to reach a nice rest stop at the junction of the Rock Wall, Harris and Shovelton trails. The three paths meet in a small clearing where a bench sits in the shade of cedar trees.

Distance: 0.7 mi.

Hiking Time: 20 to 25 minutes

Elevation Gain/Loss: +147 ft., -48 ft.

Hiking Difficulty: Easy to moderate

Location: Wade Mountain Nature Preserve, 10130 Spragins Hollow Rd. NW, Huntsville, AL 35810

Facilities: There are no facilities and no sources of potable water at the trailhead, but there is a picnic table.

Driving Directions: See page 38 and use the directions for the Spragins Hollow Trailhead.

Highlights

Mysterious Rock Wall: When you've walked almost 0.4 mi., a long span of the rock wall is visible to the right, up the slope. Some people think farmers constructed the wall to serve as a property boundary, but no one has found further evidence of a homestead near the wall.

Waypoint/Mile

Trailhead (Waypoint 20) (34.81471, -86.59498) To reach the beginning of the Rock Wall Trail, begin at the Spragins Hollow Trailhead.

At the north side of the parking lot, go to the left of the trailhead kiosk and follow the Devil's Racetrack Trail. Walk 0.7 mi. to the junction with the Rock Wall Trail, which intersects on the left. Turn left onto the Rock Wall Trail and head west.

The hike begins in an uncluttered forest of hardwoods and tall pines with hazy blue mountains on the horizon to the south. At 0.3 mi. the forest transitions to dense stands of cedars and underbrush.

20-1 (34.81610, -86.60111) (0.39 mi.) The trail passes through a break in the rock wall. To the right, the rock wall continues uphill. To the left, the wall runs down the slope.

20-2 (34.81611, -86.60194) (0.43 mi.) Look to the right and up the slope to see a long section of the rock wall, which extends some 200 ft.

Near the 0.5-mi. point, look left for a clear view of a prominent hilltop on Wade Mountain. At 0.69 mi., the path rises gradually, bordered by deep-green moss and thick woods.

21 (34.81575, -86.60622) (0.7 mi.) The Rock Wall Trail ends at a junction where you can turn right to follow the Shovelton Trail north or go straight to take the Harris Trail northwest.

Trail Facts (and Theories)

A Rock Wall Theory: The wall could have been built by Scottish or Irish farmers. As they cleared land for crops, they would pick up stones and stack them to form walls that marked boundaries for fields and served as barriers to keep animals contained.

21. Shovelton Trail

After climbing briefly, this easy path makes a long, level run along an upper flank of Wade Mountain. It's a good option if you're a trail runner looking for a fairly flat path. When you reach the end of the trail, extend your outing by taking the Devil's Racetrack Trail, which makes a level loop around the summit and offers panoramic views to the north.

Distance: 0.6 mi.

Hiking Time: 15 to 20 minutes

Elevation Gain/Loss: +83 ft., -27 ft.

Hiking Difficulty: Easy

Location: Wade Mountain Nature Preserve, 10130 Spragins Hollow Rd. NW, Huntsville, AL 35810

Facilities: There are no facilities and no sources of potable water at the trailhead, but there is a picnic table.

Driving Directions: See page 38 and use the directions for the Spragins Hollow Trailhead.

Highlights

Loop Options: This interior trail intersects with several other paths, including the Rock Wall Trail, Harris Trail, Wade Mountain Trail and Devil's Racetrack Trail. You can use the Shovelton Trail to craft a variety of loop hikes that explore the eastern side of the mountain and stay within relatively close range of the Spragins Hollow Trailhead.

Waypoint/Mile

Trailhead (Waypoint 21) (34.81575, -86.60622) To reach the Shovelton Trail, begin at the Spragins Hollow Trailhead. Take the Devil's Racetrack Trail 0.6 mi. to the junction with the Rock Wall Trail. Then walk 0.7 mi. to the junction with the Shovelton Trail and Harris Trail. Turn right onto the Shovelton Trail and begin climbing to the north.

After a short, gradual climb, the single-track path of dirt and gravel is fairly level. It begins in an open forest and soon slips into dense cedars. At 0.3 mi., the path gets a bit rockier but remains pretty level. You won't have many views until you've gone almost 0.5 mi. and a knoll to the south peeks over the tops of cedars.

21-1 (34.81865, -86.59907) (0.5 mi.) The trail enters a shady grove of cedars with a small clearing. To the left, the Harris Trail intersects and climbs to the northwest. To continue on the Shovelton Trail, go straight and travel northeast on the level path.

The trail descends a strip of flat rock to enter a drainage, where rocks and roots create a bumpy treadway.

21-2 (34.82034, -86.59801) (0.6 mi.) The Shovelton Trail ends at a wide junction where it meets the Devil's Racetrack Trail and the Wade Mountain Trail.

Trail Facts

The Shovelton Family: When you've walked 428 ft. on the trail, you'll reach a bench built by John Moser of Boy Scout Troop 634. For his Eagle Scout project, he installed the bench to honor his grandparents Corinne and Graham Shovelton.

SECTION 4:
Fleming Trail, NICA Trail and Low Peak Trail

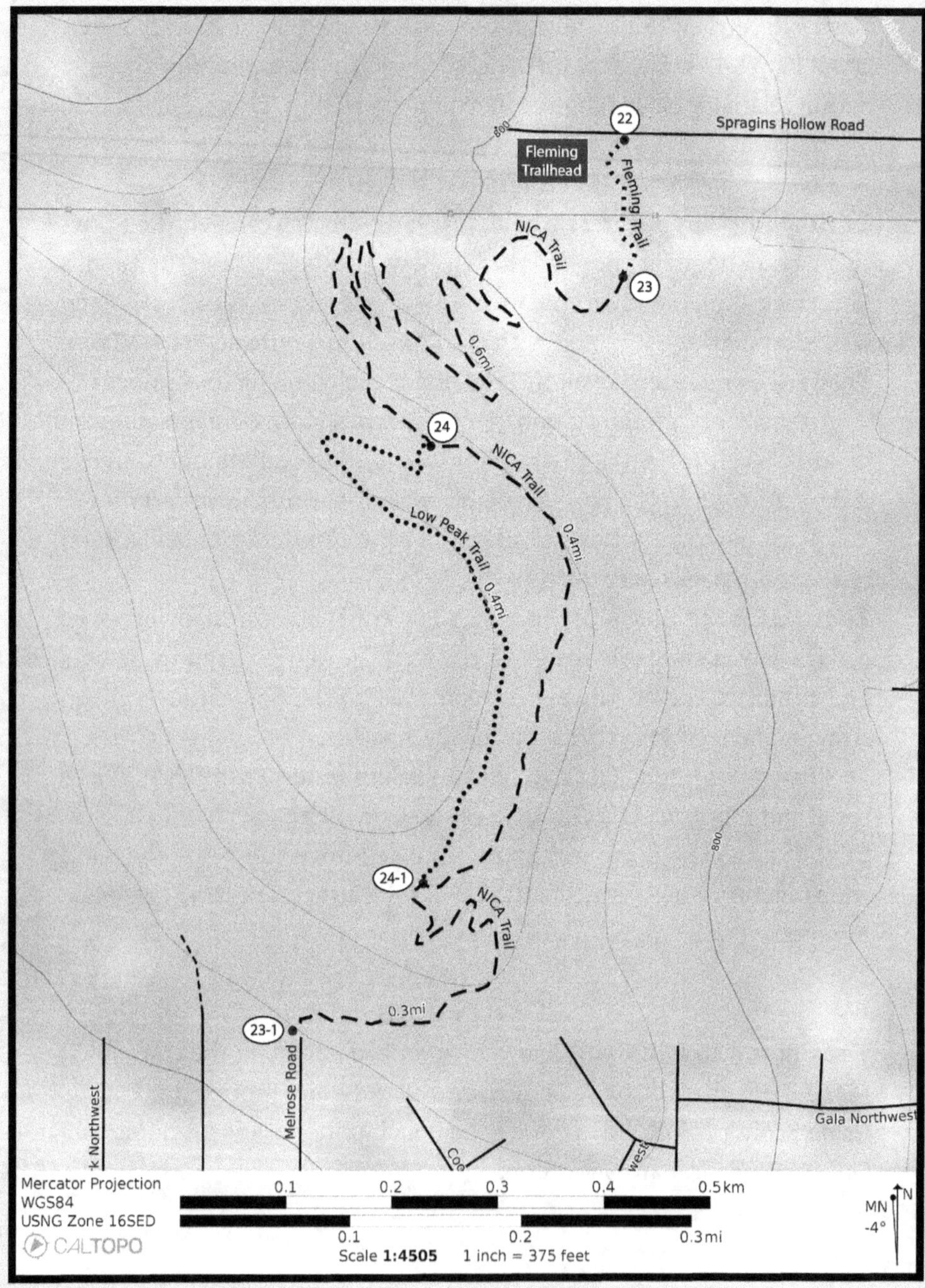

22. Fleming Trail

The Fleming Trail is a short path that connects the Fleming Trailhead area to the NICA and Low Peak trails. From the Fleming Trail, you'll walk a little more than 400 ft. to reach the NICA Trail, which is designed for technical mountain biking. If you walk 0.7 mi. on the NICA Trail, you'll reach the Low Peak Trail, which runs near the summit of Wade Mountain's lowest peak.

Distance: 0.08 mi. (466 ft.)
Hiking Time: 2 minutes
Elevation Gain/Loss: +3 ft., -10 ft.
Hiking Difficulty: Easy
Location: Wade Mountain Nature Preserve, 10130 Spragins Hollow Rd. NW, Huntsville, AL 35810
Facilities: There are no facilities and no sources of potable water at the trailhead.
Driving Directions: See page 38 and use the directions for the Spragins Hollow Trailhead.

Waypoint/Mile

Trailhead (Waypoint 22) (34.80759, -86.59909) There is no parking area near the beginning of the Fleming and NICA trails, so park at the Spragins Hollow Trailhead. Exit the parking area and turn right to go west on Spragins Hollow Road. After walking 0.5 mi., you'll see on the left a fenced area and trailhead kiosk marking the Fleming Trailhead. From the kiosk, follow the Fleming Trail south.

The Fleming Trail passes through a pine forest and at 208 ft. crosses a 100-ft.-wide powerline corridor. On the other side of the break, you'll enter dense woods.

23 (34.80647, -86.59906) (466 ft.) The Fleming Trail ends at the junction with the NICA Trail.

Trail Facts

Community Effort: This might just be a short, unremarkable path, but it represents something significant. It's part of a trail system that was made possible by many members of the Huntsville community working together. The trail is named for the Fleming family, who sold this piece of property to the Land Trust of North Alabama at a reduced rate, which really made the purchase possible. According to the Land Trust, the Alabama Department of Economic and Community Affairs provided a matching grant to help purchase the land, while the city of Huntsville, Madison County and the Land Trust also provided matching funds. It's a perfect example of a true community effort to preserve land and provide recreation opportunities.

23. NICA Trail

In 2017, the Huntsville Area Mountain Bike Riders (HAMR) and members of mountain bike teams at local schools worked with the Land Trust to construct the NICA (National Interscholastic Cycling Association) Trail. While it's designed for biking, I've included the trail in the book because hikers must travel it to reach the multiuse Low Peak Trail.

The NICA Trail is a wide path with many switchbacks and curves, including banked turns. The trail is not especially steep and makes a steady, moderate climb to a plateau that runs below a small summit on Wade Mountain. The NICA Trail terminates at the end of Melrose Road in a residential area. While you're hiking, keep your eyes and ears alert for bikers descending the trail.

Distance: 1.3 mi.
Hiking Time: 30 to 40 minutes
Elevation Gain/Loss: +172 ft., -114 ft.
Hiking Difficulty: Moderate
Location: Wade Mountain Nature Preserve, 10130 Spragins Hollow Rd. NW, Huntsville, AL 35810
Facilities: There are no facilities and no sources of potable water at the trailhead.
Driving Directions: See page 38 and use the directions for the Spragins Hollow Trailhead.

Highlights

Access to Less-Traveled Trails: The NICA Trail leads to the Low Peak Trail, which sees much less traffic than most other paths in town. Many people simply aren't aware of Wade Mountain, and they're even less aware of the Fleming Trailhead, which sits tucked away on a remote country road. During the middle of the week, or on an early weekend morning, you might have the woods to yourself as you make the quiet, peaceful climb up this humble corner of Wade Mountain.

Waypoint/Mile

Trailhead (Waypoint 23) (34.80647, -86.59906) There is no parking area near the beginning of the Fleming and NICA trails, so park at the Spragins Hollow Trailhead. Exit the parking area and turn right to go west on Spragins Hollow Road. After walking 0.5 mi., you'll see on the left a fenced area and trailhead kiosk marking the Fleming Trailhead. From the kiosk, follow the Fleming Trail south 466 ft. to the beginning of the NICA Trail. Continue straight and ascend gradually to the southwest.

The packed-earth path rises gradually through young pines and poplars. Over the next 0.5 mi., a series of banked turns provide a nice flow for riders. Periodic bumps, tight turns and rocky sections make a downhill run a bit more fun and challenging. At 0.69 mi., the forest looks a bit more interesting as a field of moss-covered boulders covers the upper slope.

24 (34.80508, -86.60093) (0.67 mi.) The Low Peak Trail intersects on the right and runs level to the northwest. To continue on the NICA Trail, bear left and travel east.

At 0.95 mi., the path reaches a plateau beneath the summit and runs level through a hallway of young trees.

24-1 (34.80150, -86.60114) (1.1 mi.) The Low Peak Trail intersects on the right (near a bench) and runs level to the north. To continue on the NICA Trail, go straight and bend to the left to travel south. Soon, the path drops and makes a series of tight turns. The surface of the trail becomes rockier as you walk near a residential area.

23-1 (34.80031, -86.60246) (1.3 mi.) The NICA Trail ends at a small berm at the end of Melrose Road.

Trail Facts

NICA's Mission: The National Interscholastic Cycling Association develops mountain biking programs for student athletes. The NICA Trail serves as a training ground to help kids on local mountain biking teams develop their skills.

24. Low Peak Trail

While the NICA Trail is designed for mountain bikers, the Low Peak Trail is more suited for hikers exploring this area. Unlike the dirt NICA Trail, the Low Peak path is more aesthetically appealing as it ascends natural, leaf-covered terrain. Portions of the trail are wide because it follows an old roadbed. But these sections are still nice, as the grassy path carries you through a mature forest with boulder fields that add visual interest.

Distance: 0.4 mi.
Hiking Time: 10 minutes
Elevation Gain/Loss: +34 ft., -24 ft.
Hiking Difficulty: Easy to moderate
Location: Wade Mountain Nature Preserve, 10130 Spragins Hollow Rd. NW, Huntsville, AL 35810
Facilities: There are no facilities and no sources of potable water at the trailhead.
Driving Directions: See page 38 and use the directions for the Spragins Hollow Trailhead.

Highlights

The Path Less Traveled: As mentioned in the NICA Trail description, the trails on this part of Wade Mountain see relatively fewer hikers, so they offer a chance to escape the crowds. Near the top of Wade Mountain, you'll not only find peace and quiet, but also an appealing forest with mature hardwoods surrounded by thick beds of leaves and boulders blanketed with emerald moss.

Waypoint/Mile

Trailhead (Waypoint 24) (34.80508, -86.60093) From the Fleming Trailhead, follow the Fleming Trail to the NICA Trail. Then follow the NICA Trail for 0.7 mi. to the junction with the Low Peak Trail, which intersects on the right and soon climbs to the south.

After you've walked a little more than 400 ft., the trail meets an old dirt and grass road. The Low Peak Trail bends to the left and climbs, heading southeast. The leaf-covered path goes through a hallway of honeysuckle. Parts of this trail follow an old roadbed, and you'll notice that the trail is unusually wide as it moves through an open hardwood forest and traverses a rocky field.

24-1 (34.80150, -86.60114) (0.4 mi.) The Low Peak Trail ends at the junction with the NICA Trail, near a bench.

Trail Facts

Trail-Building at Warp Speed: According to the Land Trust of North Alabama, it only took three to four hours to build the Low Peak Trail, thanks to the efforts of many volunteers, including a team from Whole Foods.

Chapman Mountain
Nature Preserve

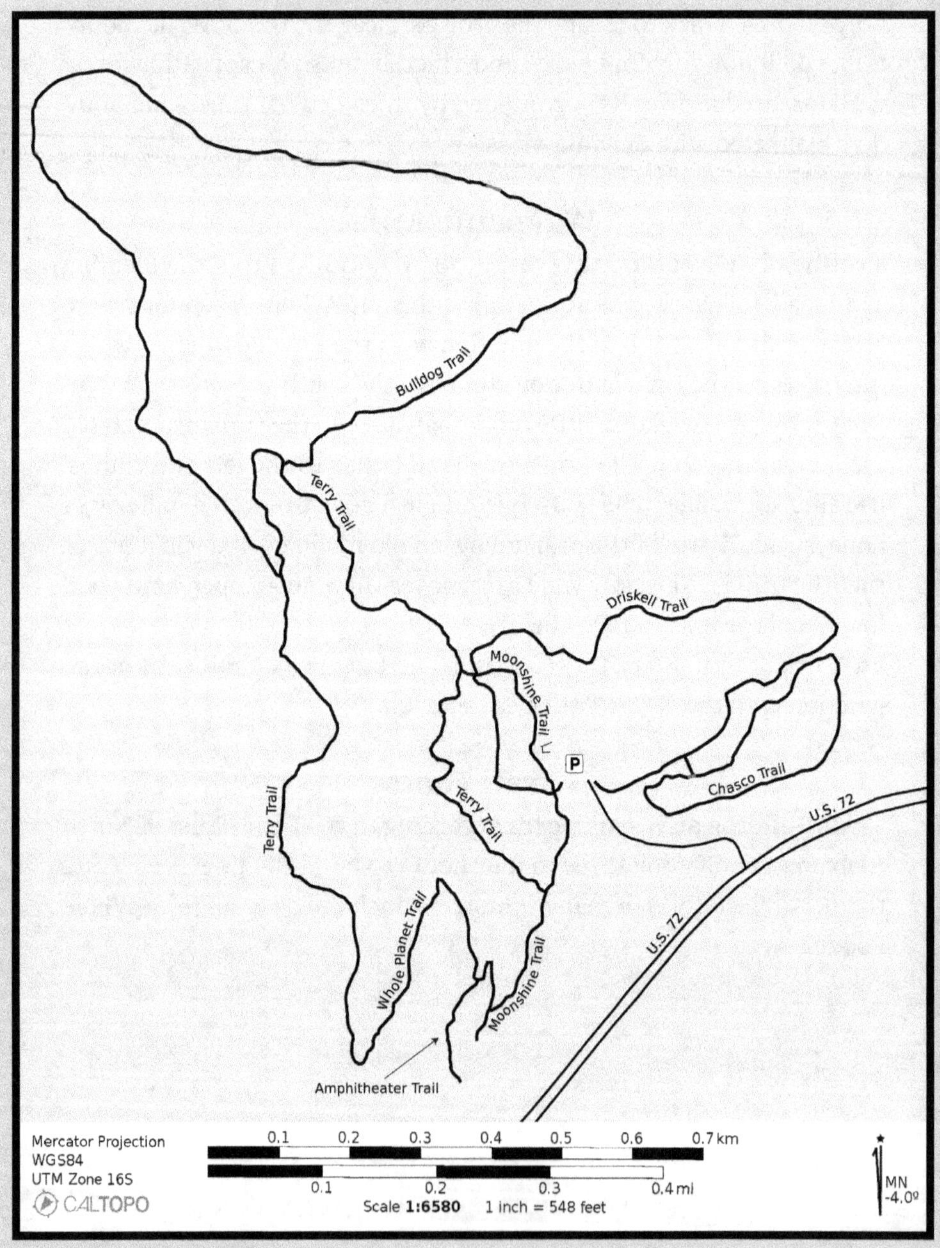

CHAPTER 5

Chapman Mountain Nature Preserve

In the 1800s, pioneers settled on Chapman Mountain, taking advantage of the diverse natural resources. A spring on the lee side of the mountain flowed with cool, clean water, while rich soil at the mountain's base nurtured their crops. A healthy forest with hickory trees and ample stones provided the timber and rock required to build structures for their homestead. But, by 1900, the land was largely uninhabited, and by the 1950s it had returned to its natural state. In 2012, the Terry family donated property on Chapman Mountain to the Land Trust of North Alabama, which established what is now a 472-acre nature preserve.

Located in east Huntsville, near Highway 72, the Chapman Mountain Nature Preserve includes seven trails that total more than four miles. While the preserve is popular with hikers, it's also open to mountain bikers and horseback riders. The paths that wind through the preserve explore mature woods with towering trees and stacks of boulders blanketed in bright moss. On your hike you'll encounter burbling streams and a spring where moonshiners secretly distilled their liquor under the cover of darkness.

Many of the paths are fairly level or not particularly steep, making them comfortable for most adults and children. A great path for kids is the Terry Trail, which takes you on a tour of nearly 50 tall, impressive trees identified by markers. (An online guided tour is also available.) As you're planning your visit, check the Land Trust website (www.landtrustnal.org) to find their calendar of environmental education programs hosted at the large pavilion located beside the parking area. (This pavilion also has restrooms, making this a more convenient spot for a family outing.)

On the east side of the preserve, you'll find one of its other unique features. The 18-hole Chapman Pines Disc Golf Course is set in a stand of tall loblolly pines. Circling the course is a wide, level path that's perfect for anyone who wants to walk or run easy terrain. Whether you want to exercise in fresh air, enjoy a round of disc golf, or explore the wild woods, you'll find what you're seeking on Chapman Mountain.

General Information

Location: 1263 U.S Hwy. 72 E., Huntsville, AL 35811
Hours: Open dawn to dusk.
Primary trail activities allowed: Hiking, biking, horseback riding
Pets: Leashed pets allowed.
Fees: There are no required fees to use the trails.
Facilities: There are restrooms at the pavilion next to the parking lot.
Information: (256) 534-5263; www.landtrustnal.org/properties/chapman-mountain-preserve/

Driving Directions

From the junction of I-565 and U.S. 231/431 (Memorial Parkway), travel northeast on I-565 for 3 mi. and then merge onto U.S. Highway 72 East. Follow U.S. Hwy. 72 for 1.9 mi. and then make a U-turn to travel west on U.S. Hwy. 72. Go 0.9 mi. and, just past the end of the metal guardrail, turn right onto the road with a Chapman Mountain Preserve sign. ***Keep a close eye out for this right turn as you're ascending the hill, because it's hard to see and sneaks up on you.* After the right turn, travel 0.16 mi. to the gravel parking area.

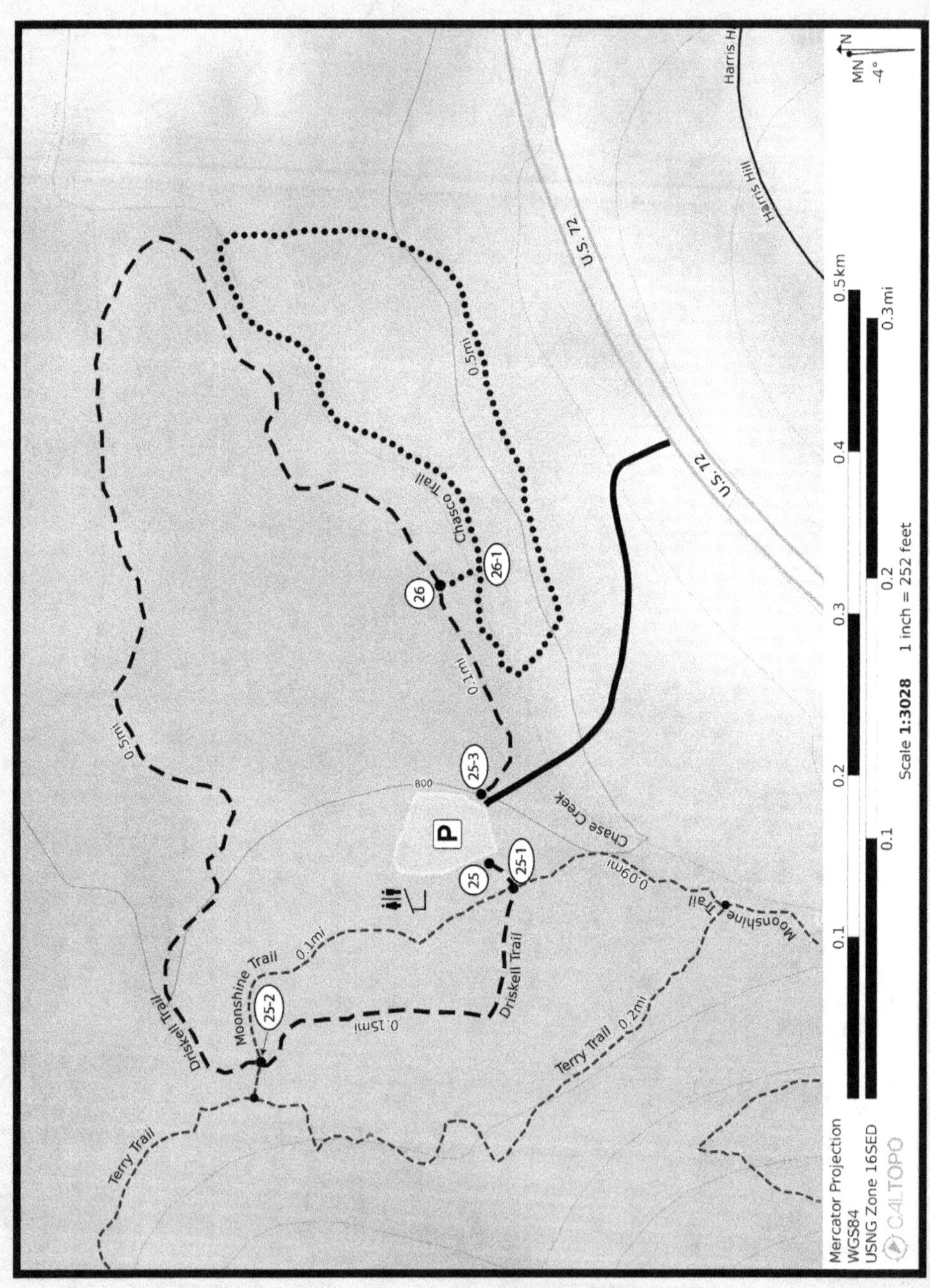

Harris H
Harris Hill
U.S. 72
U.S. 72
0.5mi
Chasco Trail
26-1
26
0.1mi
0.1mi
25-3
800
P
Chase Creek
0.5mi
25
25-1
0.09mi
Moonshine Trail
Moonshine Trail
0.1mi
Driskell Trail
Driskell Trail
25-2
0.15mi
Terry Trail
Terry Trail 0.2mi
MN
N
-4°
0.5km
0.3mi
0.4
0.3
0.2
0.1
Scale 1:3028   1 inch = 252 feet
Mercator Projection
WGS84
USNG Zone 16SED
CALTOPO

25. Driskell Trail

The Driskell Trail first runs along the base of Chapman Mountain. But after 0.1 mi., it descends to level ground and circles a large stand of tall pines that holds the Chapman Pines Disc Golf Course.

Distance: 0.8 mi.
Hiking Time: 20 to 25 minutes
Elevation Gain/Loss: +49 ft., -56 ft.
Hiking Difficulty: Easy
Location: Chapman Mountain Nature Preserve, 1263 U.S Hwy. 72 E., Huntsville, AL 35811
Facilities: There are restrooms at the pavilion next to the parking lot.
Driving Directions: See page 70.

Highlights

Level Ground for Walking and Running: While the trail rises briefly along the base of the mountain, it's mostly flat as it circles around the pines, making it ideal for people who want to walk or run on easy terrain. Also, there are almost no rocks or other obstacles along the dirt path as it loops around the disc golf course.

Waypoint/Mile

Trailhead (Waypoint 25) (34.77426, -86.55002) Begin at the trailhead kiosk at the parking area and take the path immediately to the left, traveling west.

The trail climbs gradually into dense forest for 260 ft. Then it turns right to head north over gently rolling terrain.

25-1 (34.77410, -86.55017) (111 ft.) The Driskell Trail intersects with the Moonshine Trail. To continue on the Driskell Trail, take the path that ascends to the west. The path is blazed with white diamonds marked Driskell Trail.

25-2 (34.77553, -86.55138) (0.15 mi.) The Driskell Trail intersects with the Moonshine Trail again at a four-way junction. Continue straight, traveling north on the Driskell Trail.

You'll soon drop into a basin where foliage has been cleared on each side of the path. The trail descends gradually with a creek drainage to the left. As you approach 0.3 mi., you'll see to the right a pad for the disc golf course that winds through a large stand of tall pine trees. Keep alert, as a sign warns visitors to look out for flying discs. The trail is mostly level as it loops around the island of pines and bends back to the west.

26 (34.77441, -86.54826) (0.6 mi.) The Chasco Trail intersects on the left where a wood and metal footbridge crosses Chase Creek. Continue straight, traveling west on the Driskell Trail.

25-3 (34.77422, -86.54949) (0.8 mi.) The Driskell Trail ends at the parking area.

Trail Facts

Driskell Family Donation: This trail is named in honor of Sue Terry Driskell, who, along with her brother Bob Terry, donated a significant part of the property that composes the Chapman Mountain Nature Preserve.

26. Chasco Trail

If you're hiking the Driskell Trail, the Chasco Trail is a nice diversion, as it explores Chase Creek while looping through the southeastern edge of the preserve. Also, if you're running trails in the preserve, this adds 0.5 mi. of mostly level terrain to your workout.

Distance: 0.5 mi.
Hiking Time: 15 minutes
Elevation Gain/Loss: +31 ft., -31 ft.
Hiking Difficulty: Easy
Location: Chapman Mountain Nature Preserve, 1263 U.S Hwy. 72 E., Huntsville, AL 35811
Facilities: There are restrooms at the pavilion next to the parking lot.
Driving Directions: See page 70.

Waypoint/Mile

Trailhead (Waypoint 26) (34.77441, -86.54826) Begin at the southeastern side of the parking area, where the Driskell Trail intersects with the parking lot. (As you enter the parking area, this is immediately to the right.) Take the Driskell Trail for 0.2 mi. to the junction with the Chasco Trail, which intersects on the right at the wood and metal footbridge (Waypoint 26). Turn right onto the Chasco Trail, traveling south, and following the white diamond blazes marked "Chasco Trail."

When you've walked 18 ft., a 30-ft.-long wood and metal bridge carries you across Chase Creek.

26-1 (34.77426, -86.54803) (59 ft.) After walking almost 60 ft., you'll reach a Y junction, where the Chasco Trail goes to the left and right. Because the Chasco Trail is a loop, you can go in either direction. To follow the trail description below, bear left and travel east.

At 171 ft., a wooden footbridge crosses the stream and soon passes trees wrapped in moss and a hallway of honeysuckle. At 0.14 mi., the creek is visible on the left, though dense woods stand between you and the water. The forest becomes a tangle of saplings, roots and fallen trees, though the well-maintained trail is free of obstacles.

At 0.2 mi., the trail climbs slightly, and a greater number of pines inhabit the forest, many with patches of gray-green lichen. At 0.39 mi., the path makes a mellow descent to skirt a drainage. At 0.47 mi., look to your left to check an interesting tee for the disc course: As you stand on a piece of high ground above the creek, you tee off by throwing your disc over the creek to reach the main part of the course in the stand of pines.

At 0.5 mi., you return to Waypoint 26-1. Turn left and travel 59 ft. to return to the beginning of the Chasco Trail, where it meets the Driskell Trail.

Trail Facts

What's in a Name? The Chasco Trail is named in recognition of the Boy Scouts who helped construct the trail. The name is a mashup of "CHApman" and "SCOut."

SECTION 2:
Moonshine Trail, Terry Trail, Whole Planet Trail, Amphitheater Trail and Bulldog Trail

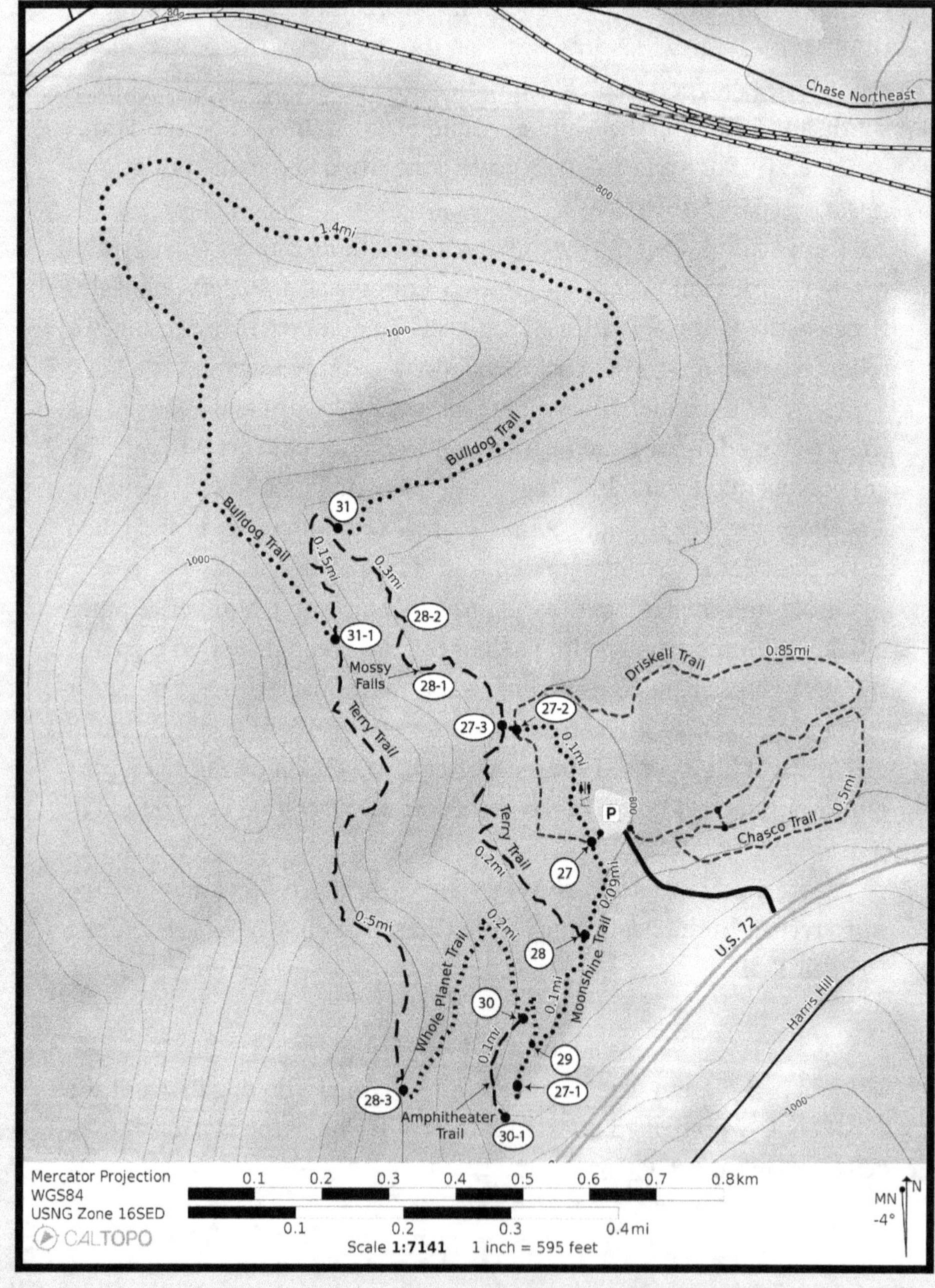

27. Moonshine Trail

The southern portion of the Moonshine Trail is one of my favorite areas in the Chapman Mountain Preserve. The path follows Chase Creek through a lush forest and ends at a burbling spring tucked away in a pocket of green woods.

Distance: 0.4 mi.
Hiking Time: 15 minutes
Elevation Gain/Loss: +57 ft., -19 ft.
Hiking Difficulty: Easy
Location: Chapman Mountain Nature Preserve, 1263 U.S Hwy. 72 E., Huntsville, AL 35811
Facilities: There are restrooms at the pavilion next to the parking lot.
Driving Directions: See page 70.

Highlights

Chase Creek Spring: The spring that feeds Chase Creek emerges from a low shelf of stone and trickles through a sublime spot in the woods. The shallow water slinks through an emerald forest with trees and rocks covered in mosses that range from bright, electric colors to deep, rich tones. A nearby bench provides the perfect place to unwind and enjoy the soothing sounds of the stream. It's rumored that a moonshine still stood here a long time ago, when this was a wild, wooded place. You can just imagine a bearded man hunkered down in this remote spot, tending to his craft under the glow of a full moon.

Waypoint/Mile

Trailhead (Waypoint 27) (34.77410, -86.55017) There's no officially designated trailhead for the Moonshine Trail. For this book, I've placed the trailhead at the junction with the Driskell Trail, near the information kiosk. To reach the Moonshine Trail, begin at the parking area information kiosk and, facing the kiosk, go left to travel west on the Driskell Trail. Walk for about 111 ft. to the junction with the Moonshine Trail, which goes northwest to the right and southeast to the left.

Moonshine Trail South

The most interesting destination on the Moonshine Trail is the spring, which lies 0.2 mi. south. To reach the spring, turn left at the trailhead (Waypoint 27) and head southeast. You'll soon cross a clearing and after traveling about 160 ft., you'll see a wooden sign that reads "Moonshine Falls." The path then leaves the clearing to enter the forest and parallel Chase Creek.

28 (34.77285, -86.55031) (518 ft.) The Terry Trail intersects on the right and climbs gradually to the northwest. Continue straight, following the creek to the southwest.

29 (34.77131, -86.55110) (0.2 mi.) The Whole Planet Trail intersects on the right and climbs north. Continue straight, continuing to climb to the southwest. Go another 200 ft. to Waypoint 27-1.

27-1 (34.77091, -86.55141) (0.25 mi.) The trail ends at a bench near the spring.

Moonshine Trail North

From the Moonshine Trail trailhead (Waypoint 27), you can also turn right to head north. This will eventually take you to junctions with the Driskell Trail and Terry Trail.

27-2 (34.77553, -86.55138) (0.14 mi.) After walking north for 0.1 mi., you'll reach a clearing and a four-way junction with the Driskell Trail. To finish the final short segment of the Moonshine Trail, continue straight and travel west to make a gradual climb.

27-3 (34.77559, -86.55161) (0.16 mi.) After walking 100 ft., you'll reach the endpoint of the Moonshine Trail, where it intersects the Terry Trail.

Trail Facts

Mountain Moonshine: Bob Terry, who donated the Chapman Mountain land to the Land Trust, says that there was indeed a still on this property at one time, but that was before his family owned the land. It would have been a good spot for distilling, as the moonshiners would have had a good source of water and plenty of tree cover to keep their operation hidden.

28. Terry Trail

Introduce kids to the great outdoors by exploring a forest full of big trees. The Terry Trail was designed to be a sort of outdoor classroom, with almost 50 stout trees with signs identifying their species. There are few steep grades on this path, so it's good for most ability levels. Plus, you can easily tailor your trip. Identified trees are located through-out the trail, so you'll encounter plenty of them whether you do a long or short trek. Before you hike, be sure to visit www.landtrustnal.org/treetour for details on the trees and other information.

Distance: 1.2 mi.
Hiking Time: 45 minutes to 1 hour
Elevation Gain/Loss: +300 ft., -112 ft.
Hiking Difficulty: Easy to moderate
Location: Chapman Mountain Nature Preserve, 1263 U.S Hwy. 72 E., Huntsville, AL 35811
Facilities: There are no facilities and no sources of potable water at the trailhead. There are restrooms at the pavilion next to the parking lot.
Driving Directions: See page 70.

Highlights

Big Trees: From towering elms to massive oaks, the Terry Trail is home to more than 40 substantial trees. Most of them stand very close to the trail, so you can easily inspect them and read the signs with species names. The online tour guide (www.landtrustnal.org/treetour) includes a map that shows the location of each tree, and this can be helpful, as some trees lie several yards away from the path. Consider carrying a phone to use the online tour or go online before your hike and print the map and tree list.

Waypoint/Mile

Trailhead (Waypoint 28) (34.77285, -86.55031) To reach the Terry Trail, begin at the trailhead kiosk at the parking area. Take the Driskell Trail—the path immediately to the left—and travel west 111 ft. to the junction with the Moonshine Trail. Turn left and travel south on the Moonshine Trail for 518 ft. (almost 0.1 mi.) to the junction with the Terry Trail (Waypoint 28), which intersects on the right. Turn right onto the Terry Trail and ascend gradually to the north.

After a little more than 50 ft., you'll reach the first identified tree, a honey locust tree. The trail rises gradually, passing an eastern red cedar, Osage orange tree, American elm and persimmon tree. The path then takes a right turn and descends gradually to the northeast. If you hike this path in spring, you might see trillium and other wildflowers in this area.

At 0.17 mi., the trail passes a massive white oak with a diameter of 38 inches. Then, at 0.2 mi., you'll encounter a towering southern red oak with the same impressive diameter.

27-3 (34.77559, -86.55161) (0.2 mi.) At the junction with the Moonshine Trail, bear left and travel north to continue on the Terry Trail. Near this area, spring hikers might see mayapple covering the ground along the trail.

28-1 (34.77628, -86.55279) (0.3 mi.) To the left is Mossy Falls, where water trickles through a jumbled pile of boulders with blankets of bright green moss.

28-2 (34.77704, -86.55330) (0.4 mi.) The trail splits and returns to being a single path after a short distance.

Over the next 0.1 mi., look for more trillium in spring. The path continues to rise gently as the forest becomes more open, with broad expanses of leaf-covered ground.

31 (34.77812, -86.55429) (0.5 mi.) The Bulldog Trail intersects on the right and descends to the east. To continue on the Terry Trail, bear left and climb, heading northwest.

After another 0.1 mi., you reach a short, steep section (it only stretches about 75 ft.) and pass by a variety of large oaks. The path soon levels out a bit and cuts across a slope, rising and falling gently. Keep an eye out for a tall pignut hickory tree, which produces a pear-shaped fruit with a thick husk that animals can open easily. Ahead are more big trees, including black oaks and a shagbark hickory with its signature bark that forms long, shaggy plates.

31-1 (34.77674, -86.55429) (0.7 mi.) The Bulldog Trail intersects on the right. To follow the Terry Trail, go straight and travel southeast.

28-3 (34.77084, -86.55346) (1.2 mi.) The Terry Trail ends at the intersection with the Whole Planet Trail.

Trail Facts

Eco Education: It's fitting that this trail serves environmental education, because Bob Terry, the man who donated the land, worked in forestry. Bob's grandfather purchased the property back in 1932 and originally planned to create a housing development. But that plan never came to fruition, and the Terry family donated the property to the Land Trust, realizing it could be a resource to educate people—especially children—about the environment.

29. Whole Planet Trail

On the Whole Planet Trail, hikers and trail runners will enjoy an easy to moderate climb and mostly smooth terrain. There are few noteworthy features on the Whole Planet Trail, and the path primarily provides a way to move between the Moonshine Trail and the Terry Trail.

Distance: 0.36 mi.
Hiking Time: 10 to 15 minutes
Elevation Gain/Loss: +146 ft., -2 ft.
Hiking Difficulty: Easy to moderate
Location: Chapman Mountain Nature Preserve, 1263 U.S Hwy. 72 E., Huntsville, AL 35811
Facilities: There are no facilities and no sources of potable water at the trailhead. There are restrooms at the pavilion next to the parking lot.
Driving Directions: See page 70.

Highlights

One Leg of an Excellent Loop Hike: The Whole Planet Trail serves as the southern leg of an excellent loop hike in the preserve. From the parking area, go south on the Moonshine Trail, and then turn right onto the Terry Trail. Enjoy the hike among the many big trees on the Terry Trail, and then take the Whole Planet Trail for an easy descent to the Moonshine Trail. After a quick side trip to visit the spring at the end of the Moonshine Trail, retrace your steps and take that path back to the parking area. The entire trip is a little less than 2 mi.

Waypoint/Mile

Trailhead (Waypoint 29) (34.77131, -86.55110) To reach the Whole Planet Trail, begin at the trailhead kiosk at the parking area. Take the Driskell Trail—the path immediately to the left—and travel west for 111 ft. to the junction with the Moonshine Trail. Turn left and travel south on the Moonshine Trail for 0.21 mi. to the junction with the Whole Planet Trail (Waypoint 29 on the map), which intersects on the right and climbs gradually to the north.

30 (34.77166, -86.55129) (320 ft.) The Amphitheater Trail intersects on the left. Turn right and ascend to the northwest to continue on the Whole Planet Trail.

The single-track path climbs gradually through an open hardwood forest. When you've gone almost 0.2 mi., you'll make a hairpin turn to the left to head southwest. After another 320 ft., you'll encounter a slightly rocky section of the trail. At 0.25 mi., the trail runs level for a short distance and then climbs again.

Near the 0.3-mi. mark, there's a short 30-ft. section where the trail becomes a bit rockier. From here, the trail enters an area with many downed trees. In winter, when the trees have lost their leaves, you can see a prominent ridge to the east. At 0.35 mi., the path turns right and curls to the northwest.

28-3 (34.77082, -86.55330) (0.36 mi.) The Whole Planet Trail ends at the intersection with the Terry Trail.

Trail Facts

Whole Foods: According to the Land Trust of North Alabama, "Volunteers from Whole Foods Huntsville contributed a significant amount of time working with the Land Trust to build trails at Chapman Mountain before the preserve opened. Because of this contribution, we gave them the opportunity to name one of the trails they worked so hard to create."

30. Amphitheater Trail

Stretching just 0.1 mi., this is the shortest trail in the preserve. As you explore the extreme southern end of the preserve, you'll climb gradually for half the length of the trail. Then you'll ease down into an alcove where the surrounding terrain forms a natural amphitheater.

Distance: 0.1 mi.
Hiking Time: 3 to 5 minutes
Elevation Gain/Loss: +28 ft., -14 ft.
Hiking Difficulty: Easy
Location: Chapman Mountain Nature Preserve, 1263 U.S Hwy. 72 E., Huntsville, AL 35811
Facilities: There are no facilities and no sources of potable water at the trailhead. There are restrooms at the pavilion next to the parking lot.
Driving Directions: See page 70.

Waypoint/Mile

Trailhead (Waypoint 30) (34.77166, -86.55129) To reach the Amphitheater Trail, take the Moonshine Trail to the Whole Planet Trail. Then walk 320 ft. on the Whole Planet Trail to its junction with the Amphitheater Trail at Waypoint 30. Head southwest on the Amphitheater Trail, climbing gradually on a narrow, packed earth path that runs through a hallway of honeysuckle.

30-1 (34.77049, -86.55160) (0.1 mi.) The Amphitheater Trail ends near a stack of boulders in an alcove.

31. Bulldog Trail

The Bulldog Trail loops through the quiet, remote northern section of the Chapman

Mountain Nature Preserve. For nearly 1 mi., the path remains fairly level as it traverses the flank of the mountain and tours an open forest of hardwoods and cedars. Near its end, the path makes a brief, moderate climb and then drops to meet the Terry Trail, which will carry you back to your starting point.

Distance: 1.4 mi.
Hiking Time: 45 minutes
Elevation Gain/Loss: +123 ft., -59 ft.
Hiking Difficulty: Easy
Location: Chapman Mountain Nature Preserve, 1263 Hwy 72 E., Huntsville, AL 35811
Facilities: There are no facilities and no sources of potable water at the trailhead. There are restrooms at the pavilion next to the parking lot.
Driving Directions: See page 70.

Highlights

A Quiet Walk in Remote Woods: This trail runs deep into the northernmost section of Chapman Mountain, carrying you far away from the preserve's more active areas. As you move into the heart of the Bulldog Trail, you'll notice that it feels very isolated. On many occasions I've found this to be the quietest, most peaceful trail in the preserve.

Waypoint/Mile

Trailhead (Waypoint 31) (34.77812, -86.55429) To reach the Bulldog Trail, begin at the trailhead kiosk at the parking area. Take the Driskell Trail—the path immediately to the left—and travel west 111 ft. to the junction with the Moonshine Trail. Turn right and travel north on the Moonshine Trail for 0.16 mi. to the junction with the Terry Trail at Waypoint 27-3. Turn right onto the Terry Trail and travel north 0.3 mi. to the junction with the Bulldog Trail. Turn right and head east on the Bulldog Trail.

The narrow path of packed earth rises gradually in an open hardwood forest. To the southeast, you can see the high pines that house the disc golf course. Beyond the towering trees, a high ridge with a distinct saddle stretches across the horizon. As the path bends to the west, you lose the southeastern views, but it's still an appealing stretch of trail. The route takes you along the high flank of a hill, allowing clear views of the forest floor below on the right. As the path proceeds, it widens and rolls along easily, with few changes in elevation.

At 0.8 mi., the trail bends to the west and passes through stands of tall cedars. At 0.96 mi., the trail turns left and changes in character quite a bit. You leave the wide track of packed earth and follow a narrow path across rocky ground. When you've walked about 1 mi., you'll climb gradually and skirt a hilltop. The path tops out at 962 ft. of elevation and then drops for a little more than 0.1 mi. to meet the Terry Trail.

31-1 (34.77674, -86.55429) (1.4 mi.) The Bulldog Trail intersects the Terry Trail. If you turn left, you can follow the Terry Trail for about 0.1 mi. to return to the beginning of the Bulldog Trail.

Trail Facts

Why the "Bulldog" Trail? The Land Trust doesn't actually own the property that the Bulldog Trail explores—Alabama A&M University does. The university and the Land Trust made an agreement to construct a trail that would create access to 226 acres of Alabama A&M land on the east side of the campus. So the trail is named for the University's mascot, the bulldog.

U.S. Space & Rocket Center

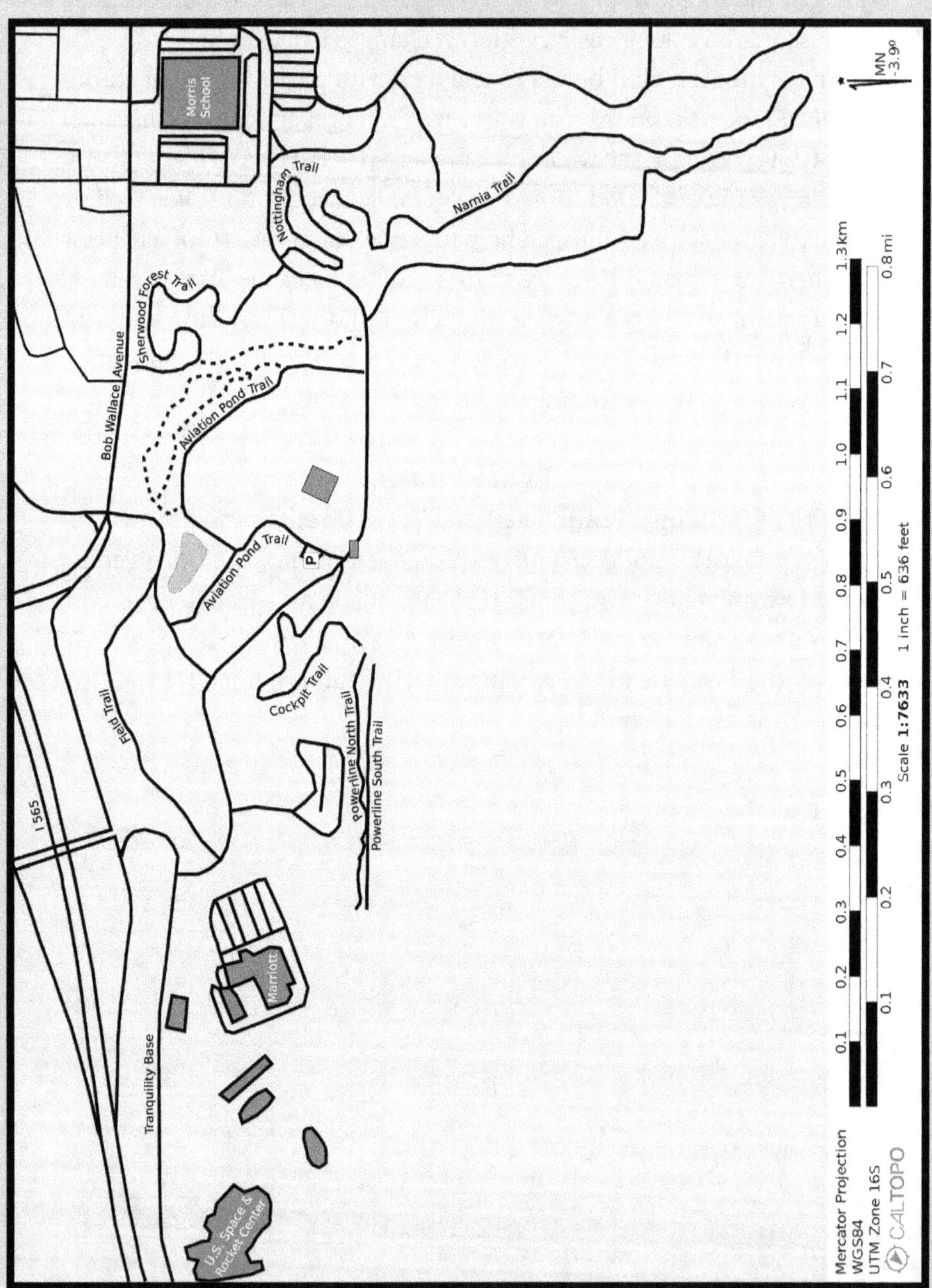

CHAPTER 6

U.S. Space & Rocket Center

Drawing as many as 600,000 visitors each year, the U.S. Space & Rocket Center is Huntsville's most recognized tourist destination. The replica of a Saturn V rocket is the city's most iconic landmark, and anyone exploring Huntsville will no doubt see the towering structure. But people willing to investigate a bit further will find many other intriguing, though less obvious, attractions on the grounds near the Space & Rocket Center.

Winding through the woods east and south of the center are eight trails covering more than 3.5 miles. The majority of the paths are level and cross easy terrain, making them accessible to most people. This is an especially good place to hike or bike with kids, not only because the trails are easy, but also because interesting objects lie tucked away in the forest.

As the Cockpit Trail implies, it's home to the shell of an airplane cockpit. That's just one of the many odd artifacts you'll find in the surrounding woods. Other trails to the east are home to even stranger attractions, including the weathered hulls of small aircraft and the remains of old rockets. On the east side of the property, trails have more fanciful names, indicating that hikers are entering a strange realm. On the Sherwood and Nottingham trails, you won't find Robin and his merry band of thieves, but you will see weird stuff, like military-style forest outposts draped in camouflage, which are used for the U.S. Space & Rocket Center's Aviation Challenge programs. While walking the Narnia Trail, kids will be fascinated with a whimsical wooden statue of a large rabbit.

Not so much a trail as a gravel path, the Aviation Pond Trail is also worth your time. It will give you a close-up view of the training grounds for participants in the Aviation Challenge. As you pass Aviation Pond, you can imagine learning to ditch your plane by soaring down the 150-foot zipline to splash into the water.

General Information

Location: 1 Tranquility Base, Huntsville, AL 35805
Hours: Open daily, 9 a.m.-5 p.m.
Primary trail activities allowed: Hiking, biking
Pets: Leashed pets allowed.
Fees: There are no required fees to use the trails.
Information: (800) 637-7223; www.rocketcenter.com

Driving Directions

S&RC Field Trail

Traveling East on I-565: Use the right lane to take Exit 15 toward Madison Pike/Sparkman Drive/Bob Wallace Avenue. Travel 0.2 mi., and then keep to the right, following signs for the Space & Rocket Center. Travel 331 ft. to where the road becomes Tranquility Base. Go another 243 ft. on Tranquility Base, and then turn left onto the unnamed road that leads to the RV park. Go 240 ft., and the trail begins on the left side of the road. Note that there is no trailhead sign and no designated parking area for this trail. The nearest parking area is the Marriott hotel lot about 180 ft. to the immediate southwest.

Traveling West on I-565: Use the right lane to take Exit 15 for Bob Wallace Avenue. Go 0.2 mi., and when you reach a fork, stay in the lane second from the left and follow signs for Bob Wallace Ave./Old Madison Pike/Space & Rocket Center. Go 0.2 mi. and turn left onto Madison Pike. Go 0.2 mi. to where Madison Pike turns right and becomes Tranquility Base. Go another 243 ft. on Tranquility Base, and then turn left onto the unnamed road that leads to the RV park. Go 240 ft., and the trail begins on the left side of the road. Note that there is no trailhead sign and no designated parking area for this trail. The nearest parking area is the Marriott hotel lot about 180 ft. to the immediate southwest.

Aviation Challenge Parking Area

Traveling East on I-565: Use the right lane to take Exit 15 toward Madison Pike/Sparkman Drive/Bob Wallace Avenue. Travel 0.2 mi., and then keep to the right, following signs for the Space & Rocket Center. Travel 331 ft. to where the road becomes Tranquility Base. Go another

243 ft. on Tranquility Base, and then turn left onto the unnamed road that leads to the RV park. Travel 0.2 mi. to where a road intersects on the left. Continue straight for another 0.2 mi., and then turn left into the parking lot near the Aviation Challenge area.

Traveling West on I-565: Use the right lane to take Exit 15 for Bob Wallace Avenue. Go 0.2 mi., and when you reach a fork, stay in the lane that's second from the left and follow signs for Bob Wallace Ave./ Old Madison Pike/Space & Rocket Center. Go 0.2 mi. and turn left onto Madison Pike. Go 0.2 mi. to where Madison Pike turns right and becomes Tranquility Base. Go another 243 ft. on Tranquility Base, and then turn left onto the unnamed road that leads to the RV park. Travel 0.4 mi., passing the RV park on the way, and then turn left into a parking lot just before you reach the Aviation Challenge buildings.

S&RC Field Trail, Cockpit Trail, Powerline North Trail, Powerline South Trail and Aviation Pond Trail

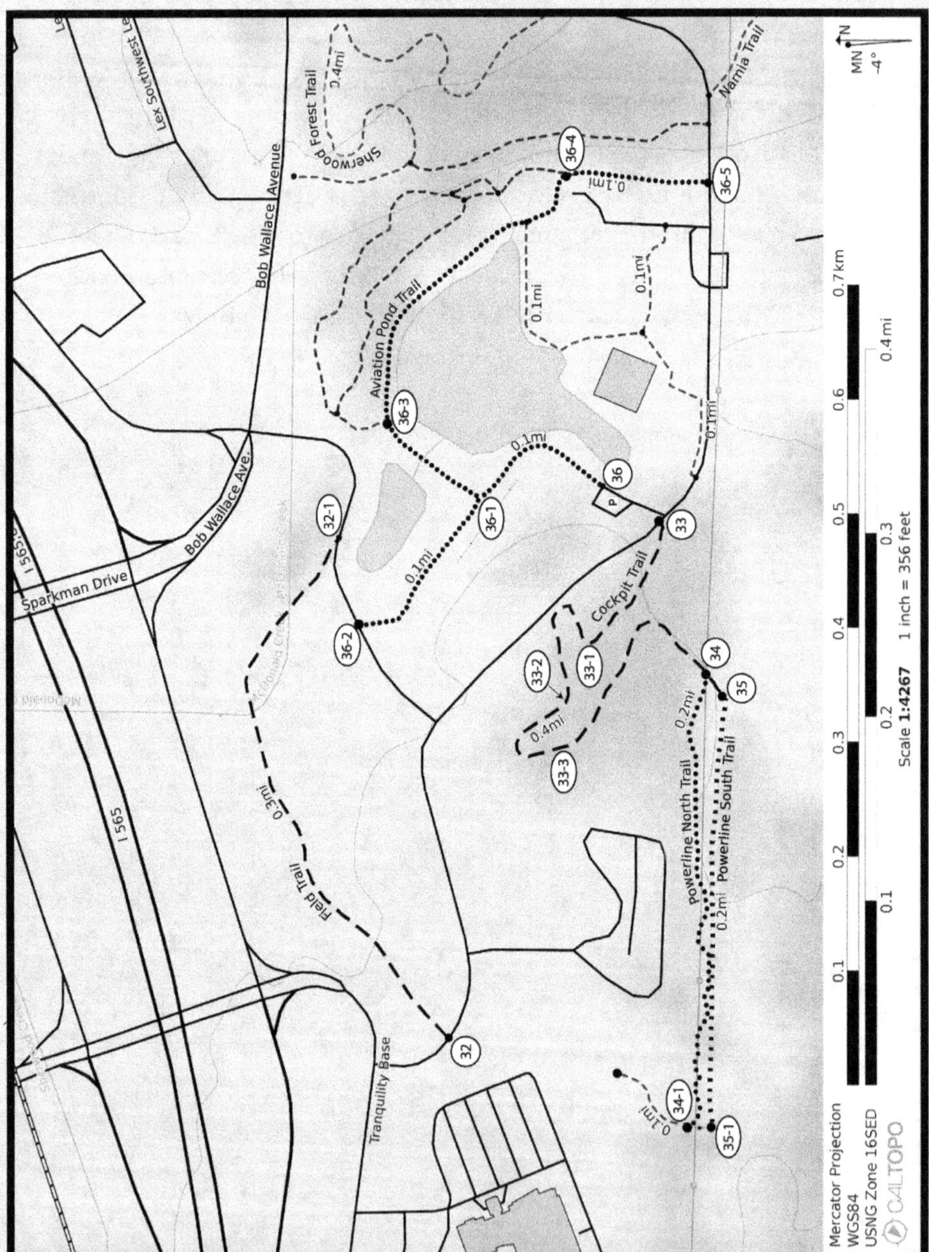

32. S&RC Field Trail

This path is mostly used by people who walk or run the Space Center trails for exercise. People who park at the Marriott can use this easy path to cross a grassy field and then walk a short distance on a road to reach the Aviation Pond Trail.

Distance: 0.3 mi.
Hiking Time: 5 to 10 minutes
Elevation Gain/Loss: +0 ft., -26 ft.
Hiking Difficulty: Easy
Location: U.S. Space & Rocket Center, 1 Tranquility Base, Huntsville, AL 35805
Facilities: There are no facilities and no sources of potable water at the trailhead.
Driving Directions: See page 88 and use the directions for the S&RC Field Trail.

Waypoint/Mile

Trailhead (Waypoint 32) (34.71164, -86.64775) The S&RC Field Trail begins beside the road that leads to the U.S. Space & Rocket Center RV park. From Tranquility Base, travel south for about 220 ft. on the road that leads to the RV park. The S&RC Field Trail is on the left: a faint, narrow dirt path that runs northeast between two stands of trees.

The trail descends slightly as it crosses a wide field. To the right is a stand of tall pines, and to the left a dense corridor of trees separates the field and the nearby highway. At 0.2 mi., the path bends to the right to head southeast toward a road.

32-1 (34.71256, -86.64321) (0.3 mi.) The trail ends at the junction with the road. If you want to extend your walk, turn right and travel west on the road for 212 ft. to access the Aviation Pond Trail. (See page 95 for information on the Aviation Pond Trail.)

33. Cockpit Trail

Hikers, trail runners and mountain bikers frequent this entertaining trail that winds through shaded woods and passes the remnants of an airplane cockpit.

Distance: 0.44 mi.
Hiking Time: 10 to 15 minutes
Elevation Gain/Loss: +22 ft., -18 ft.
Hiking Difficulty: Easy
Location: U.S. Space & Rocket Center, 1 Tranquility Base, Huntsville, AL 35805
Facilities: There are no facilities and no sources of potable water at the trailhead.
Driving Directions: See page 88 and use the directions for the Aviation Challenge Parking Area.

Highlights

A cockpit hull sits beside the trail.

Aircraft Cockpit: When you've walked nearly 0.3 mi., you'll reach a wide area of the trail where you will find a weathered airplane cockpit. The dingy hull is an odd sight for sure, and it's just one of several aircraft remnants scattered throughout the surrounding woods. It's likely that these relics were once used by the Space & Rocket Center or NASA, though their exact origins seem lost to history.

Waypoint/Mile

Trailhead (Waypoint 33) (34.70985, -86.64287) Exit the south end of the parking area to cross the road you came in on. Head toward the sign that says, "Welcome to the Energy Greenway." Immediately after crossing the road, look to the right to see white trail blazes on the trees and go west to enter a tunnel of foliage.

33-1 (34.71054, -86.64407) (485 ft.) At the T junction, turn right and travel east.

At 0.1 mi., the trail turns left to skirt the road but soon reenters the forest. As the trail continues, there are no major changes in elevation, but occasional dips and bumps make it an entertaining ride for mountain bikers.

33-2 (34.71063, -86.64454) (0.18 mi.) At the Y junction, bear right and travel east.

33-3 (34.71070, -86.64500) (0.27 mi.) At the Y junction, bear right to walk past the old space shuttle cockpit and travel south.

34 (34.70953, -86.64432) (0.43 mi.) The Powerline North Trail intersects on the right and drifts back toward the tree line, heading northwest. This path stretches 0.26 mi. and leads to a short connector trail. This will take you to a path that lies between the Marriott and the RV park. From Waypoint 34, you can also continue across the powerline break for 70 ft. to meet the Powerline South Trail at Waypoint 35.

35 (34.70934, -86.64450) (0.44 mi.) The Cockpit Trail ends at the junction with the Powerline South Trail, which heads west through the heart of the powerline corridor for 0.25 mi.

34. Powerline North Trail

This easy trail rises gradually as it passes through a powerline corridor and parallels the educational Energy Greenway. (Signs along this greenway provide information on sustainable ways of living.) At the end of the Powerline North Trail, a connector trail cuts through the woods to meet a road that runs beside the Marriott. If you've parked at the Marriott to explore the trail system, you can use the Powerline trails and the connector to return to your vehicle.

Distance: 0.26 mi.
Hiking Time: 5 to 7 minutes
Elevation Gain/Loss: +34 ft., -4 ft.
Hiking Difficulty: Easy
Location: U.S. Space & Rocket Center, 1 Tranquility Base, Huntsville, AL 35805

Facilities: There are no facilities and no sources of potable water at the trailhead.

Driving Directions: See page 88 and use the directions for the Aviation Challenge Parking Area.

Waypoint/Mile

Trailhead (Waypoint 34) (34.70953, -86.64432) To reach the Powerline North Trail, begin at the parking lot immediately west of the Aviation Challenge area. From the southeast corner of the parking area, cross the main road that leads to the Aviation Challenge. Once across, immediately turn right to follow the Cockpit Trail. (The path begins between trees marked with white blazes.) Travel 0.43 mi. on the Cockpit Trail to the powerline corridor, where the Powerline North Trail intersects on the right. Turn right onto the Powerline North Trail and travel northwest, heading back toward the forest you just exited.

34-1 (34.70969, -86.64853) (0.26 mi.) The Powerline North Trail intersects with the Powerline South Trail (on the left) and a connector trail (on the right). The connector trail goes north for 263 ft. and ends at a path that runs between the Marriott and the RV park.

35. Powerline South Trail

This trail rises gradually as it moves through the powerline corridor and runs beside the educational Energy Greenway. (Signs along this greenway provide information on sustainable ways of living.) At the end of the Powerline South Trail, you can continue straight to follow a short connector trail that cuts through the woods and meets a road that runs beside the Marriott. If you've parked at the Marriott to explore the trail system, you can use the Powerline trails and the connector trail to return to your vehicle.

Distance: 0.25 mi.
Hiking Time: 5 minutes
Elevation Gain/Loss: +33 ft., -3 ft.
Hiking Difficulty: Easy
Location: U.S. Space & Rocket Center, 1 Tranquility Base,

Huntsville, AL 35805

Facilities: There are no facilities and no sources of potable water at the trailhead.

Driving Directions: See page 88 and use the directions for the Aviation Challenge Parking Area.

Waypoint/Mile

Trailhead (Waypoint 35) (34.70934, -86.64450) To reach the Powerline South Trail, begin at the parking lot immediately west of the Aviation Challenge area. From the southeast corner of the parking area, cross the main road that leads to the Aviation Challenge. Once across, immediately turn right to follow the Cockpit Trail. (The path begins between trees marked with white blazes.) Travel 0.44 mi. on the Cockpit Trail to the junction with the Powerline South Trail, which intersects on the right near the far side of the powerline corridor. Turn right onto the Powerline South Trail and head west through the middle of the powerline break.

35-1 (34.70939, -86.64866) (0.24 mi.) Make a sharp turn to the right to head north toward the forest.

34-1 (34.70969, -86.64853) (0.25 mi.) The Powerline South Trail ends near the edge of the forest. If you continue straight, you'll follow a 263-ft. connector trail that ends at a path that runs between the Marriott and the RV park.

36. Aviation Pond Trail

This level and wide gravel path runs around a pond used for training during Aviation Challenge programs offered by the U.S. Space & Rocket Center. This path also provides access to about 0.3 mi. of unofficial trails that wind through the woods immediately northwest of the pond.

Distance: 0.4 mi.
Hiking Time: 5 to 10 minutes
Elevation Gain/Loss: +0 ft., -15 ft.
Hiking Difficulty: Easy

Location: U.S. Space & Rocket Center, 1 Tranquility Base, Huntsville, AL 35805
Facilities: There are no facilities and no sources of potable water at the trailhead.
Driving Directions: See page 88 and use the directions for the Aviation Challenge Parking Area.

Highlights

Aviation Pond: The Aviation Pond serves as a training ground for the U.S. Space & Rocket Center's Aviation Challenge programs. As part of their five-day adventure, participants learn what it takes to be a fighter pilot. This includes getting a taste of what it's like to ditch your plane over a body of water. For this challenge, students ride a 150-ft. zipline that ends with a water landing in the pond.

Access to Unofficial Trails: At the north end of the pond, a connector trail leads to about 0.3 mi. of unofficial trails that wind through the woods between the Aviation Pond and McDonald Creek. Whether you're a hiker, biker or trail runner, you can use these trails to add a bit of distance to your outing and enjoy more time in a forest environment.

Waypoint/Mile

Trailhead (Waypoint 36) (34.71047, -86.64268) The Aviation Pond Trail begins immediately west of the Aviation Pond and the Aviation Challenge area of the U.S. Space & Rocket Center. At the northeast corner of the parking area, follow the Aviation Pond Trail, which is a gravel path that heads northeast toward the pond.

36-1 (34.71136, -86.64266) (436 ft.) At Waypoint 36-1, the Aviation Pond Trail goes in two directions. If you continue straight, traveling northwest, you'll walk almost 70 ft. to where the path ends at the road at **Waypoint 36-2** (34.71226, -86.64382). If you turn right at Waypoint 36-1 and head northeast, you can continue exploring the pond area.

***Mileage numbers below refer to a hike where you turn right at Waypoint 36-1.*

36-3 (34.71207, -86.64191) (0.15 mi.) A path intersects on the left and heads north to trails that loop through the woods near the pond and McDonald Creek. Bear right and travel east to continue on the Aviation

Pond Trail and parallel the northeast bank of the pond.

36-4 (34.71061, -86.63955) (0.34 mi.) A path intersects on the left and goes north to connect with unofficial trails north and east of the pond. Continue straight and walk south to continue on the Aviation Pond Trail.

36-5 (34.70957, -86.63961) (0.4 mi.) The Aviation Pond Trail ends at the road.

Trail Facts

Aviation Challenge: The Aviation Challenge programs offer kids ages 9-18 the opportunity to play the role of fighter pilots. During five-day camps, participants experience flight simulators, practice basic water- and land-survival skills, and learn about civilian and military careers in aviation. For information, visit www.spacecamp.com/aviation.

SECTION 2:
Sherwood Forest Trail, Nottingham Trail and Narnia Trail

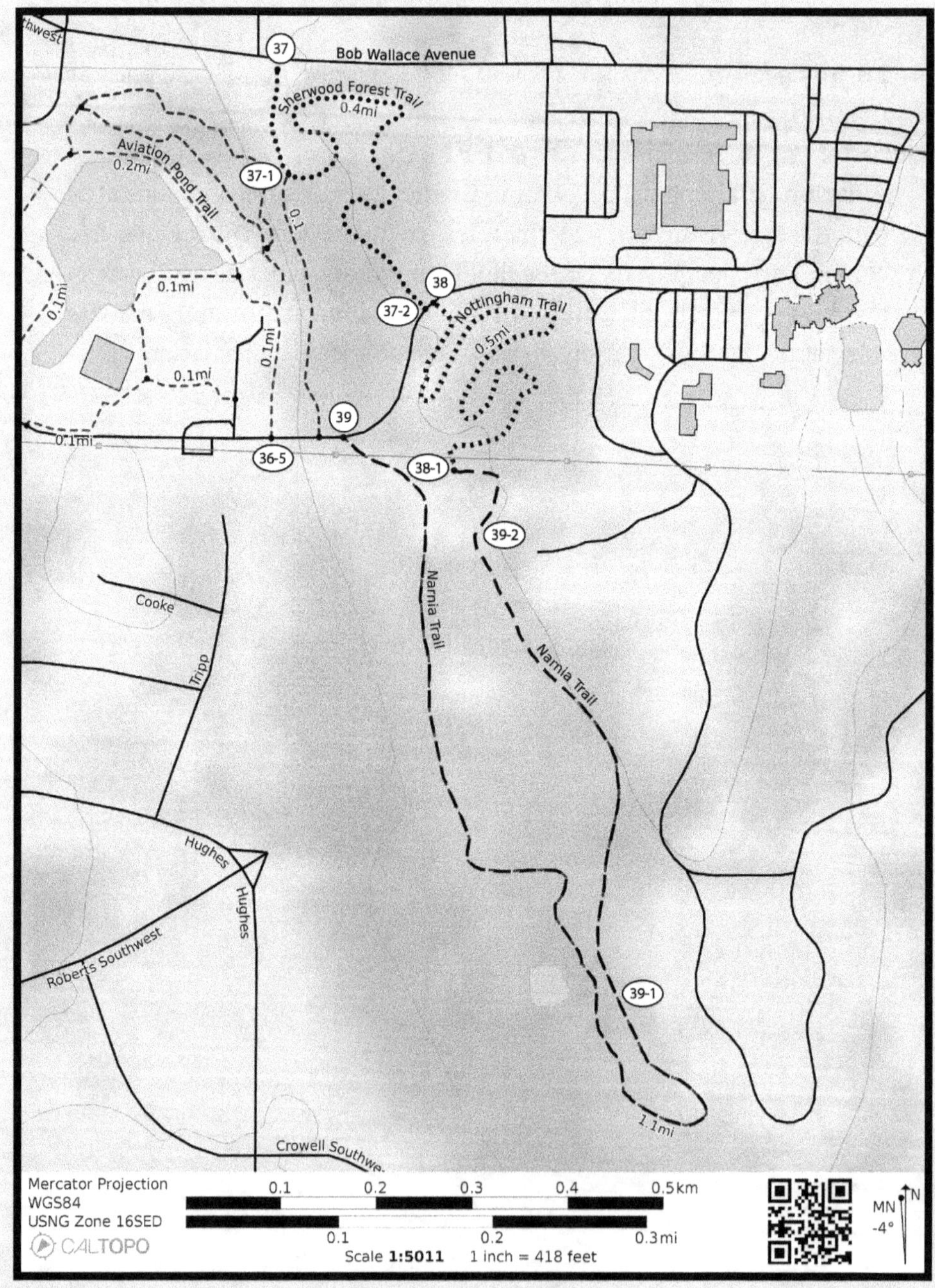

37. Sherwood Forest Trail

The Sherwood Forest Trail rollercoasters through dense woods, offering occasional bumps, dips and modest changes in elevation to keep hikers, runners and riders entertained. Along the way, you'll encounter military-style outposts and encampments used for the U.S. Space & Rocket Center's Aviation Challenge program.

Distance: 0.45 mi.
Hiking Time: 10 to 15 minutes
Elevation Gain/Loss: +64 ft., -54 ft.
Hiking Difficulty: Easy
Location: U.S. Space & Rocket Center, 1 Tranquility Base, Huntsville, AL 35805
Facilities: There are no facilities and no sources of potable water at the trailhead.
Driving Directions: See page 88 and use the directions for the Aviation Challenge Parking Area.

Highlights

Odd Objects in the Woods: Many years ago, this property served as a training ground for the military. It has also been a dumping ground for old military and aviation hardware. As you explore the forest, you'll encounter several oddities, including the weathered shells of old aircraft and rockets.

Waypoint/Mile

Trailhead (Waypoint 37) (34.71279, -86.63957) The Sherwood Forest Trail begins on the south side of Bob Wallace Avenue, across from the junction of Bob Wallace Ave. and Lex Drive. But there is no convenient parking area near the trailhead. Your best option is to park in the lot near the Aviation Challenge facility and then follow the Aviation Pond Trail to where it ends at a road (marked Waypoint 36-5 on the map). From here, turn left and walk about 170 ft. to an unofficial trail on the left. To continue to the trailhead at Waypoint 37, follow this trail north for 0.23 mi. If you begin at Waypoint 37, you'll go south and walk to the

Aircraft remnants along the Sherwood Forest Trail

left of the building toward the forest.

37-1 (34.71184, -86.63944) (366 ft.) Turn left and travel east, leaving the wide path and entering the forest on a single-track path.

The trail runs through dense woods, and after 0.1 mi. it begins a long, gradual descent. The path then rises and turns east to parallel Bob Wallace Avenue. More moderate elevation changes lie ahead as the path mixes in a few bumps and dips. At 0.38 mi., look to the side of the trail to see the metal carcass of a small aircraft.

37-2 (34.71060, -86.63789) (0.45 mi.) The Sherwood Forest Trail ends at the road. To continue exploring nearby trails, turn left onto the road. Go northwest 40 ft. and look to the right for the Nottingham Trail, a narrow path that enters dense woods.

38. Nottingham Trail

The Nottingham Trail twists through a forest of hardwoods and pines for 0.5 mi. to meet the Narnia Trail. Tucked away in these woods are Aviation Challenge training sites.

Distance: 0.5 mi.

Hiking Time: 10 to 15 minutes

Elevation Gain/Loss: +40 ft., -29 ft.

Hiking Difficulty: Easy

Location: U.S. Space & Rocket Center, 1 Tranquility Base, Huntsville, AL 35805

Facilities: There are no facilities and no sources of potable water at the trailhead.

Driving Directions: See page 88 and use the directions for the Aviation Challenge Parking Area.

Highlights

Relics of the Past: Scattered about the woods are small clearings that appear to be military camps or training stations. Camouflage netting drapes over decaying structures, and old boxes and barrels lie strewn about.

Waypoint/Mile

Trailhead (Waypoint 38) (34.71064, -86.63769) To reach the Nottingham Trail, begin at the parking area near the Aviation Challenge facility. Then follow the Aviation Pond Trail to where it ends at a road at Waypoint 36-5. Turn left and walk east on the road for 0.15 mi. You'll see the entrance to the Nottingham Trail on the right.

The Nottingham Trail begins in a tangled forest of young trees and brush. But wide openings in the tree canopy allow ample light to flood the woods. At 400 ft., the hardwoods give way to pines, and a plush bed of needles blankets the ground. The pine thicket soon ends as you move into a dense hardwood forest, and road noise echoes in the woods. The trail twists through more pines and passes the remains of old military training stations.

38-1 (34.70865, -86.63699) (0.5 mi.) The Nottingham Trail ends at the junction with the Narnia Trail.

39. Narnia Trail

Stretching a little more than 1 mi., this is the longest of the Space & Rocket Center trails. As with the other trails in the area, it's relatively flat and allows you to stroll comfortably through shaded woods. For a 2-mi. loop, begin with the Narnia Trail and combine it with the Nottingham and Sherwood Forest trails. When you reach Waypoint 37-1 on the Sherwood Forest Trail, head south on the 0.17-mi. connector path that ends at the road immediately west of the Narnia trailhead.

A stand of bamboo on the Narnia Trail

Distance: 1.1 mi.
Hiking Time: 30 minutes
Elevation Gain/Loss: +45 ft., -33 ft.
Hiking Difficulty: Easy
Location: U.S. Space & Rocket Center, 1 Tranquility Base, Huntsville, AL 35805
Facilities: There are no facilities and no sources of potable water at the trailhead.
Driving Directions: See page 88 and use the directions for the Aviation Challenge Parking Area.

Highlights

Trailside Attractions: With a name like Narnia, you'd expect this trail to lead to a strange, fantastic world. Well, it's not exactly like stepping through a wardrobe, but the path is home to a few odd attractions, including a bamboo forest and a large wooden sculpture of a rabbit.

Waypoint/Mile

Trailhead (Waypoint 39) (34.70948, -86.63879) To reach the beginning of the Narnia Trail, start in the Aviation Challenge parking area. At the northeast corner of the parking lot, follow the Aviation Pond Trail, which is a gravel path that heads northeast toward the pond. Walk around the pond completely and go to where the trail ends at a road at Waypoint 36-5. Turn left and walk down the road 250 ft. to where the Narnia Trail begins at Waypoint 39.

The wide path soon crosses a powerline corridor and becomes a mixture of dirt and gravel. The trail narrows and runs level until the 0.4-mi. mark, where it traverses undulating terrain. In a shady forest of hardwoods and cedar you'll cross a berm, which is one of a few terrain features along the path that mountain bikers must negotiate. Not far beyond the 0.5-mi. mark, the trail turns north, and the boughs of trees arc over the trail to form natural tunnels.

39-1 (34.70439, -86.63537) (0.7 mi.) Look to the right to see the wooden rabbit sculpture.

You'll encounter another series of small rises and dips and enter an area with widely spaced mature pines. Around 0.9 mi., you'll pass the shell of an old rocket.

39-2 (34.70865, -86.63699) (1 mi.) The path enters a stand of large bamboo and soon exits the trees to cross a powerline corridor.

38-1 (34.70865, -86.63699) (1.1 mi.) The Narnia Trail ends at the junction with the Nottingham Trail.

Trail Facts

Rabbit Statue: The wooden rabbit sculpture was once a display in the neighboring Huntsville Botanical Garden. It was likely moved to the trail as the path was being prepped for a mountain bike race many years ago.

This rabbit statue is one of several odd objects occupying Space Center trails.

Harvest Square Nature Preserve

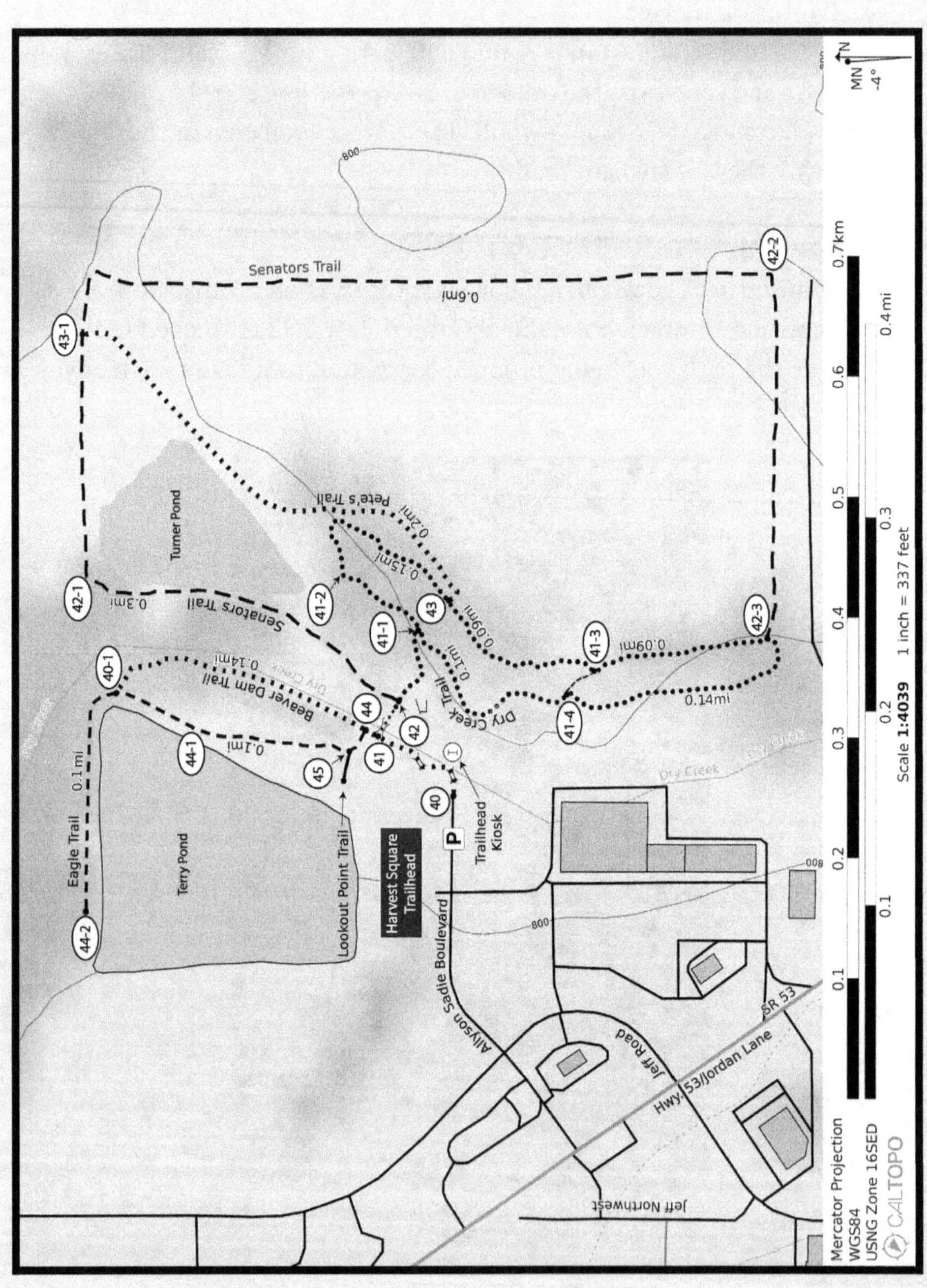

CHAPTER 7

Harvest Square Nature Preserve

There are nearly 9 million acres of farmland in Alabama, and agriculture contributes about $70 billion to the state's economy each year. The Harvest Square Nature Preserve celebrates Alabama's farming heritage with trails that explore 69 acres of rural land in the small community of Harvest, which is about 12 miles northwest of Huntsville.

As the Harvest Square Shopping Center was being built in 2009, the developers donated a portion of the adjacent land to the Land Trust of North Alabama. In 2011, the Land Trust opened the Harvest Square Nature Preserve, which includes six trails covering a total of 2.3 miles. These trails explore 36 acres of land still used for farming and 33 acres of lowland woods. Most of the trails are level, and some have a gravel surface, making this a good destination for people of all ability levels to walk, run and ride bikes.

If you enjoy viewing wildlife, there's plenty to see in the preserve. The farm fields, the neighboring forest, and a creek that flows through the preserve provide habitat for deer, foxes and beavers, as well as many species of birds (including turkeys), amphibians and reptiles. When the shopping center was built, two borrow pits were created, and these have been transformed into two ponds that are now home to a variety of fish and draw several species of migratory birds.

The Harvest Square Nature Preserve is also a good place to introduce kids to the outdoors. The gravel paths and dirt forest trails make for easy walking. If you want to teach a youngster to fish, you can follow the Eagle Trail to the easily accessible Terry Pond, which is naturally stocked. For kids who want to explore the woods, the Dry Creek Trail has interpretive signs that identify trees and provide information about the surrounding forest and farmland. During your outing with the kids, you can take a break and enjoy a picnic meal at the Dale W. Strong Community Pavilion near the parking area.

Whether you're looking for a place to take young ones or just want a mellow place to enjoy nature and get some exercise, you'll find what you're seeking among the fields and woodlands of Harvest Square.

General Information

Location: 111 Allyson Sadie Blvd., Harvest, AL 35749
Hours: Open dawn to dusk.
Primary trail activities allowed: Hiking, biking
Pets: Leashed pets allowed.
Fees: There are no required fees to use the trails.
Facilities: There are no restrooms and no sources of potable water at the trailhead.
Information: (256) 534-5263; www.landtrustnal.org/properties/harvest-square-preserve/

Driving Directions

From the junction of U.S. 72 (University Drive) and AL 53 (Jordan Lane), travel north on AL 53 for 9.1 mi. and then turn right onto Jeff Road. (You'll see a Publix supermarket on the right.) Travel 0.1 mi. on Jeff Rd., passing a Burger King on the right, and then turn right onto Allyson Sadie Boulevard. Go 489 ft. to reach the parking area for Harvest Square Nature Preserve.

Beaver Dam Trail, Dry Creek Trail, Senators Trail, Pete's Trail, Eagle Trail and Lookout Point Trail

40. Beaver Dam Trail

This short path runs along Dry Creek and explores an area where beavers build dams that flood the ground after periods of rain. If you hike this trail within a few days of a good rain, consider wearing boots to keep your feet dry.

Distance: 0.2 mi.
Hiking Time: 5 minutes
Elevation Gain/Loss: +7 ft., -3 ft.
Hiking Difficulty: Easy
Location: Harvest Square Nature Preserve, 111 Allyson Sadie Blvd., Harvest, AL 35749
Facilities & Driving Directions: See page 106.

Highlights

Evidence of Beaver Dams: When you see water flooding the trail, it's evidence that beavers have been diligent in constructing dams across Dry Creek. Beavers build these dams to create pools of deep water. Inside the pool, they create a dry living space, known as a "lodge," that gives them protection from predators and serves as a place to store food.

Waypoint/Mile

Trailhead (Waypoint 40) (34.84761, -86.70989) At the east end of the parking area, take the gravel path to begin the Beaver Dam Trail. After walking 80 ft., you'll reach the trailhead kiosk. Turn left and follow the gravel path, traveling north.

41 (34.84816, -86.70941) (284 ft.) At a wooden footbridge, the Dry Creek Trail intersects on the right and leads to a pavilion. Go straight and travel northeast to continue on the Beaver Dam Trail.

44 (34.84830, -86.70933) (333 ft.) The Eagle Trail intersects on the left.

To stay on the Beaver Dam Trail, continue straight on the wide gravel path and parallel Dry Creek.

Small streams feed into the slow-flowing Dry Creek on your right. When I hiked this area during a rainy period in winter, water from the creek had partially flooded the Beaver Dam Trail. As the path heads north, it's flanked by dense woods thick with underbrush and vines. **40-1** (34.85018, -86.70893) (0.2 mi.) The Beaver Dam Trail ends at the junction with the Eagle Trail, near the bank of Terry Pond.

41. Dry Creek Trail

Over a relatively short distance, the Dry Creek Trail covers diverse areas within the preserve. One minute you're in a stand of pines or skirting a vast farm field, and the next you're in a shady corridor of hardwoods covered in deep-green moss. Along the way, interpretive signs explain the evolution of the landscape and call out a variety of trees found in the forest.

Distance: 0.65 mi.
Hiking Time: 15 minutes
Elevation Gain/Loss: +30 ft., -22 ft.
Hiking Difficulty: Easy
Location: Harvest Square Nature Preserve, 111 Allyson Sadie Blvd., Harvest, AL 35749
Facilities & Driving Directions: See page 106.

Highlights

Get to Know the Local Trees: This is a good trail if you like to combine your hiking with eco-education. Signs along the trail identify several varieties of trees common to Southern woods, such as shagbark hickory, sweet gum, southern red oak and hackberry. Plus, the signs share interesting facts about each type of tree.

Waypoint/Mile

Trailhead (Waypoint 41) (34.84816, -86.70941) At the east end of the parking area, take the gravel path, which is the Beaver Dam Trail. After walking 80 ft., you'll reach the trailhead kiosk. Turn left and follow the gravel path, traveling north, for 316 ft. to reach the junction with a wooden footbridge on the right, marked Waypoint 41. Turn right onto the Dry Creek Trail and cross the bridge. After you cross, continue straight across the open grassy area north of the pavilion.

42 (34.84803, -86.70901) (100 ft.) After about 100 ft., the Senators Trail intersects on the left. Go straight to continue across the grassy clearing north of the pavilion. After walking another 75 ft., you'll reach a 14-ft.-long wooden footbridge at the edge of the dense woods. Cross the footbridge, traveling southeast.

41-1 (34.84785, -86.70837) (350 ft.) At the T junction, you can go left or right on the Dry Creek Trail. Turn left and head northeast. After 20 ft., you'll see an interpretive sign identifying a shagbark hickory.

41-2 (34.84849, -86.70792) (0.1 mi.) On the left side of the trail is a path that leads to Lookout Point. Be aware that this path might be flooded and difficult to identify and follow. To continue, go straight and follow the Dry Creek Trail as it bends to the right and heads east.

Over the next 200 ft., keep an eye out for interpretive signs identifying a sweet gum tree and a southern red oak.

43 (34.84762, -86.70812) (0.2 mi.) On the left, a Madison County Agriculture sign sits before an opening in trees that affords a view of the large

Moss blankets the base of trees on the Dry Creek Trail.

farm field that is still in use. At the break in the trees, two benches face the field and the trailhead for Pete's Trail.

41-3 (34.84652, -86.70878) (0.3 mi.) On the right is a short connector trail that runs northwest through a pine thicket and meets the western side of the Dry Creek Trail. At Waypoint 41-3, bear left and continue to skirt the large field, traveling southeast.

At 0.34 mi., an interpretive sign explains the evolution of a "natural succession" forest, which is what surrounds hikers exploring the Harvest Square Nature Preserve. Ahead, more pine trees populate the woods, and a peaceful scene unfolds to the left as ridges stretch across the horizon beyond the vast fields.

42-3 (34.84522, -86.70846) (0.4 mi.) At the Y junction, the Senators Trail goes left to head east and skirt the field. To continue on the Dry Creek Trail, turn right and go south to enter the woods.

The path soon bends to the north. On your left, commercial buildings come into view, while thick woods on the right stand between the trail and the large field to the east. Near 0.5 mi., the pines lay down a thick layer of needles on the trail.

41-4 (34.84675, -86.70894) (0.5 mi.) On the right, the connector trail intersects and heads southeast. Bear left and travel northwest to continue on the Dry Creek Trail.

At 0.6 mi., a stout loblolly pine towers over the path on the right, and the trail soon arrives back at Waypoint 41-4. Turn left to retrace your steps to the trailhead.

Trail Facts

Why "Dry Creek"? For much of the year, Dry Creek lives up to its name. But after periods of rain, the creek fills up and occasionally floods the surrounding land. Dry Creek now serves as a natural source of water to replenish the two man-made ponds in the preserve.

42. Senators Trail

The most interesting part of this trail is within the first 0.2 mi. First, the trail crosses the flood zone for Dry Creek. After a hard rain, this area can flood, so you might have some interesting hiking as you negotiate ankle-deep water. But then you reach the most attractive part of the trail, as a wood walkway skirts Turner Pond and provides broad views of the water. Beyond the pond, the trail runs along the perimeter of a working farm field.

Distance: 0.9 mi.
Hiking Time: 20 minutes
Elevation Gain/Loss: +18 ft., -13 ft.
Hiking Difficulty: Easy
Location: Harvest Square Nature Preserve, 111 Allyson Sadie Blvd., Harvest, AL 35749
Facilities & Driving Directions: See page 106.

Highlights

A Stroll Along the Pond: A few hundred feet into the hike, a wooden walkway carries you over the western edge of Turner Pond. It's quiet and peaceful in this central part of the preserve. A bench on the walkway provides a good spot to sit, gaze out over the riffling water, and watch the breeze blowing through the trees encircling the pond.

Waypoint/Mile

Trailhead (Waypoint 42) (34.84807, -86.70903) At the east end of the parking area, take the gravel Beaver Dam Trail for 316 ft. to reach a wooden footbridge, which intersects on the right. Turn right to take the Dry Creek Trail and cross the bridge. Walk another 100 ft. to the junction with the Senators Trail, which intersects on the left at Waypoint 42. Turn left onto the Senators Trail, which is a wide, grassy path that heads northeast.

When I hiked this trail during a particularly rainy winter, it was flooded for the first 0.1 mi. At 338 ft., a wood walkway extending nearly 500 ft. carried me over a portion of Turner Pond. Beyond the walkway, I hiked in ankle-deep water. At 0.17 mi., a wood bench faces the pond and provides a peaceful spot to relax and view the many types of birds that visit the preserve.

42-1 (34.85044, -86.70789) (0.19 mi.) The trail reaches a large field and turns right to travel east along the edge of the field.

43-1 (34.85049, -86.70567) (0.3 mi.) Pete's Trail intersects on the right and cuts across the field to the southwest. Continue straight, heading east. Walk to the eastern edge of the field, and just before you reach a gravel road, turn right to walk south along the field.

42-2 (34.84519, -86.70518) (0.7 mi.) At the bench, turn right and head west to follow the edge of the field.

42-3 (34.84529, -86.70852) (0.9 mi.) The Senators Trail ends at the junction with the Dry Creek Trail.

Trail Facts

Sparkman Senators: Sparkman High School students volunteered to help develop this trail, so it's named in honor of their school mascot.

43. Pete's Trail

Pete's Trail essentially crosses a large field and briefly skirts Turner Pond to meet the Senators Trail. When I walked this trail, the path was not clearly defined, so you might want to carry a map to stay on course. No matter your exact route, if you cross the large field, you will eventually intersect with the Senators Trail.

Distance: 0.2 mi.
Hiking Time: 5 minutes
Elevation Gain/Loss: +7 ft., -14 ft.
Hiking Difficulty: Easy
Location: Harvest Square Nature Preserve, 111 Allyson Sadie Blvd., Harvest, AL 35749
Facilities & Driving Directions: See page 106.

Waypoint/Mile

Trailhead (Waypoint 43) (34.84764, -86.70808) To reach the beginning of Pete's Trail, follow the Dry Creek Trail loop, traveling clockwise. At the 0.2-mi. mark, Pete's Trail intersects on the left at an opening in the woods that offers a view of the large field (Waypoint 43). At this junction, you'll also see an interpretive sign for Madison County Agriculture. Turn left to walk toward the field, and when you reach it turn left. After walking about 330 ft. along the perimeter of the field, you'll see a marker identifying this as Pete's Trail.

A little beyond 0.1 mi., the path runs along the edge of Turner Pond. A narrow strip of cedars and low brush shrouds your view of the water.

43-1 (34.85049, -86.70567) (0.2 mi.) Pete's Trail ends at the junction with the Senators Trail.

Trail Facts

For Pete's Sake: According to the Land Trust of North Alabama, "Pete was one of the early volunteers who helped the Land Trust get Harvest Square Nature Preserve started. He worked diligently to garner support from Sparkman High School students and their track club to assist with trail construction."

44. Eagle Trail

Enjoy a comfortable stroll on this wide, level path that skirts Terry Pond and visits a small fishing pier.

Distance: 0.2 mi.
Hiking Time: 5 to 10 minutes
Elevation Gain/Loss: +7 ft., -0 ft.
Hiking Difficulty: Easy
Location: Harvest Square Nature Preserve, 111 Allyson Sadie Blvd., Harvest, AL 35749
Facilities & Driving Directions: See page 106.

Highlights

A small pier provides a good fishing spot on Terry Pond.

A Great Fishing Spot for Kids: If you want to introduce a kid to fishing, this is an ideal place. The Eagle Trail runs immediately beside Terry Pond, so little ones don't have to walk far to reach a fishing spot. Plus, the path is right next to the water, so there are several convenient places to cast a line. Just be aware that you'll need an Alabama fishing license.

Waypoint/Mile

Trailhead (Waypoint 44) (34.84830, -86.70933) To reach the Eagle Trail, begin at the east end of the parking area and take the gravel path 80 ft. to the trailhead kiosk. Turn left and follow the gravel Beaver Dam Trail north for about 250 ft. to reach Waypoint 44. Turn left onto the Eagle Trail and head northwest toward Terry Pond.

45 (34.84841, -86.70953) (66 ft.) The Lookout Point Trail intersects on the left and heads west for 135 ft. to end at the edge of the pond. Bear right to stay on the Eagle Trail.

44-1 (34.84966, -86.70927) (0.1 mi.) After walking 533 ft., you'll see to the left a small, short pier that juts out into the pond to provide a good platform for fishing. Note the sign with rules for fish cleaning. Go another 217 ft. to reach Waypoint 40-1.

40-1 (34.85018, -86.70893) (0.14 mi.) The Beaver Dam Trail intersects on the right. Bear left and head west to continue on the Eagle Trail and walk along the northern bank of the pond.

44-2 (34.85044, -86.71095) (0.2 mi.) The Eagle Trail ends at the terminus of the gravel path, at the northwest corner of the pond. You'll find two benches that face the pond.

Trail Facts

Eagle Project: This trail is named in honor of local Boy Scouts who played a major role in developing trails and infrastructure in the preserve. Much of their work was part of an Eagle Scout project.

45. Lookout Point Trail

As you're hiking the Eagle Trail, take this short path to the edge of Terry Pond for a broad view of the water.

Distance: 135 ft.
Hiking Time: 1 minute
Elevation Gain/Loss: +3 ft., -0 ft.
Hiking Difficulty: Easy
Location: Harvest Square Nature Preserve, 111 Allyson Sadie Blvd., Harvest, AL 35749
Facilities & Driving Directions: See page 106.

Waypoint/Mile

Trailhead (**Waypoint 45**) (34.84841, -86.70953) To reach the Lookout Point Trail, begin at the east end of the parking area and take the gravel path 80 ft. to the trailhead kiosk. Turn left and follow the gravel Beaver Dam Trail north for 253 ft. to reach Waypoint 44. Turn left onto the Eagle Trail and head northwest toward the pond. After walking 66 ft., you'll reach the beginning of the Lookout Point Trail, which intersects on the left and heads west toward the pond.

Rainbow Mountain Preserve

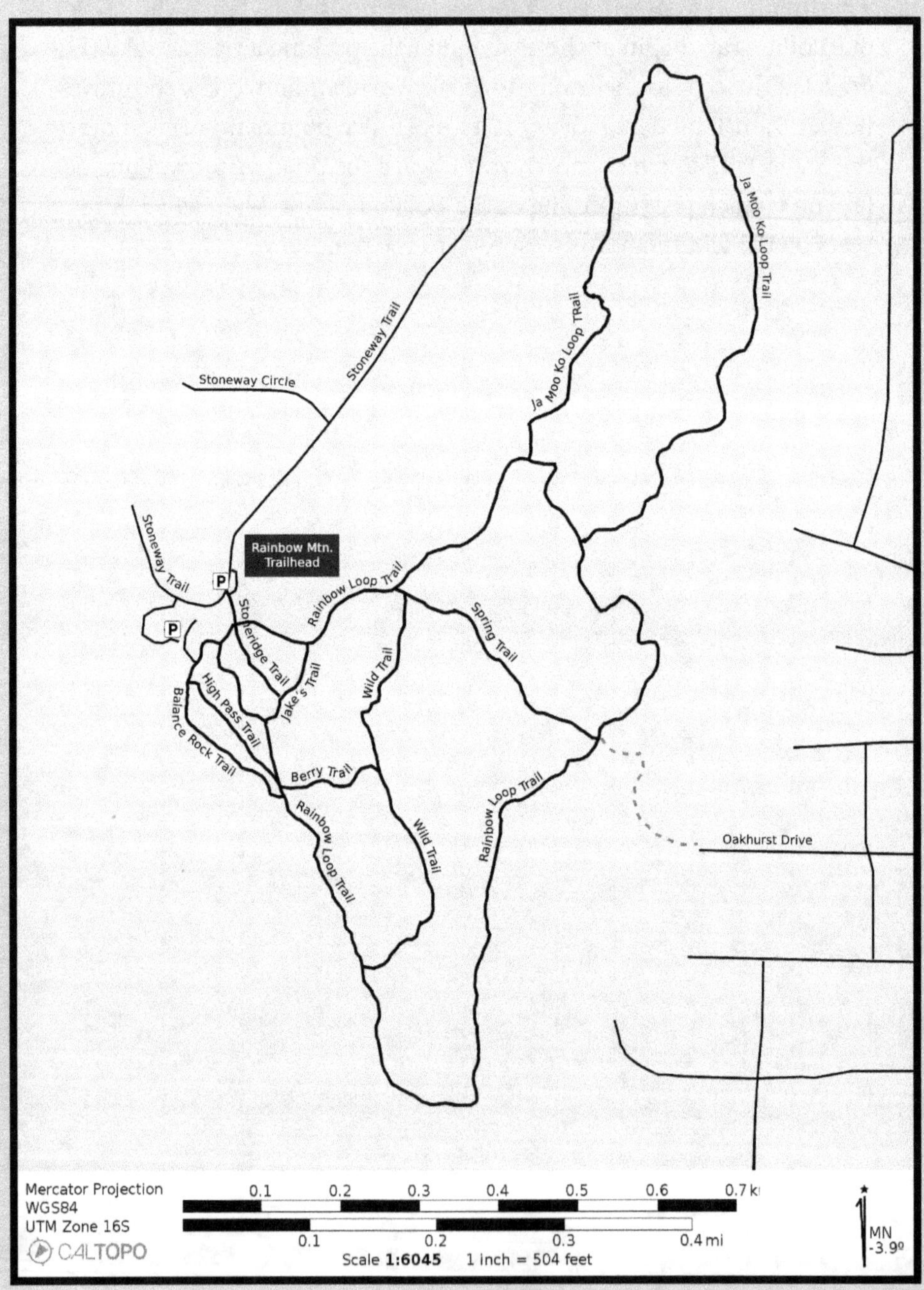

CHAPTER 8

Rainbow Mountain Nature Preserve

Covering only about 147 acres, the Rainbow Mountain Nature Preserve is a relatively small hiking area, but it packs plenty of adventure into a modest space. Located in northeast Madison, the preserve includes nine trails that total about 3.5 miles. The diverse trails traverse high ridges and rocky slopes and descend to a stream basin with a burbling spring. With its wide variety of terrain, the preserve offers something for every kind of hiker. At the top of the mountain, a number of trails cross easy ground and lead to fascinating rock formations. Lower down, a series of challenging trails crawl up and down the rugged mountainside. Whether you're a beginner or an experienced hiker, you'll find a route that suits your desires.

A main attraction on Rainbow Mountain is Balance Rock. The fairly level Balance Rock Trail leads to a rock formation where erosion has created the optical illusion of a boulder precariously balanced on a smaller boulder. From this trail, you can easily reach the High Pass Trail, which traverses a ridge. Big boulders atop the ridge make for fun scrambling and provide the perfect perch to relax and enjoy inspiring views.

Hikers seeking a longer trek over demanding terrain should check out the Rainbow Loop Trail. This 1.5-mi. path tromps down boulder-strewn drainages and dives down to a stream basin, where a small spring-fed waterfall flows into a clear pool. From there, the path climbs back to the top of the ridge and passes Baby Balance Rock, where erosion has created another geological magic trick. From the Rainbow Loop Trail, you can also access several other paths to do a variety of loops and lengthen your trek.

While Rainbow Mountain draws plenty of hikers, the preserve is also a popular place to entertain kids. Near the parking lot there's a playground and a pavilion with picnic tables.

General Information

Location: 230 Stoneway Trail, Madison, AL 35758

Hours: Open dawn to dusk.

Primary trail activities allowed: Hiking, biking

Pets: Leashed pets allowed.

Fees: There are no required fees to use the trails.

Facilities: There is a pavilion with picnic tables and a portable toilet near the trailhead.

Information: (256) 534-5263; www.landtrustnal.org/properties/rainbow-mountain-preserve/

Driving Directions

Traveling East on I-565: Take Exit 9. Travel 0.3 mi. on the on-ramp and keep left at the fork to follow signs for Madison. Go another 249 ft. and turn left onto Wall Triana Highway. Go 0.3 mi. on Wall Triana Hwy. and then turn right onto Madison Boulevard. Travel 1.1 mi. on Madison Blvd. and use the left two lanes to turn left onto Hughes Road. Drive 3.9 mi. on Hughes Rd., and then turn right onto Thomas Drive. Go 0.4 mi., and then turn left onto Concord Drive. Travel 0.1 mi., and then turn right onto Stoneway Trail. Go another 1.2 mi. to the paved parking area for the Rainbow Mountain Nature Preserve on the left. If the small lot near the trailhead is full, continue another 200 ft. to a second paved parking area on the left.

Traveling West on I-565: Take Exit 13 for Madison Boulevard. Go 0.7 mi., and then keep left to continue on Madison Blvd. Travel 2.5 mi. on Madison Blvd., and then turn right onto Hughes Road. Drive 3.9 mi., and then turn right onto Thomas Drive. Go 0.4 mi., and then turn left onto Concord Drive. Travel 0.1 mi., and then turn right onto Stoneway Trail. Go another 1.2 mi. to the paved parking area for the Rainbow Mountain Nature Preserve on the left. If the small lot near the trailhead is full, continue another 200 ft. to a second paved parking area on the left.

SECTION 1:
Stoneridge Trail, Jake's Trail, Balance Rock Trail and High Pass Trail

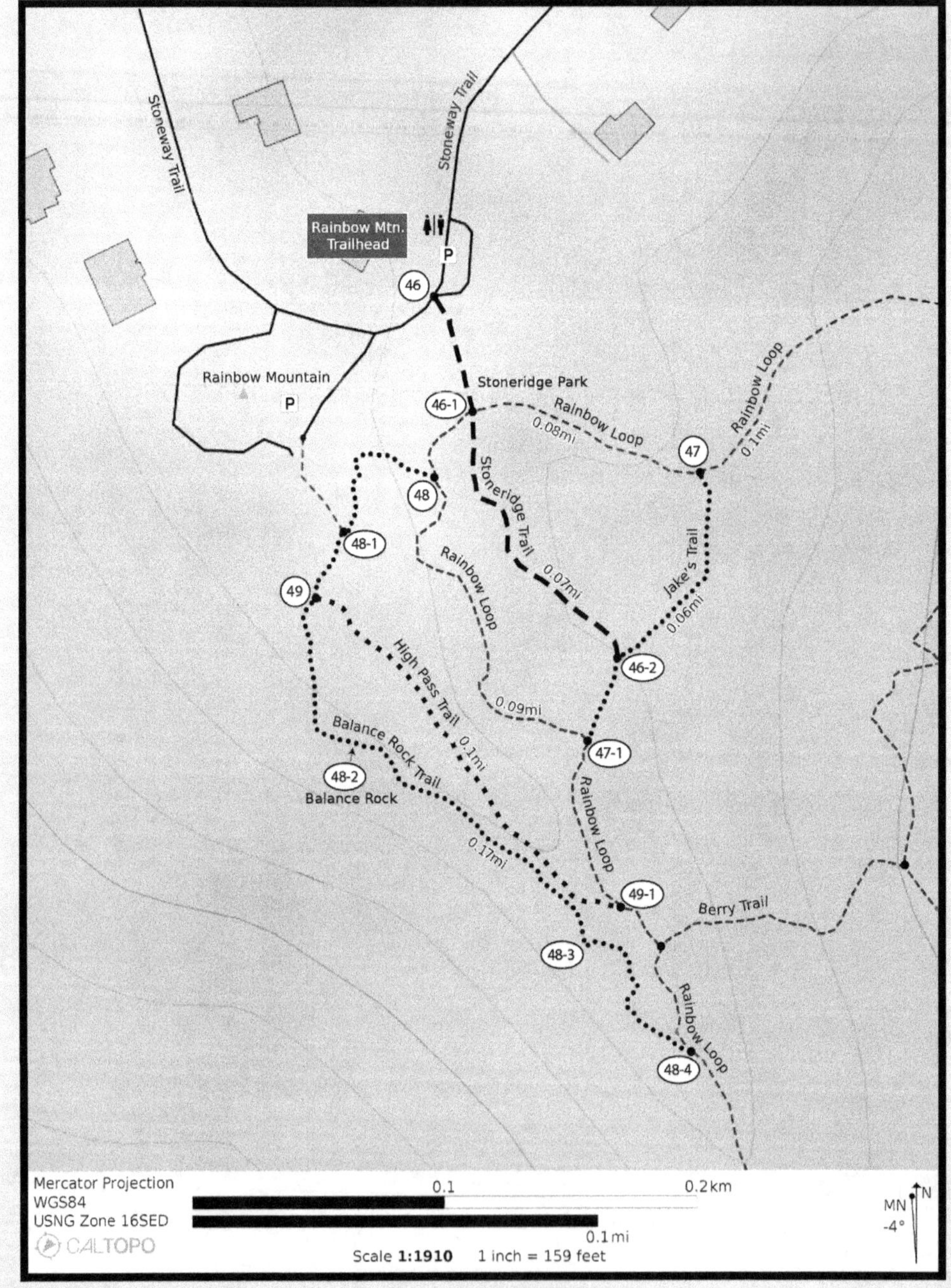

46. Stoneridge Trail

The Stoneridge Trail leads to the Stoneridge Park playground area and the Rainbow Loop Trail. It then continues on to meet Jake's Trail near a boulder formation. From this rocky vantage point, you can see for miles and catch partial views of Huntsville.

Distance: 0.1 mi.
Hiking Time: 2 minutes
Elevation Gain/Loss: +2 ft., -41 ft.
Hiking Difficulty: Easy
Location: Rainbow Mountain Nature Preserve, 230 Stoneway Trail, Madison, AL 35758
Facilities & Driving Directions: See page 120.

Highlights

Playtime for the Kids: For a nice outing with the kids, take them to the Stoneridge Park playground, and add an easy nature walk on the nearby trails.

Waypoint/Mile

Trailhead (Waypoint 46) (34.73426, -86.72780) This hike begins at the Rainbow Mtn. Trailhead parking area. From the parking lot, go to the right of the kiosk and head south to descend the Stoneridge Trail, which leads to the playground.

46-1 (34.73387, -86.72761) (133 ft.) The Stoneridge Trail crosses the Rainbow Loop Trail. To continue on the Stoneridge Trail, go to the right side of the playground and continue south.

46-2 (34.73297, -86.72699) (0.1 mi.) The Stoneridge Trail ends at the junction with Jake's Trail. From this junction, you can turn left onto Jake's Trail, traveling northeast, and descend 275 ft. to meet the Rainbow Loop Trail. Or you can turn right onto Jake's Trail, traveling southwest, to climb for about 100 ft. and meet the western side of the Rainbow Loop Trail.

47. Jake's Trail

Jake's Trail is an interior path that connects the western and northern sections of the Rainbow Loop Trail. It's mellow for the first 300 ft. or so and then makes a moderate to steep climb to the top of a ridge to meet the Rainbow Loop Trail.

Distance: 0.09 mi.
Hiking Time: 3 to 5 minutes
Elevation Gain/Loss: +35 ft., -12 ft.
Hiking Difficulty: Easy
Location: Rainbow Mountain Nature Preserve, 230 Stoneway Trail, Madison, AL 35758
Facilities & Driving Directions: See page 120.

Highlights

Loop Hike Options: One of the best aspects of the Rainbow Mountain trail system is that there are many options for loop hikes. Many of the paths, including Jake's Trail, intersect several other trails, creating long and short loops. This means you can design a hike to suit whatever you are in the mood forwhether it's a short hike with the kids or a long solo trek.

Bluff View: At the junction of Jake's Trail and the Rainbow Loop Trail (Waypoint 47), there is a stack of boulders. If you look beyond these rocks, you can see portions of Huntsville, including the replica of the Saturn V rocket, which is about 4 mi. away as the crow flies.

Waypoint/Mile

Trailhead (Waypoint 47) (34.73366, -86.72663) You can access Jake's Trail from the Stoneridge Trail (see page 123) and from the Rainbow Loop Trail. To reach it from the Rainbow Loop Trail, begin at the Rainbow Mtn. Trailhead parking area and follow the Stoneridge Trail to the junction with the Rainbow Loop Trail near the playground. Then go left (east) and follow the Rainbow Loop Trail for 437 ft. to reach the junction with Jake's Trail, which intersects on the right at Waypoint 47.
46-2 (34.73297, -86.72699) (317 ft.) The Stoneridge Trail intersects on

the left. Continue straight, traveling southwest, and pass through a stand of tall pines.

47-1 (34.73267, -86.72715) (0.09 mi.) Jake's Trail intersects with the Rainbow Loop Trail.

Trail Facts

A Dog Named Jake: You'll see the profile of a dog on the blazes marking Jake's Trail. This path is named for Jake, a dog owned by Land Trust volunteer Nat Berry, who played a key role in developing the trails on Rainbow Mountain.

48. Balance Rock Trail

This trail runs along a bluff and passes Balance Rock, one of the most iconic features of the Rainbow Mountain trail system. From there, the path continues along the bluff, and side trails allow hikers to explore the base of tall rock formations. Finally, the path crawls along the ridge to meet the Rainbow Loop Trail.

Distance: 0.2 mi.
Hiking Time: 5 to 10 minutes
Elevation Gain/Loss: +47 ft., -57 ft.
Hiking Difficulty: Easy
Location: Rainbow Mountain Nature Preserve, 230 Stoneway Trail, Madison, AL 35758
Facilities & Driving Directions: See page 120.

Highlights

Balance Rock: Weathering and erosion have stripped away portions of this sandstone and shale formation, making it appear that an oblong boulder is impossibly perched atop another rock. As the Land Trust explains, "Balance Rock was created when softer layers of rock eroded below and around a denser rock." If you look at the base of the top rock, you'll see that its foot is incredibly small, heightening the illusion that the stone is perfectly balanced.

Waypoint/Mile

Balance Rock atop Rainbow Mountain

Trailhead (Waypoint 48) (34.73361, -86.72777) The Balance Rock Trail begins a short distance down the west side of the Rainbow Loop Trail. To reach it, begin at the Rainbow Mtn. Trailhead parking area. From the parking lot, go to the right of the kiosk and head south to descend the Stoneridge Trail. At the junction with the Rainbow Loop Trail near the playground, turn right and travel south-west on the Rainbow Loop Trail. At 0.15 mi., the Balance Rock Trail intersects on the right. Turn right onto the Balance Rock Trail and travel west.

48-1 (34.73340, -86.72816) (225 ft.) A path to the right leads to the upper parking area.

49 (34.73323, -86.72835) (315 ft.) The High Pass Trail intersects on the left. Continue straight, traveling south along the edge of the bluff.

48-2 (34.73267, -86.72812) (0.1 mi.) Balance Rock is on the right. From this point, continue walking southeast along the bluff. You'll walk another 400 ft. to reach Waypoint 48-3.

48-3 (34.73200, -86.72712) (0.18 mi.) A path to the right drops down to explore the base of the bluff. The actual Balance Rock Trail bears left and passes between two boulders.

After you walk another 120 ft., to the right and below you'll see a small slot in the rocks that's big enough to pass through and explore the area further.

48-4 (34.73164, -86.72665) (0.22 mi.) The Balance Rock Trail ends at the junction with the Rainbow Loop Trail.

Trail Facts

Balance Rock: This rock formation is an erosional remnant of a body of rock known as the Hartselle Formation, which includes layers of sandstone, conglomerate, shale and coal.

49. High Pass Trail

Allow some time to linger on this short but impressive trail. As you walk along a narrow ridge, you'll have dramatic views of the surrounding lowlands. Relax on a bench or scramble to the top of a boulder to enjoy a snack and the inspiring scenery.

Distance: 0.1 mi.
Hiking Time: Less than 5 minutes
Elevation Gain/Loss: +1 ft., -27 ft.
Hiking Difficulty: Easy
Location: Rainbow Mountain Nature Preserve, 230 Stoneway Trail, Madison, AL 35758
Facilities & Driving Directions: See page 120.

Highlights

Beautiful Ridge Top Walk: The High Pass Trail traverses a narrow spine atop Rainbow Mountain, offering views of the surrounding valleys. Mature cedars, rock outcrops and large boulder formations make this mountaintop beautifully rugged.

Waypoint/Mile

Trailhead (Waypoint 49) (34.73323, -86.72835) To reach the northern end of the High Pass Trail, begin at the Rainbow Mtn. Trailhead parking area and take the Stoneridge Trail to the Rainbow Loop Trail. Turn right and go southwest on the Rainbow Loop Trail for 0.15 mi., and then turn right onto the Balance Rock Trail. Walk 315 ft. to the junction with the High Pass Trail, which intersects on the left at Waypoint 49.

The trail runs level along the knife-edge ridge, and then drops gradually to pass several spots where you can relax and enjoy the view. You might stop at a bench flanked by cedars or find a perch atop one of the many large boulders.

49-1 (0.12 mi.) At the southern end of the High Pass Trail, the path crosses over the ridge top and intersects with the Rainbow Loop Trail.

Trail Facts

Top of the Rainbow: Reaching an elevation of 1,140 ft., this trail crosses the highest point of the Rainbow Mountain Nature Preserve.

SECTION 2:
Rainbow Loop Trail, Spring Trail, Wild Trail and Berry Trail

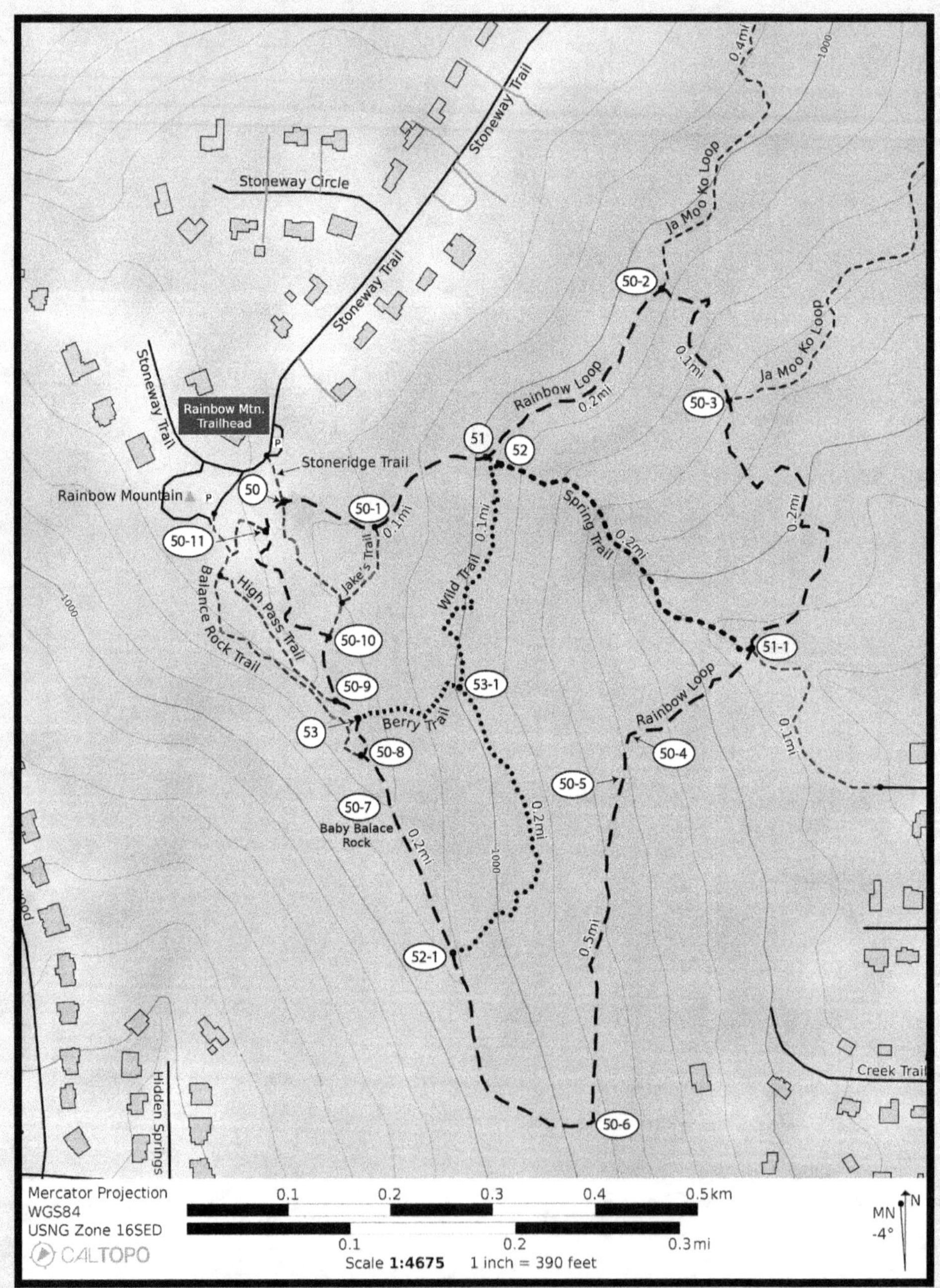

50. Rainbow Loop Trail

When you hike something dubbed the "Rainbow Loop," you might envision skipping along, all smiles, admiring the butterflies. But this 1.5-mi. loop will challenge many hikers due to a few rocky, rugged sections and steep terrain. As it swings though a great deal of the preserve, the Rainbow Loop allows you to access the other trails in the system, so you can add a variety of side trips and loops.

Distance: 1.5 mi.
Hiking Time: 1 hour
Elevation Gain/Loss: +422 ft., -422 ft.
Hiking Difficulty: Moderate to strenuous
Location: Rainbow Mountain Nature Preserve, 230 Stoneway Trail, Madison, AL 35758
Facilities & Driving Directions: See page 120.

Highlights

Creek and Waterfall: One of the prettiest and most peaceful spots on the trail lies a little more than 0.5 mi. in. At the junction of the Rainbow Loop Trail and the Spring Trail, the path eases into a small clearing, where a small waterfall flows into a shallow pool. A nearby bench provides the ideal spot to soak up some sun and doze off to the hypnotic sounds of the trickling water.

Baby Balance Rock: Baby Balance Rock is smaller and less impressive than its older sibling, Balance Rock, but it's still a nice feature. A thick, flat stone sits atop a bench of boulders, and erosion and weathering have carved away some of the stone between the top and bottom rocks. It creates a slight effect that the top rock is balanced with one end hovering. The illusion is not as dramatic as Balance Rock, but this formation is lower, so you can scramble onto it and enjoy nice views to the west.

Waypoint/Mile

Trailhead (Waypoint 50) (34.73394, -86.72756) This hike begins at the Rainbow Mtn. Trailhead parking area. From the parking lot, go to the right of the kiosk and head south to descend the Stoneridge Trail, which leads to the playground. Go to the northeast side of the playground (the far-left corner) and take the Rainbow Loop Trail, which descends to the southeast. The path soon makes a steep descent through boulders.

50-1 (34.73364, -86.72669) (437 ft.) At the T junction, Jake's Trail intersects on the right. To continue on the Rainbow Loop Trail, turn left and travel northeast. At this junction, you can peer over the highest boulder in front of you to see the Saturn V rocket replica to the east.

51 (34.73423, -86.72538) (0.1 mi.) The Spring Trail intersects on the right and descends to the southeast. Continue straight and travel northeast to stay on the Rainbow Loop Trail.

50-2 (34.73575, -86.72354) (0.3 mi.) At the T junction, the Ja Moo Ko Loop Trail intersects on the left and makes a rocky ascent to the northwest. To stay on the Rainbow Loop Trail, go right and descend to the south on a narrow path that's extremely rocky and rooted.

50-3 (34.73473, -86.72275) (0.4 mi.) The Ja Moo Ko Loop Trail intersects on the left and heads east. Continue straight to head southeast and descend gradually through more rocks and roots. The forest soon becomes denser, and the trail transitions back to packed earth.

51-1 (34.73258, -86.72251) (0.6 mi.) This is a nice area at the creek, with a bench and small falls. Across the creek bed, you'll reach a four-way junction. To the right, the Spring Trail climbs to the northwest. Straight ahead, across the creek, is an unofficial trail that goes 0.1 mi. and ends at a residential area. To continue on the Rainbow Loop Trail, go straight after you cross the creek and begin a steep climb, heading south.

50-4 (34.73183, -86.72386) (0.7 mi.) As you're ascending the slope, you'll reach a Y junction. To stay on the official trail, go right and climb to the west. If you go left at the Y, you'll follow an unofficial trail that ascends to meet the Rainbow Loop Trail at **Waypoint 50-5** (34.73144, -86.72402).

50-6 (34.72853, -86.72428) (1 mi.) At the trail junction, the Rainbow Loop Trail goes right and climbs over rocky terrain. If you continue straight, you'll reach a dead end after 50 ft.

After walking another 200 to 300 ft., you'll reach a high point on this portion of Rainbow Mountain. A bench beneath old hardwoods and cedars makes a nice spot to catch your breath and enjoy the breeze blowing over the crest of the mountain.

52-1 (34.73008, -86.72583) (1.1 mi.) The Wild Trail intersects on the right and drops to the east. Continue straight, traversing the top of the ridge.

50-7 (34.73129, -86.72659) (1.2 mi.) On the left is Baby Balance Rock.

50-8 (34.73167, -86.72671) (1.3 mi.) The Balance Rock Trail intersects on the left. Continue straight, crossing the ridge top. Walk another 150 ft. to Waypoint 53.

53 (34.73199, -86.72680) (1.33 mi.) The Berry Trail intersects on the right and descends. Continue straight, hugging the rocks on your left and traveling northwest.

50-9 (34.73212, -86.72702) (1.34 mi.) The High Pass Trail intersects on the left. Continue straight to stay on the Rainbow Loop Trail.

50-10 (34.73270, -86.72711) (1.39 mi.) At the Y junction, Jake's Trail intersects on the right. Bear left to stay on the Rainbow Loop Trail.

50-11 (34.73361, -86.72777) (1.48 mi.) The Balance Rock Trail intersects on the left. Continue straight on the Rainbow Loop Trail, which soon bends to the right and heads northeast. After another 100 ft., you'll arrive back at the playground.

51. Spring Trail

This steep and rocky path dives down a creek drainage to meet the Rainbow Loop Trail. At this junction, a small waterfall trickles into a pool to create one of the most peaceful spots in the preserve.

Distance: 0.2 mi.
Hiking Time: 10 to 15 minutes
Elevation Gain/Loss: +0 ft., -253 ft.
Hiking Difficulty: Moderate to strenuous
Location: Rainbow Mountain Nature Preserve, 230 Stoneway Trail, Madison, AL 35758
Facilities & Driving Directions: See page 120.

Highlights

Resting Spot and Waterfall: At the southeastern end of the Spring Trail, the creek forms a small waterfall that flows over mossy rocks to collect in a shallow, tea-colored pool. This water feature sits next to a small clearing that's relatively flat. Several steep trails surround this spot, so the level ground and attractive water feature make it a popular rest stop.

Waypoint/Mile

Trailhead (Waypoint 51) (34.73423, -86.72538) Begin at the Rainbow Mtn. Trailhead parking area and take the Stoneridge Trail to the Rainbow Loop Trail. Travel east on the Rainbow Loop Trail a little more than 0.1 mi. to the junction with the Spring Trail, which intersects on the right. Turn right onto the Spring Trail and descend to the southeast.

52 (34.73417, -86.72530) (35 ft.) The Wild Trail intersects on the right and gradually rises to the south. Continue straight to head southeast on the Spring Trail.

As you descend gradually on the rocky path, breaks in the tree foliage reveal distant ridges to the east. At 430 ft., a bench provides a place for people ascending this trail to stop and catch their breath. Near 0.1 mi., the path crosses a small stream, and then crosses again after another 40 ft. Then you'll begin a steep, rocky descent. At 0.17 mi., your knees and legs get a break as the trail levels out. Soon, the path descends on a gentle grade and transitions from packed earth to flat stone.

51-1 (34.73258, -86.72251) (0.2 mi.) The Spring Trail ends at the junction with the Rainbow Loop Trail beside the creek. While the Spring Trail officially ends here, you can continue straight on an unofficial path that continues southeast. After a little more than 0.1 mi., this path ends at a cul-de-sac on Oakhurst Drive.

52. Wild Trail

The Wild Trail traverses a boulder-strewn slope to connect northern and southwestern sections of the Rainbow Loop Trail. The walk isn't too challenging for the first 0.28 mi. But the trek concludes with a steep, short (less than 0.1 mi.) climb to the ridge top.

Distance: 0.36 mi.

Hiking Time: 10 to 15 minutes

Elevation Gain/Loss: +100 ft., -46 ft.

Hiking Difficulty: Moderate to strenuous

Location: Rainbow Mountain Nature Preserve, 230 Stoneway Trail, Madison, AL 35758

Facilities & Driving Directions: See page 120.

Highlights

Wild Rock Features: While contemplating the meaning behind the trail's "Wild" name, I noticed a sinkhole near the path and several other intriguing rock features along the way. A couple of moss-covered boulders with small openings reminded me of the "elf houses" I encountered in Iceland. In that country, many folks believe that rocks are home to magical "hidden people." It seemed to me that a place named Rainbow Mountain should house its own fantastic creatures. The many rock gardens and stone pockets along this path certainly look like good hiding places for wild things.

Waypoint/Mile

Trailhead (Waypoint 52) (34.73415, -86.72531) To reach the trailhead, begin at the Rainbow Mtn. Trailhead parking area and take the Stoneridge Trail to the Rainbow Loop Trail. Travel east on the Rainbow Loop Trail a little more than 0.1 mi. to the junction with the Spring Trail. Follow the Spring Trail for 35 ft. to the junction with the Wild Trail, which intersects on the right. Turn right onto the Wild Trail and climb gradually to the southwest.

After a quick rise, the path drops and becomes

mostly level as it traverses a boulder-strewn slope thick with cedars and hardwoods. After about 390 ft., the trail climbs through a rocky landscape, and the forest is a bit more open.

53-1 (34.73225, -86.72574) (0.1 mi.) The Berry Trail intersects on the right and climbs to the west. To continue on the Wild Trail, go left and descend, traveling southeast.

The narrow path makes a mellow descent in scraggly woods littered with jumbles of rocks. As you continue, keep an eye out for a sinkhole to the right of the trail. Ahead, the trail runs along a rock shelf, and you can imagine what wild things might scurry through small openings in the trailside boulders. At 0.28 mi., the trail heads west and begins a moderate to steep climb.

52-1 (34.73008, -86.72583) (0.3 mi.) After consistent climbing, you reach the end of the Wild Trail where it meets the Rainbow Loop Trail atop the ridge.

53. Berry Trail

This interior trail begins atop the ridge and makes a moderate to steep descent to meet the Wild Trail. If you plan to hike this in reverse and climb to the top of the ridge, be prepared for a short but steep hike.

Distance: 385 ft.
Hiking Time: 5 minutes
Elevation Gain/Loss: +0 ft., -103 ft.
Hiking Difficulty: Moderate (Strenuous if hiked from Waypoint 53-1 to Waypoint 53)
Location: Rainbow Mountain Nature Preserve, 230 Stoneway Trail, Madison, AL 35758
Facilities & Driving Directions: See page 120.

Waypoint/Mile

Trailhead (Waypoint 53) (34.73197, -86.72680) To reach the beginning of the Berry Trail, begin at the Rainbow Mtn. Trailhead parking area and take the Stoneridge Trail to the Rainbow Loop Trail. Turn right to travel southwest on the Rainbow Loop Trail almost 0.2 mi. At Waypoint 53, the Wild Trail intersects on the left and descends from the top of the ridge.

53-1 (34.73225, -86.72574) (385 ft.) After a descent that measures 385 ft., the Berry Trail ends at the intersection with the Wild Trail.

SECTION 3:
Ja Moo Ko Loop Trail

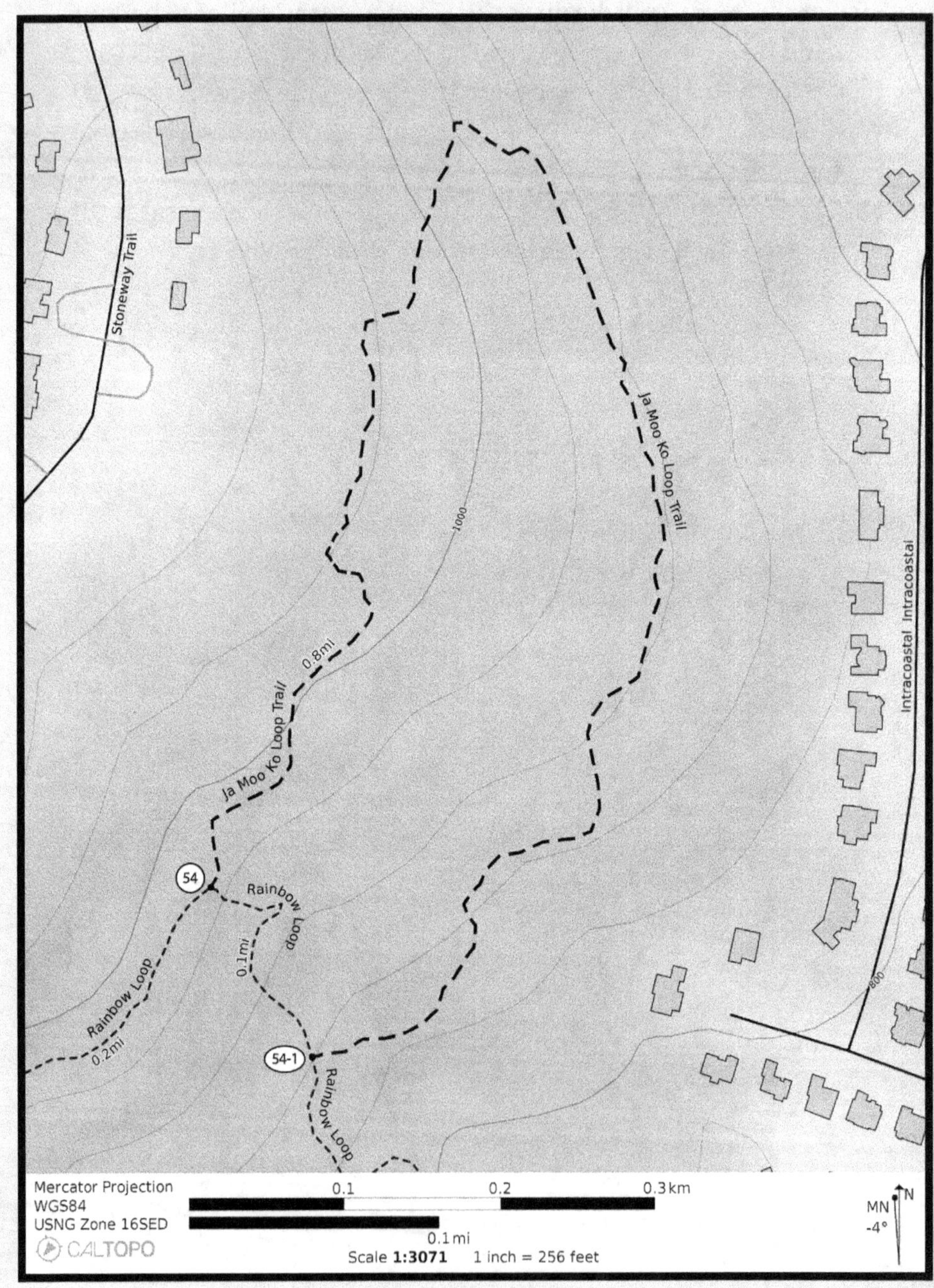

54. Ja Moo Ko Loop Trail

The Ja Moo Ko Loop Trail crosses rocky terrain as it loops through the northeastern corner of the preserve. When hiking this trail, you should wear shoes or boots with good traction, because you could encounter many slippery stones.

Distance: 0.86 mi.
Hiking Time: 30 minutes
Elevation Gain/Loss: +136 ft., -226 ft.
Hiking Difficulty: Moderate
Location: Rainbow Mountain Nature Preserve, 230 Stoneway Trail, Madison, AL 35758
Facilities & Driving Directions: See page 120.

Highlights

Rocky Ground: While traveling this trail, you won't encounter stellar views or remarkable natural features. However, if you're seeking a challenge, you can up your game by adding this rugged stretch of trail to your hike or run.

Waypoint/Mile

Trailhead (Waypoint 54) (34.73575, -86.72354) To reach the beginning of the Ja Moo Ko Loop Trail, begin at the Rainbow Mtn. Trailhead parking area and take the Stoneridge Trail to the Rainbow Loop Trail. Turn left and travel east on the Rainbow Loop Trail. At 0.4 mi., turn left at the T junction to take the Ja Moo Ko Loop Trail, which ascends to the northwest over stepped rocks. The path is marked with white blazes, and additional red arrows point the way.

At 0.14 mi., the trail continues to move up a rocky slope. Be on the lookout for a red arrow that directs you to go left. After the left turn, the trail scrambles over rocks and climbs through stands of cedars. At 0.2 mi., the trail moves down a slope, and in winter you can see beyond the bare trees the lowlands of west Huntsville and distant ridges to the east.

When you've hiked 0.25 mi., you'll begin a downhill run that lasts a little more than 0.1 mi. Near 0.4 mi., you'll finish that descent and turn right to head southeast. The trail drops off a low rock ledge to once again wind its way downward, wandering through rocky fields.

A little beyond 0.5 mi., the hike becomes less appealing. Downed trees and dense brush fill the forest, and neighboring houses come into view. Fortunately, after a few hundred feet the trail turns to the west to escape the residential area. As you near 0.8 mi., a red arrow directs you to follow the narrow rocky path to the left, which winds through dense brush.

The trail then begins a moderate descent through more rocks. As the trail traverses a rock shelf, the surface of the path becomes stone. At 0.82 mi., you'll begin a final climb to rejoin the Rainbow Loop Trail. **54-1** (34.73485, -86.72300) (0.86 mi.) The Ja Moo Ko Loop ends at the T junction with the Rainbow Loop Trail.

Trail Facts

Dog Tales: As mentioned earlier in the chapter, Nat Berry, a volunteer with the Land Trust of North Alabama, named Jake's Trail after his dog. Preferring not to slight his other dogs, he named this path Ja Moo Ko, which is a mashup of Jake, Moose and Kodiak.

Dallas W. Fanning Preserve

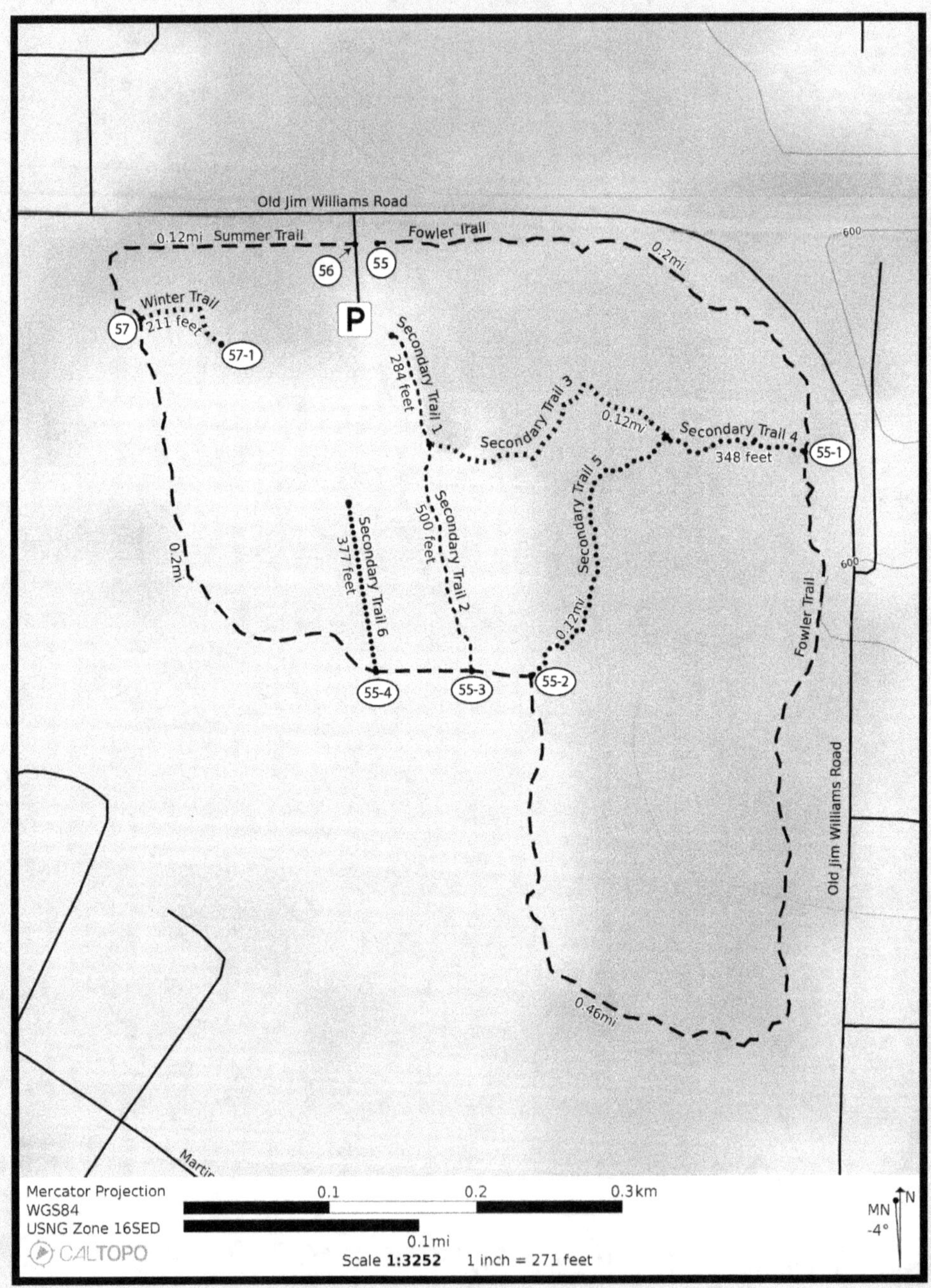

CHAPTER 9

Dallas W. Fanning Nature Preserve

Most of Huntsville's hiking areas are on the eastern side of the city. But in the summer of 2020, the city of Huntsville opened its first nature preserve on the west end of town. The Dallas W. Fanning Nature Preserve is located south of I-565, just east of Wall Triana Boulevard, on Old Jim Williams Road. The 58-acre preserve includes nearly 1.7 miles of trails that wind through a low-lying wetland area.

The trails in the preserve are flat and primarily made of gravel covered in soft mulch, which provides a comfortable surface for walking, trail running and biking. People on the west side of town venture here to get exercise and enjoy a peaceful escape from the city. Plus, many people bring their young children here to take advantage of the stroller-friendly paths.

Many of the trails explore dense, shaded woods, but low brush occupies the heart of the preserve. This creates a broad area with open sky, and ample sunlight washes over the wide trails bordered by clusters of wildflowers. At the northern end of the preserve, a large grassy area dotted with trees provides a comfortable spot to relax in the shade or catch a few rays.

Before the preserve opened, builders harvested topsoil from this land and used it as a dumpsite for construction waste. It's commendable that the preserve's namesake, Dallas W. Fanning, led the effort to rehabilitate and preserve this plot of land. When Fanning was development director for the city of Huntsville, he championed the town's western expansion. With Huntsville's explosive growth, he recognized the importance of creating green spaces to provide a respite from the urban sprawl. As City Administrator John Hamilton said, this space not only preserves a slice of the local environment, but also provides residents with a "sanctuary space to connect with nature."

General Information

Location: 258 Old Jim Williams Rd. SW, Huntsville, AL 35824

Hours: Open dawn to dusk.

Primary trail activities allowed: Hiking, biking

Pets: Leashed pets allowed.

Fees: There are no fees to use the trails.

Facilities: There are no facilities and no sources of potable water at the trailhead.

Information: (256) 532-5326; www.huntsvilleal.gov/environment/green-team/nature-preserves/dallas-w-fanning-nature-preserve/

Driving Directions

Traveling West on I-565: Take Exit 9, go 0.2 mi., and keep left at the fork to follow signs for Triana. Merge onto Wall Triana Highway. Travel 1.7 mi. on Wall Triana Hwy., and then turn left onto Trademark Drive. Go 0.1 mi., and then turn left onto Old Jim Williams Road. Go 0.3 mi. and turn right to enter the parking area for the Dallas W. Fanning Nature Preserve.

Traveling East on I-565: Take Exit 9, go 0.3 mi., and then keep right at the fork to follow signs for Triana. Merge onto Wall Triana Highway. Travel 1.1 mi., and then turn left onto Trademark Drive. Go 0.1 mi., and then turn left onto Old Jim Williams Road. Go 0.3 mi. and turn right to enter the parking area for the Dallas W. Fanning Nature Preserve.

Fowler Trail, Fowler Trail Secondary Trails 1-6, Summer Trail and Winter Trail

55. Fowler Trail

Measuring 1 mi., the Fowler Trail is the longest path in the preserve. It's frequented by trail runners, people walking for exercise, and folks getting their kids out for some fresh air. As it loops around the preserve, the trail remains level, allowing a wide range of people to travel it comfortably. It's even stroller-friendly. Plus, the surface of the trail is soft earth and bark, so it reduces impact for runners.

Distance: 1 mi.
Hiking Time: 20 to 30 minutes
Elevation Gain/Loss: +34 ft., -28 ft.
Hiking Difficulty: Easy
Location: Dallas W. Fanning Nature Preserve, 258 Old Jim Williams Rd. SW, Huntsville, AL 35824
Facilities & Driving Directions: See page 144.

Waypoint/Mile

Trailhead (Waypoint 55) (34.65524, -86.74724) To reach the beginning of the Fowler Trail, begin in the parking lot and walk toward the entrance to the parking area. When you've walked about 140 ft., you'll see on the right a sign with "Start" and a red arrow, as well as a sign that says, "Steve Fowler Trail." Enter the wide, leaf-covered path, which is slightly higher than the surrounding ground.

The level path begins in extremely dense woods, though Old Jim Williams Road is visible on the left.

55-1 (34.65408, -86.74405) (0.2 mi.) Secondary Trail 4 (the Black

The Dallas W. Fanning Preserve's green field

Trail) intersects on the right and is marked with black blazes. (Black Trail details are below.) Go straight to stay on the Fowler Trail, which continues south.

The path runs parallel to Old Jim Williams Road in a shady corridor of maples and oaks. At 0.36 mi., the trail descends gradually; this is one of the few places in the preserve where you can discern a change in elevation. At 0.4 mi., you can see the road as well as a few houses. Near 0.5 mi., the trail hooks to the right and heads away from the road, running northwest.

Exploring the interior of the Dallas W. Fanning Preserve

55-2 (34.65270, -86.74623) (0.69 mi.) At the junction, the Black Trail goes to the right and heads northeast back into the forest. The Fowler Trail turns left and moves into more open land. After you turn left, you'll go another 123 ft. to reach Waypoint 55-3.

55-3 (34.65273, -86.74659) (0.72 mi.) Secondary Trail 2 (the Blue Trail) intersects on the right and heads north across open terrain to end at the parking area. (More Blue Trail details below.) To continue on the Fowler Trail, go straight and head west.

55-4 (34.65269, -86.74728) (0.76 mi.) Secondary Trail 6 (the Orange Trail) intersects on the right and goes northwest for 377 ft. to end at a large grassy clearing. (More Orange Trail details below.) To stay on the Fowler Trail, go straight and bend to the right, heading northwest.

As the path proceeds west and north, it takes a wide arc and passes through pines growing from red clay earth. Near the 0.9-mi. mark, the trees provide some shade, and to the right you'll see the parking area on the opposite side of the grassy field.

57 (34.65485, -86.74906) (1 mi.) The Fowler Trail ends at the junction with the Winter Trail and Summer Trail. If you continue straight at this junction, you'll follow the Summer Trail, which returns to the parking area after a little more than 0.1 mi. If you go right at the junction, you'll follow the Winter Trail, which dead-ends at the edge of the large field after about 200 ft.

Trail Facts

Steve Fowler: The trail is named for Steve Fowler, a supervisor for the city of Huntsville's Landscape Management Maintenance group. Fowler helped design the trails in the Dallas W. Fanning Nature Preserve, and he did carpentry for the benches and signs. (*Source: al.com*)

Fowler Trail Secondary Trails 1-6

These six paths, coded by number and color, are offshoots of the Fowler Trail that explore the interior of the preserve. If you're walking the Fowler Trail, you can use these paths to extend your outing by walking though the center of the preserve. These secondary trails also allow you to create a variety of loop hikes.

Location: Dallas W. Fanning Nature Preserve, 258 Old Jim Williams Rd. SW, Huntsville, AL 35824
Facilities & Driving Directions: See page 144.

Secondary Trails 1 & 2 (Blue Trail)

Connecting the parking area with the Fowler Trail, the Blue Trail traverses one of the more attractive areas in the preserve. The wide path is surrounded by low brush rather than dense succession forest. On clear days, hikers walk beneath a broad blue sky with ample sunshine on their shoulders.

Distance: 0.14 mi.
Hiking Time: 2 to 3 minutes
Elevation Gain/Loss: +/-0 ft.
Hiking Difficulty: Easy

Secondary Trail 3 (Purple Trail)

This wide and level path winds through shaded woods as it cuts across the heart of the preserve. This trail, as well as the Purple and Black trails, allows you to do a variety of loops and extend your outing. As is the case with the Fowler Trail, the bark-covered path provides some welcome cushioning. When you've walked 330 ft. on the Purple Trail, you exit the shaded woods and enter open land in the center of the preserve.

Distance: 0.12 mi.
Hiking Time: 2 to 3 minutes
Elevation Gain/Loss: +3 ft., - 3 ft.
Hiking Difficulty: Easy

Secondary Trails 4 & 5 (Black Trails)

Like the eastern part of the Fowler Trail, the Black Trail moves through the shade of thick forest. About 250 ft. down the trail, the woods briefly allow in more light where a wooden bench sits in a small clearing. Similar to other paths in the preserve, the Black Trail has a soft, bark-covered surface and explores level terrain. Because this trail intersects the Purple and Blue trails, as well as the Fowler Trail, you can use it to hike a few loops.

Distance: 0.18 mi.
Hiking Time: 5 minutes
Elevation Gain/Loss: +0 ft., -16 ft.
Hiking Difficulty: Easy

Secondary Trail 6 (Orange Trail)

This very wide path goes north for 377 ft. to end at a grassy clearing dotted with pines, which is a great spot to relax. A bench sits in the shade of a pine tree, and the broad field, dotted with trees, creates a pastoral backdrop.

Distance: 377 ft.
Hiking Time: 1 to 2 minutes
Elevation Gain/Loss: +/-0 ft.
Hiking Difficulty: Easy

56. Summer Trail

If you'd like to walk the entire loop around the preserve, take this short but very rocky path that connects to the Fowler Trail. At its end, the Summer Trail also links to the Winter Trail, which stretches just a couple of hundred feet.

Distance: 0.12 mi.
Hiking Time: 2 to 3 minutes
Elevation Gain/Loss: +7 ft., -0 ft.
Hiking Difficulty: Easy
Location: Dallas W. Fanning Nature Preserve, 258 Old Jim Williams Rd. SW, Huntsville, AL 35824
Facilities & Driving Directions: See page 144.

Waypoint/Mile

Trailhead (Waypoint 56) (34.65519, -86.74756) To reach the beginning of the Summer Trail, begin at the parking area and walk about 140 ft. back toward the entrance. Go left and enter the woods to take the Summer Trail, which heads west.

The Summer Trail begins in a more mature section of woods, and the path is quite rocky. As you proceed through this shaded corridor, watch your footing, as there are more stones beneath a bed of leaves.

57 (34.65485, -86.74906) (0.12 mi.) The Summer Trail ends at the junction with the Winter Trail, which goes left, and the Fowler Trail, which goes right and heads south.

57. Winter Trail

Measuring just over a couple of hundred feet, this short path skirts the northwest corner of the large open field in the preserve.

Distance: 211 ft.
Hiking Time: 1 minute
Elevation Gain/Loss: +0 ft., -3 ft.
Hiking Difficulty: Easy
Location: Dallas W. Fanning Nature Preserve, 258 Old Jim Williams Rd. SW, Huntsville, AL 35824
Facilities & Driving Directions: See page 144.

Waypoint/Mile

Trailhead (Waypoint 57) (34.65485, -86.74906) To reach the Winter Trail, begin at the parking area and walk about 140 ft. back toward the entrance. Go left and enter the woods to take the Summer Trail, which heads west. Follow the Summer Trail 0.12 mi. to the junction with the Winter Trail and Fowler Trail. Turn left onto the Winter Trail at Waypoint 57 and head east.

The path drops into shaded forest, and after 136 ft. it takes a sharp right toward the field.

57-1 (34.65469, -86.74858) (211 ft.) The Winter Trail ends at the northwestern edge of the grassy field.

Huntsville Metro Area Greenways

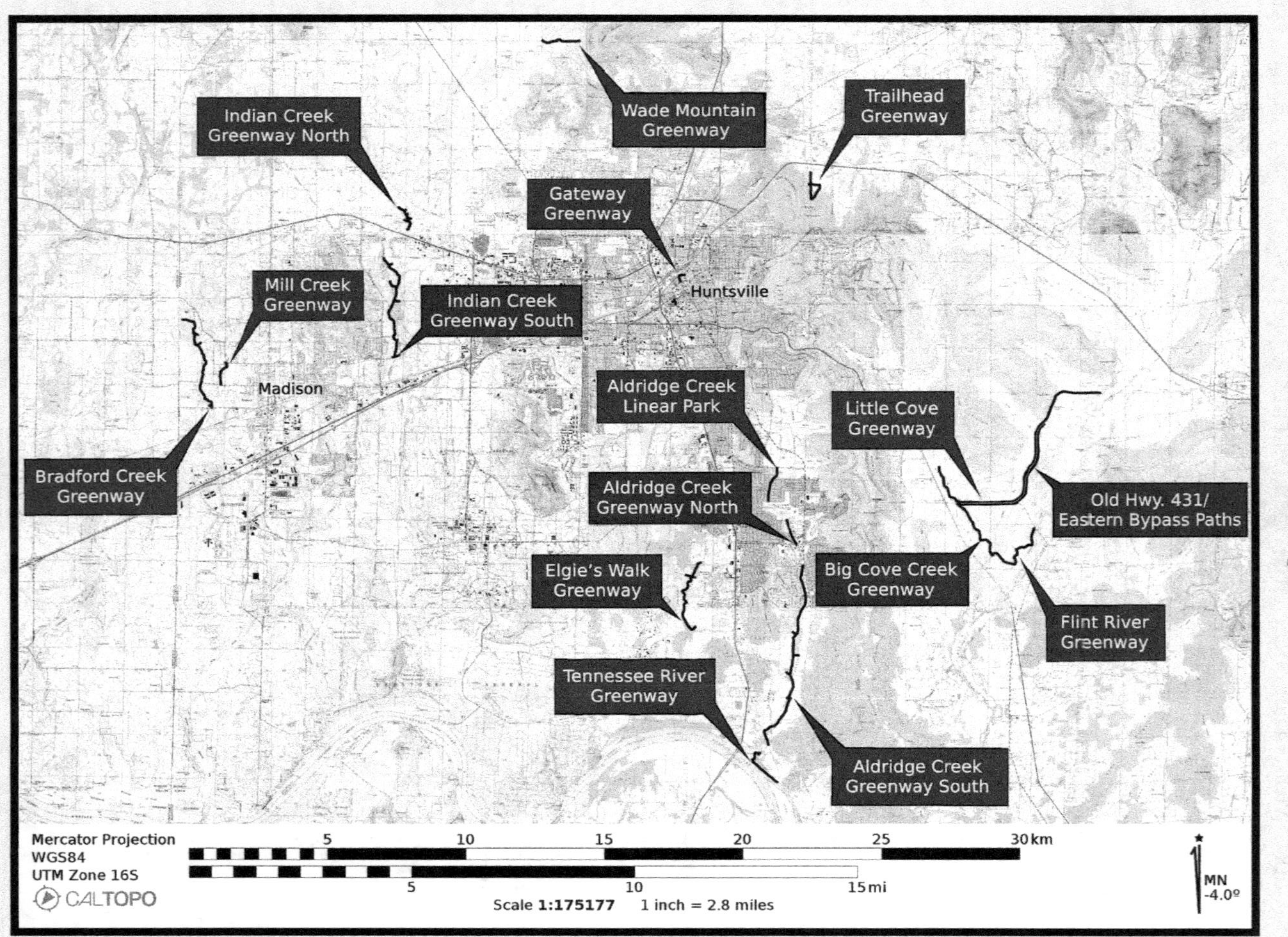

CHAPTER 10

Greenways

In 1868, architect Frederick Law Olmsted created the first greenway in the United States in Buffalo, New York. Olmsted, who had designed New York's Central Park a decade earlier, believed it was important to create corridors of natural land and water in cities to not only preserve the environment but also bring together people in communities.

More than 150 years later, greenways are thriving as more and more communities are recognizing their benefits. The cities of Huntsville and Madison have created more than a dozen greenways, realizing that they build connections between people, promote exercise and healthy living, and even increase home values.

There are many definitions for the term "greenway," but it's basically a strip of undeveloped land that runs through an urban area. Some greenways traverse forests and follow creeks, while others pass through old railroad corridors. The paths that run through greenways can have natural surfaces, but many are paved, as is the case with most greenways in Huntsville and Madison.

Our local greenway trails are not only paved but also mostly level. This makes these recreation areas accessible to a wide range of people and activities. On any given day, it's common to see people walking, running, biking and even skating on the greenways. Another benefit of greenways is that they are generally protected from surrounding streets, so they're great places to safely walk and bike with kids.

In Huntsville, Madison, and other nearby communities, there are at least 13 official greenways, measuring more than 27 miles, and they offer a wide range of experiences. Madison's Bradford Creek Greenway explores an extensive section of uninterrupted woods, making this trek feel particularly wild. The Flint River Greenway in Owens Cross Roads, southeast of Huntsville, has a similar feel as it winds among vast farm fields and dense woodlands and skirts the Flint River. On the other hand, some trails, such as the Little Cove Road Greenway and the Gateway Greenway, run through a more urban landscape, and they're closer to roads, neighborhoods and commercial areas.

While we're fortunate to have an abundance of greenways, the metro population is growing rapidly, so we're going to need even more natural escapes. Fortunately, city officials intend to create dozens of more miles of greenways in the area. This includes development of the Singing River Trail, which will eventually include 70 miles of paths linking Huntsville, Madison, Decatur and Athens.

General Information

Hours: Most greenways open 1 hour before sunrise and close 1 hour after sunset, unless otherwise posted.

Primary trail activities allowed: Walking, biking

Pets: Leashed pets allowed.

Fees: There are no required fees to use the trails.

Information: Huntsville greenways: www.huntsville.org/things-to-do/outdoors/parks-greenways/; Madison greenways: www.madisonal.gov/681/Greenways-Trails

Owens Cross Roads Greenways:
Big Cove Creek Greenway (South and North Sections), Little Cove Road Greenway, Old Hwy. 431/Eastern Bypass Paths and Flint River Greenway

58. Big Cove Creek Greenway
(South and North Sections)

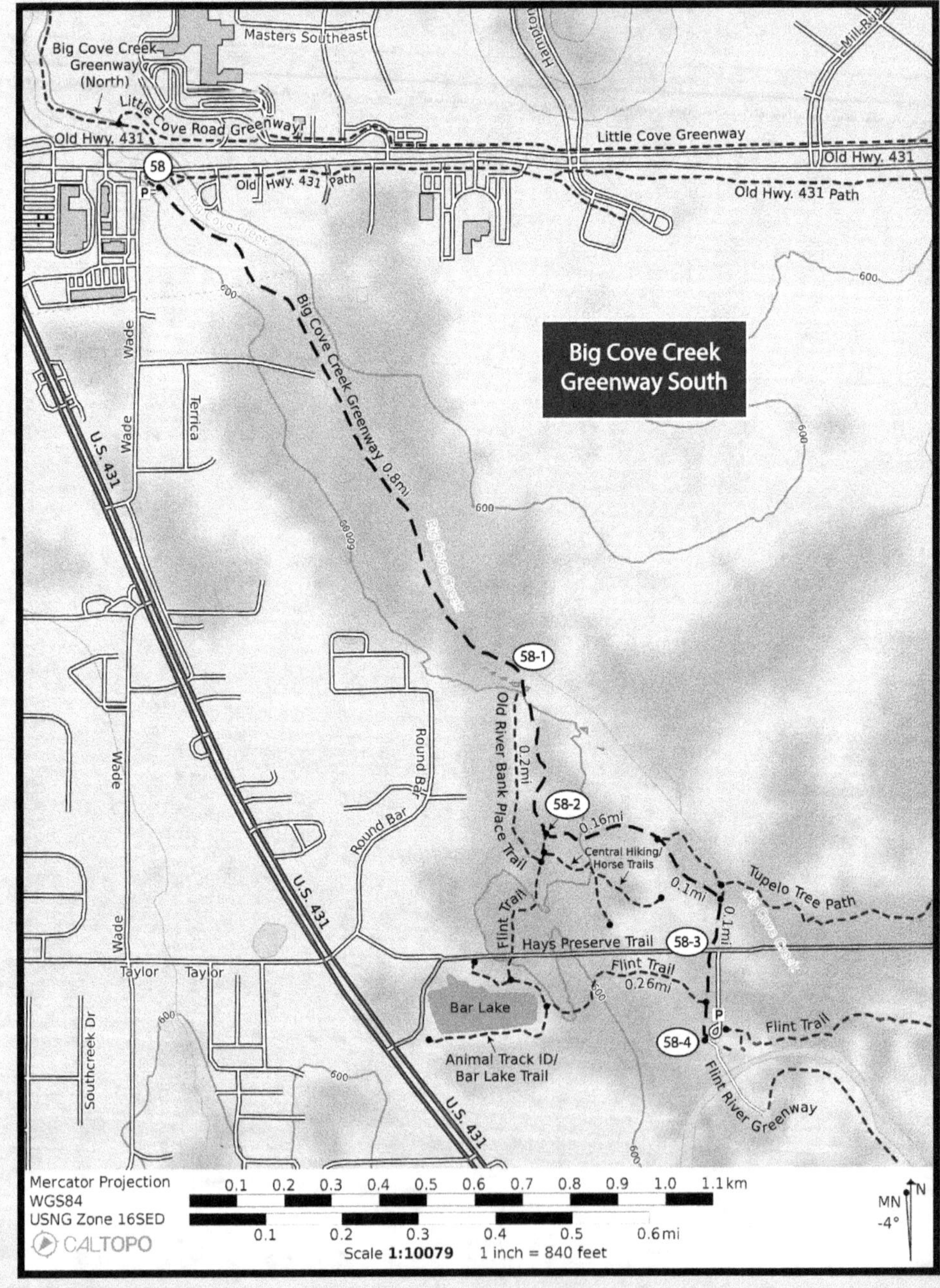

Big Cove Creek Greenway South
(Old Hwy. 431 to Hays Nature Preserve)

This paved and mostly level path steers you away from civilization to explore a quiet forested corridor. Portions of this greenway feel remote and wild, especially the section that snakes through a bottomland forest in the Hays Nature Preserve. Your hike ends at an attractive spot where a handsome wood and metal bridge spans a wide section of the Flint River.

Distance: 1.5 mi.

Hiking Time: 30 to 40 minutes

Elevation Gain/Loss: +37 ft., -37 ft.

Hiking Difficulty: Easy

Location: 327 Old Hwy. 431, Owens Cross Roads, AL 35763

Facilities: At the trailhead, there are no facilities and no sources of potable water.

Driving Directions: From the junction of U.S. 231/431 (Memorial Parkway) and U.S. 431/Governors Drive, travel east on U.S. 431 for 8.4 mi. Then use the second from the left lane to turn left onto Old Highway 431. Go 0.3 mi., and then turn right onto Wade Road. Go another 157 ft., and then turn left into the parking area for the Big Cove Creek Greenway. The parking area is not large. If all spaces are full, you can usually park in the lot for the State Farm Agency on the opposite side of Wade Rd.

Highlights

Long Forested Passageways: Thick woods and green fields flank the greenway for most of its length, allowing you to immerse yourself in nature as you walk, run or ride.

Hays Nature Preserve: For more than 0.5 mi., this southern section of the greenway explores the Hays Nature Preserve. (See page 13 for more on the preserve.) Covering some 375 acres, the preserve includes large tracts of undisturbed wetlands and hardwood forest. At its southern end, the greenway meets a bridge that spans the Flint River. If you have time, turn left and cross the parking area to explore the north riverbank. Grab a seat at a riverside picnic table and enjoy an excellent view of the bridge and its rust-colored arches hovering over the emerald river.

Waypoint/Mile

Trailhead (Waypoint 58) (34.65961, -86.47914) The trailhead lies near the east end of the Big Cove Creek Greenway parking lot. From the trailhead, head southeast to parallel Big Cove Creek, which will be on your left.

A narrow band of trees separates the trail and the creek, and the path soon arcs away from the water. At about 0.2 mi., the trail returns to skirt the slow-flowing creek, which is visible beyond a veil of trees. For the next 0.5 mi., the trail explores an especially attractive and wild corridor flanked by pines and hardwoods.

58-1 (34.65082, -86.47098) (0.8 mi.) You reach a sign marked "STOP/ Entering Hays Nature Preserve." But there's no need to stop, because the greenway continues through the preserve.

As the trail enters the preserve, the character of the surrounding forest changes quite a bit. In this floodplain, Big Cove Creek runs shallow and creeps through bottomland woods with flooded areas that resemble a swamp. As you approach 1 mi., the trail is not as flat as the typical greenway path, as it rises a few feet and soon drops. The brief sections of twisting, undulating terrain add some unexpected flair to this part of the greenway.

58-2 (34.64774, -86.47027) (1 mi.) On the right is a sign marked "Old Riverbank Place/1,000' to Flint Trail and Main Road." The trail on the right is a wide dirt path that runs south through the preserve. To continue on the Big Cove Creek Greenway, bear left to stay on the paved trail and travel east.

A narrow channel of water slides by on the left and runs through thick stands of spindly trees wrapped in ivy, while a few mature trees hug the trail. At 1.1 mi., a golf course comes into view on the left, while a field to the right creates a wide break with open sky.

58-3 (34.64569, -86.46658) (1.3 mi.) Cross the Hays Preserve Trail road and continue south in a shady corridor of woods.

58-4 (34.64393, -86.46654) (1.48 mi.) The Big Cove Creek Greenway ends at the beginning of the concrete bridge with a metal railing.

Long stretches of the Big Cove Creek Greenway feel remote and wild.

Big Cove Creek Greenway North

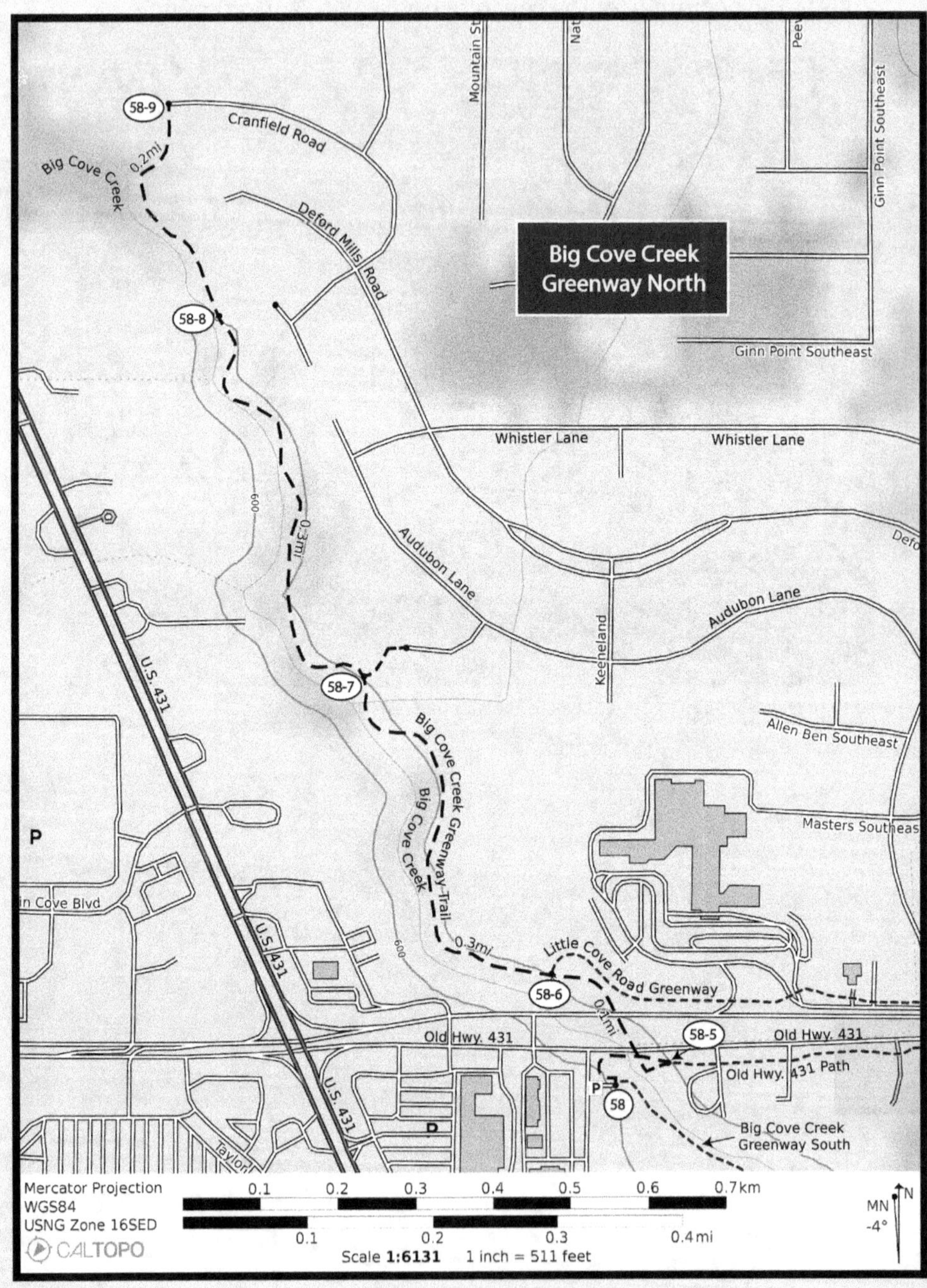

Big Cove Creek Greenway North
(Old Hwy. 431 to Cranfield Rd.)

From the trailhead, this paved path climbs briefly and then dips to run beneath Old Highway 431. The trail levels out as it skirts the grounds of Hampton Cove Elementary School and then heads northwest to parallel Big Cove Creek. You'll get intermittent views of the creek, but this is more of an urban walk that takes you along the edge of a neighborhood.

Distance: 1.1 mi.
Hiking Time: 30 to 40 minutes
Elevation Gain/Loss: +79 ft., -65 ft.
Hiking Difficulty: Easy
Location: 327 Old Hwy. 431, Owens Cross Roads, AL 35763
Facilities & Driving Directions: See page 157 and use the information for Big Cove Creek Greenway South.

Highlights

Nearly a Mile of Easy Walking: After the trail passes the elementary school, there is very little change in elevation, allowing an extended walk on mostly level ground. This is a great out-and-back trip for anyone who only has an hour or so to walk and prefers easier terrain.

Waypoint/Mile

Trailhead (Waypoint 58) (34.65961, -86.47914) The trailhead lies at the east end of the Big Cove Creek Greenway parking lot. From the trailhead, go west toward Wade Road, ascending the paved path that curls back to the east and crosses Big Cove Creek.

58-5 (34.65979, -86.47847) After walking 420 ft., bear right at the Y junction and follow the paved path as it curls back to the north to pass beneath Old Highway 431.

58-6 (34.66077, -86.48012) (0.2 mi.) The Little Cove Road Greenway path intersects on the right. Continue straight, traveling northwest to skirt the large field that stands between the greenway path and Hampton Cove Elementary School.

Standing more than 1,400 ft. high, Drake Mountain dominates the scene to the north. At 0.33 mi., you leave the edge of the field and bend toward Big Cove Creek. As you continue north, a narrow island of trees stands between the trail and the neighborhood on the right. At 0.36 mi., the creek becomes visible as you round a bend in the path. After another 320 ft., the greenway trail bends around a pond.

58-7 (34.66414, -86.48269) (0.5 mi.) On the right, a greenway access path stretches 144 ft. and leads to Kincade Circle.

At 0.6 mi., the backyards of homes are immediately to the right, while trees lining the left side of the path shroud the nearby creek. At 0.7 mi., you'll get your first really good view of the creek, while more backyards lie to the right.

58-8 (34.66820, -86.48475) (0.8 mi.) On the right, a greenway access path stretches 250 ft. to Kentshire.

58-9 (34.67054, -86.48546) (1.1 mi.) The greenway path ends at the end of Cranfield Road.

Skirting a pond on the northern section of the Big Cove Creek Greenway

Map 1
Little Cove Road Greenway &
Old Hwy. 431/Eastern Bypass Paths

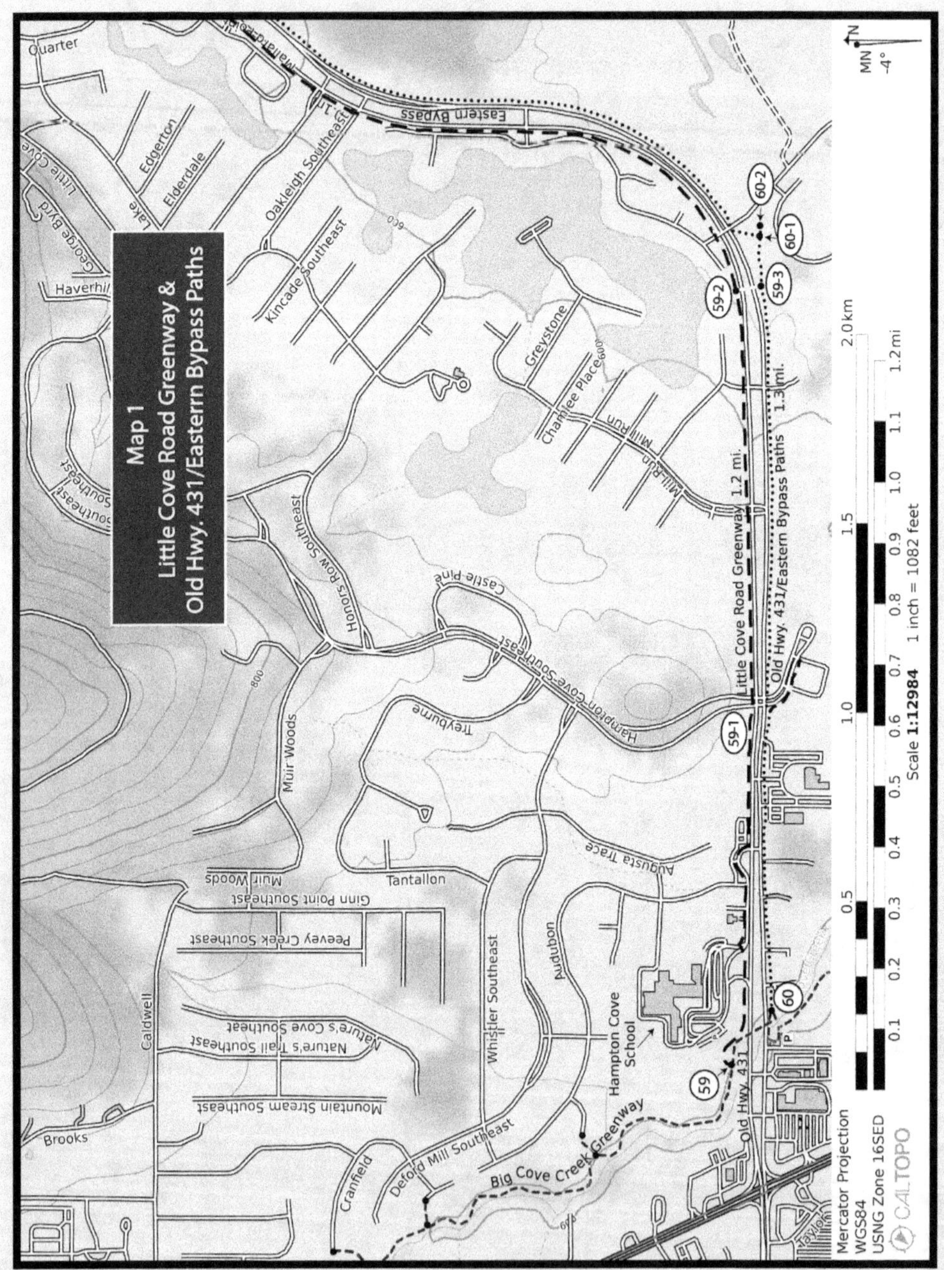

Map 2
Little Cove Creek Greenway &
Old Hwy. 431/ Eastern Bypass Paths

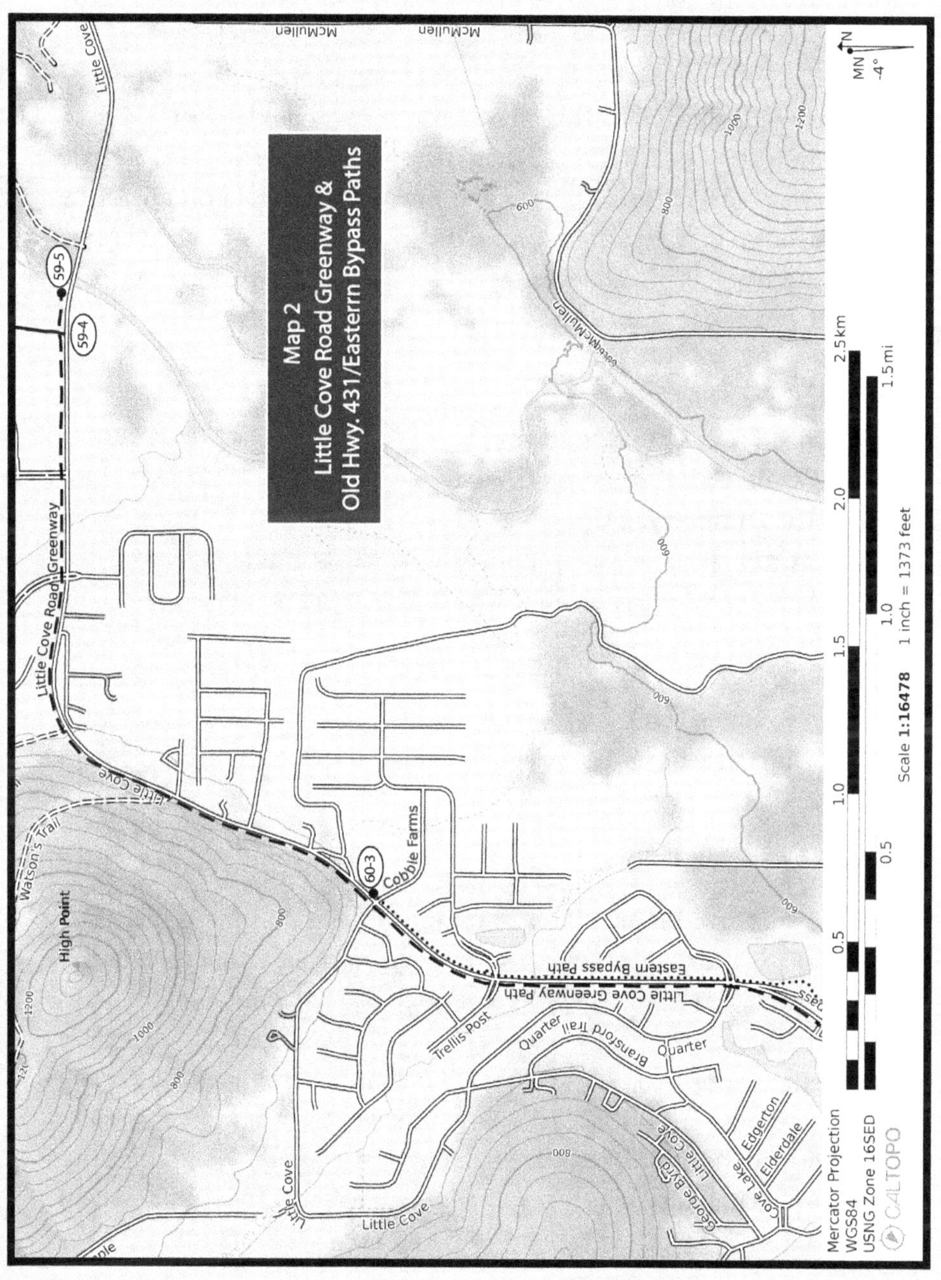

59. Little Cove Road Greenway

Stretching 5 mi. from Hampton Cove to a field just southeast of McMullen Cove, this is one of the longest paved paths in the Huntsville area. Hampton Cove residents primarily walk, run and bike on the first couple of miles of the trail, where it stays fairly level as it skirts Old Highway 431 and the Eastern Bypass. After the first 2 mi., the trail climbs gradually and then moderately to run along the foot of Drake Mountain and a peak called High Point. The trail then drops into Little Cove to parallel Little Cove Road and runs level for about 0.5 mi. At the end of the greenway path in Little Cove, there is no designated parking area. But if you want to place a vehicle at each end of the trail, it's possible to park a car in a field beside Little Cove Road.

Distance: 5 mi.
Hiking Time: 1.5 to 2 hours
Elevation Gain/Loss: +169 ft., -172 ft.
Hiking Difficulty: Easy
Location: The trailhead is immediately west of Hampton Cove Elementary School, 261 Old Hwy. 431, Owens Cross Roads, AL 35763.
Facilities: There are no facilities and no sources of potable water at the trailhead.
Driving Directions: See page 157 and use the directions for Big Cove Creek Greenway South.

Highlights

Hampton Cove Waterfall and Community: As you approach 0.6 mi. and the junction with Hampton Cove Way, look left to see the multi-tiered Hampton Cove Waterfall cascading down the hill. This artificial waterfall runs between the 18th hole and the first hole tee boxes of the Highlands Course, an 18-hole championship course that's part of the Robert Trent Jones Golf Trail. When the course was constructed in the early 1990s, it sparked development of the greater Hampton Cove planned community, which covers some 2,800 acres and includes more than 2,000 homes.

Map 1

(See map on page 164 for Waypoints 59 through 59-3)

Waypoint/Mile

Trailhead (Waypoint 59) (34.66060, -86.47923) From the south end of the Hampton Cove Elementary School parking lot, take the paved path that bends to the right to head southwest toward Old Highway 431. After walking about 130 ft., you'll reach a junction where the Big Cove Creek Greenway ends and the Little Cove Road Greenway begins. Turn left and travel southeast to take the Little Cove Road Greenway.

59-1 (34.66029, -86.46996) (0.59 mi.) When you've traveled almost 0.6 mi., you'll reach the junction with Hampton Cove Way on the left. This is a major entrance to the Hampton Cove residential area, and if you look left and up the hill, you'll see the Hampton Cove Waterfall. It makes a great backdrop for a photo, so it's worth a side trip to see it. From Waypoint 59-1, continue east on the paved greenway path that parallels Old Highway 431.

59-2 (34.66068, -86.45770) (1.2 mi.) A path on the right runs beneath Old Highway 431, stretching 230 ft. to meet a paved walkway on the south side of the highway.

59-3 (34.66007, -86.45756) (1.28 mi.) The path that runs under Old Highway 431 ends at the junction with the paved path on the south side of the highway. If you turn right at this junction, you can return to the Big Cove Creek Greenway parking area and complete a loop that measures 2.4 mi.

From Waypoint 59-2, the Little Cove Road Greenway continues to the northeast, following the Eastern Bypass road and climbing gradually. At 1.6 mi., you'll reach a bench where you can take a breather.

Map 2

(See map on page 165 for Waypoints 59-4 through 59-5)

Waypoint/Mile

At 2.2 mi., there's a nice section of trail where you begin to get glimpses of mountains to the northwest. More benches lie ahead, and at 3.3 mi. Cobble Farms Drive intersects on the right, while Little Cove Road intersects on the left. At this point, the Eastern Bypass becomes Little

Cove Rd. and begins a steeper climb.

At 3.8 mi., there's a nice view to the right with the Flint River valley in the foreground and Keel Mountain rising in the distance. At 4 mi., the path bends to the east and drops gradually, hugging Little Cove Road.

59-4 (34.69692, -86.42433) (5 mi.) The greenway path crosses a dirt road that provides access to Little Cove Road. If you're using a shuttle, this is the best spot for someone to pick you up. If you continue east for about another 400 ft., you'll reach the end of the greenway path.

59-5 (34.69686, -86.42283) (5 mi.) The path ends at the edge of the trees that line the Flint River.

Trail Facts

Hampton Cove's Original Name: In the 1800s, when the Hampton Cove area was just a rural community with open farmland, it was named Horse Cove. It got the name because, during the Civil War, locals hid their horses there to prevent the Union Army from seizing them.

Exploring the eastern end of the Little Cove Road Greenway

60. Old Hwy. 431/Eastern Bypass Paths

This paved path begins in Hampton Cove and runs along the southern side of Old Hwy. 431 and the eastern side of the Eastern Bypass. Similar to the Little Cove Road Greenway, this path is a popular running, walking and biking route for Hampton Cove residents. However, it's shorter than the Little Cove Road Greenway and ends at the base of the hill known as High Point, rather than stretching all the way into Little Cove.

Distance: 1.3 mi.
Hiking Time: 30 minutes
Elevation Gain/Loss: +37 ft., -43 ft.
Hiking Difficulty: Easy
Location: 327 Old Hwy. 431, Owens Cross Roads, AL 35763
Facilities: There are no facilities and no sources of potable water at the trailhead.
Driving Directions: See page 157 and use the information for Big Cove Creek Greenway South.

Map 1

(See map on page 164 for Waypoints 60 through 60-2)

Waypoint/Mile

Trailhead (Waypoint 60) (34.65979, -86.47851) The trailhead lies near the east end of the Big Cove Creek Greenway parking lot. From the trailhead, head west toward Wade Road. The path curls back to the east to carry you over Big Cove Creek. When you've walked about 430 ft., you'll reach a junction with a paved path on the right. Continue straight, heading east along Old Highway 431.

The paved path rises very gradually as it runs beside Old Highway 431 and passes two churches. When you've gone 0.5 mi., you'll cross an entrance road for a golf course. This is the Hampton Cove "River Course," which occupies old soybean fields in the Flint River floodplain.

59-3 (34.66007, -86.45756) (1.2 mi.) A path on the left runs beneath the highway for 230 ft. to meet the Little Cove Road Greenway. If you take this path, you can loop back to the Big Cove Creek Greenway parking area and complete a 2.4-mi. loop. At Waypoint 59-3, go straight to continue on the Old Hwy. 431/Eastern Bypass paths.

60-1 (34.66010, -86.45614) (1.3 mi.) A paved path intersects on the left. Turn left onto this path and head north toward Old Highway 431. (If you continue straight from Waypoint 60-1, you'll reach the end of the paved path after a little more than 100 ft. at **Waypoint 60-2** (34.66008, -86.45581).

Once you reach Old Highway 431, turn right to go northeast. At this point, the divided highway becomes the Eastern Bypass. As you continue, you'll see Robinson Mill Creek flowing on the right.

At 1.6 mi., the mountains to the north come into view, adding some visual interest to this urban walk. On the right side of the path lies Little Cove, a lowland area tucked between the highway and Keel Mountain. A pond appears on the right side of the path, and up ahead the trail skirts a wetland area with more ponds.

Map 2

(See map on page 165 for Waypoint 60-3)

Waypoint/Mile

The path climbs gradually, and at 2.2 mi. you gain enough height to get a good view to the east. Just below is the valley where the Flint River flows. The lowlands stretch east to meet Keel Mountain, and your vantage point offers a clear view of a forested ridge.

60-3 (34.68704, -86.44507) (3.3 mi.) The paved path crosses Cobble Farms Drive, and then ends after about another 50 ft.

Ponds flank an attractive stretch of the Old Hwy. 431/Eastern Bypass Path

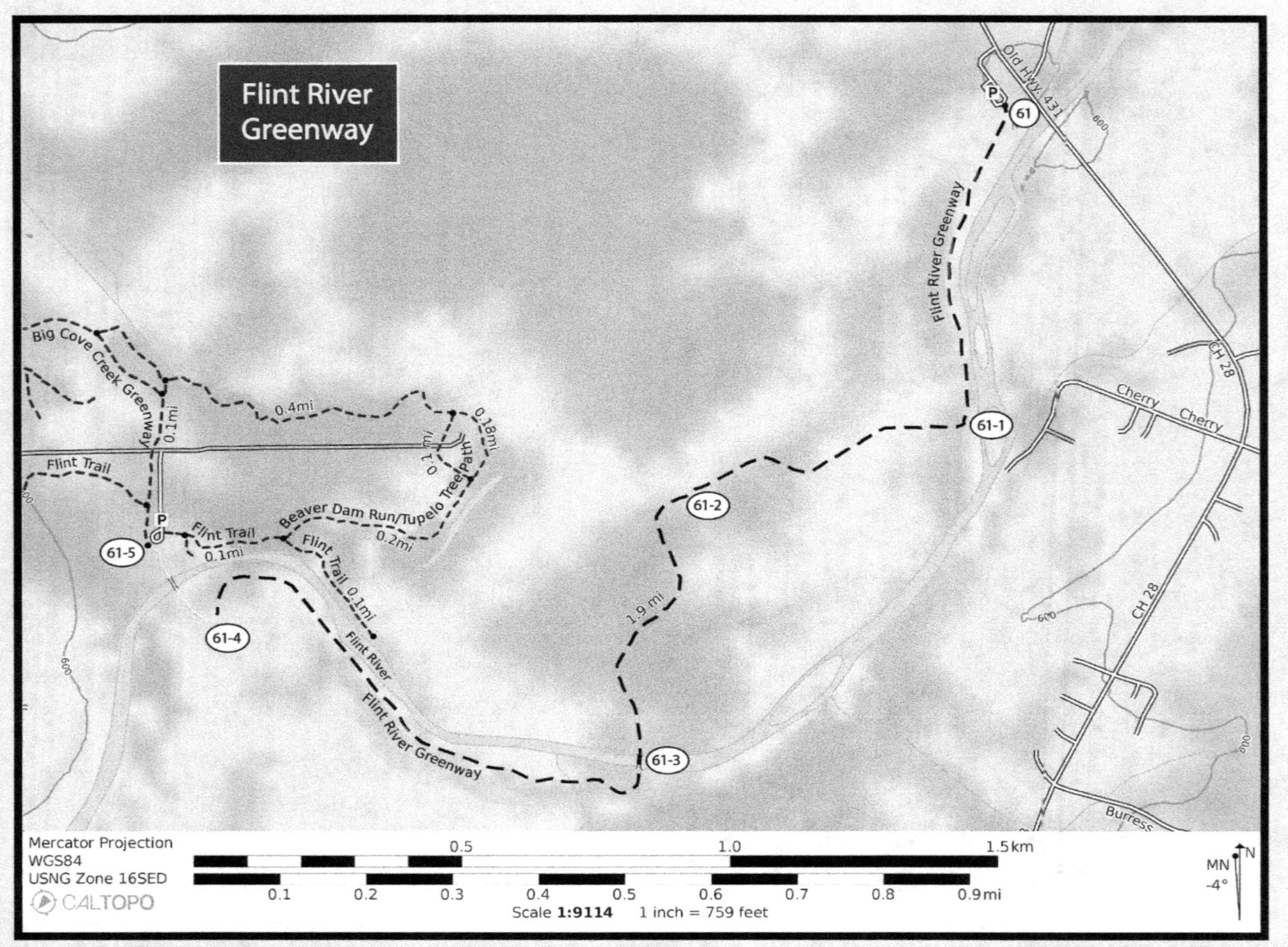

Flint River Greenway
Flint River Greenway
Old Hwy. 431
P
61
600
Flint River Greenway
CH 28
Cherry
Cherry
CH 28
Big Cove Creek Greenway
0.4mi
0.18mi
0.1 mi
61-1
Flint Trail
0.1mi
61-2
Beaver Dam Run/Tupelo TreePath
0.2mi
P
Flint Trail
61-5
0.1mi
Flint Trail 0.1mi
1.9 mi
600
Flint River
61-4
Flint River Greenway
61-3
600
Burress
Mercator Projection
WGS84
USNG Zone 16SED
CALTOPO
0.5
1.0
1.5 km
0.1
0.2
0.3
0.4
0.5
0.6
0.7
0.8
0.9mi
Scale 1:9114   1 inch = 759 feet
MN
-4°
N

61. Flint River Greenway

While parts of the Flint River Greenway skirt a golf course, much of the route feels wild and remote. The trail is mostly surrounded by hardwood forest and broad, green fields. In quiet, shaded corridors, the paved path hugs wide channels of the Flint River. When you reach the western end of the greenway, you enter the interior of the Hays Nature Preserve, reinforcing the feeling that civilization is far away. Because the entire path is paved and pretty level, it's a good place for kids to enjoy a walk (or bike ride) that's a bit wilder, but still safe and accessible.

Distance: 1.9 mi.
Hiking Time: 45 minutes
Elevation Gain/Loss: +26 ft., -29 ft.
Hiking Difficulty: Easy
Location: 7153 SE Old Hwy. 431, Owens Cross Roads, AL 35763
Facilities: There are no facilities and no sources of potable water at the trailhead.
Driving Directions: From the junction of U.S. 231/431 (Memorial Parkway) and U.S. 431 (Governors Drive), travel east on U.S. 431. Go 8.4 mi., and then use the left two lanes to turn left onto Old Highway 431. Travel 1.6 mi., and then bear right to stay on Old Hwy. 431. Go another 0.7 mi. and turn right into the large parking area for the Flint River Greenway.

****Special Note:** *As this book was being published, access to the main Flint River Greenway trailhead was blocked due to a road closure. If this is still the case, you can park and access the Flint River Greenway from the Hays Nature Preserve. For driving directions for the Hays Nature Preserve, see page 14.*

Highlights

Flint River: Of course, the centerpiece of this greenway is the Flint River, which begins in Lincoln County, Tennessee, and flows 65.7 mi., running through Madison County to feed into the Tennessee River. On each end, the greenway runs near the river, providing a beautiful backdrop for hiking, biking and running. Also, kayaking and canoeing are popular on the Flint River, and many sections are suitable for beginners when the river isn't running high. Some people launch boats at Hays Nature Preserve, but there are many other put-in options. If you're not familiar with the Flint River, check out North Alabama Canoe & Kayak (nacktrips.com). This popular outfitter will not only provide you information, but they also rent boats and run a shuttle service.

Wildlife Watching: The Flint River Greenway and the Hays Nature Preserve are home to a wide variety of bird species. "Species to look for along the river include great blue and green herons, belted kingfishers, and in winter, Wilson's snipe," reports alabamabirdingtrails.com. Along the edges of the woodlands, look for "eastern bluebirds, song sparrows, and numerous other resident and migrant species."

Waypoint/Mile

Trailhead (Waypoint 61) (34.65159, -86.44912) To reach the trailhead, walk to the information kiosk at the southeast end of the Flint River Greenway parking area. From the kiosk, head south on the paved path and walk along the edge of a large field with the Flint River on your left.

After walking almost 0.2 mi., you'll move beyond the first large field and enter a more shaded corridor with trees lining each side of the path. You'll soon enter one of the most tranquil parts of the trail and stroll along a wide section of the Flint River.

61-1 (34.64608, -86.44998) (0.4 mi.) The path makes a sharp turn to the right to run west and lead you away from the river.

For 0.2 mi., the trail winds among broad green fields and runs near the southern end of the Hampton Cove Golf Course.

61-2 (34.64480, -86.45561) (0.7 mi.) Cross a golf cart path and continue following the narrow paved path to the southwest.

61-3 (34.64044, -86.45656) (1.1 mi.) An attractive metal and concrete bridge, measuring 164 ft., carries you across the Flint River.

At 1.29 mi., a short concrete bridge crosses a stream that feeds into the Flint River. The path soon hugs the edge of a large field, and at 1.4 mi. a bench beside the path faces the field. Even though the golf course is not far away to the northeast, this quiet, pastoral part of the greenway feels remote and peaceful.

Not far beyond the 1.6-mi. mark, the path emerges from the shade of hardwoods to skirt another large field. In the spring, marsh marigolds transform the green field into a sea of golden color.

61-4 (34.64264, -86.46524) (1.8 mi.) Turn right onto a path that climbs gradually toward the bridge. Then follow the bridge across the Flint River.

61-5 (34.64401, -86.46652) (1.9 mi.) The Flint River Greenway ends where the paved path drops to meet a circular pathway near the Hays Nature Preserve parking area.

The Flint River Greenway meanders among vast green fields.

Huntsville Greenways:

Aldridge Creek Greenway Linear Park Trail; Aldridge Creek Greenway South; Aldridge Creek Greenway North; Tennessee River Greenway; Elgie's Walk Greenway; Gateway Greenway, Patriots Walkway and Battlefield Memorial Walkway; Indian Creek Greenway North; Indian Creek Greenway South; Wade Mountain Greenway; and Trailhead Greenway

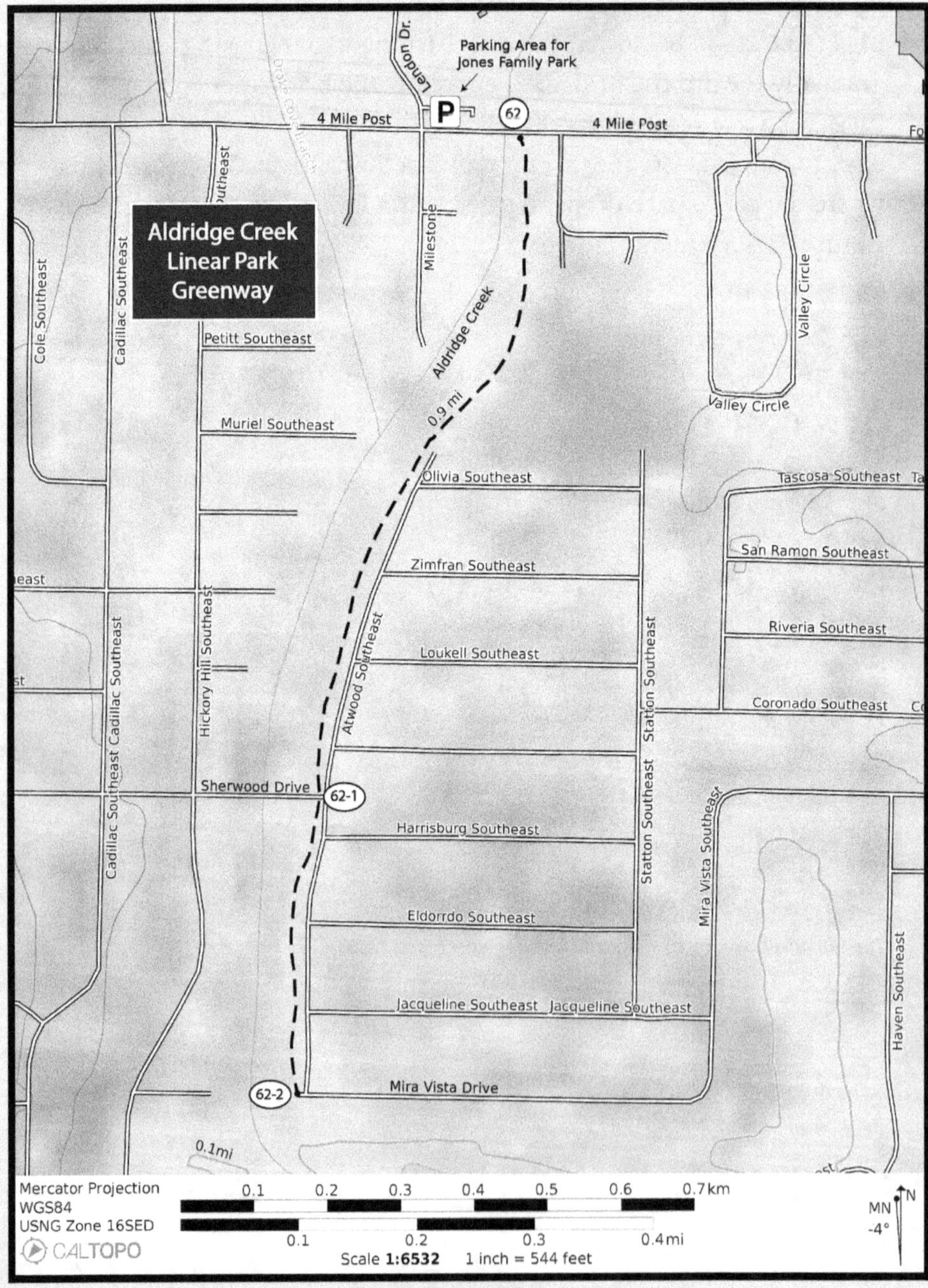

62. Aldridge Creek Greenway Linear Park Trail

Perfect for a brief walk or run, this narrow greenway in the Jones Valley area runs between Jones Family Park and Valley Hill Country Club. For most of the way, the greenway passes through a neighborhood, so this is definitely more of an urban walk. Still, it's a low-key and fairly quiet corridor where you can enjoy a quick escape.

Distance: 0.9 mi.
Hiking Time: 20 minutes
Elevation Gain/Loss: +6 ft., -15 ft.
Hiking Difficulty: Easy
Location: 4 Mile Post Rd. (about 440 ft. east of the junction with Lendon Park Dr. and Milestone Dr.), Huntsville, AL 35803
Facilities: There are no facilities and no sources of potable water at the trailhead.
Driving Directions: The nearest parking area is the lot for the Jones Family Park, near the junction of 4 Mile Post Road and Lendon Park Drive. From the junction of U.S. 231/431 (Memorial Parkway) and Martin Road, travel east on Martin Rd. for 0.4 mi. Then turn left onto Whitesburg Drive. Go 0.3 mi., and then turn right onto 4 Mile Post Rd. Travel 1 mi., and then turn left onto Lendon Park Dr. Go about 90 ft., and then turn right into the parking area for the Jones Family Park.

Highlights

A Long, Easy Walk: You'll hardly notice any elevation change as you travel this greenway, so it's ideal for walkers or runners looking to avoid hilly terrain.

Waypoint/Mile

Trailhead (Waypoint 62) (34.67203, -86.55042) To reach the trailhead, begin at the Jones Family Park parking area on the north side of 4 Mile Post Road. From the parking area, cross 4 Mile Post Rd., turn left and walk east for 440 ft. The Aldridge Creek Greenway path intersects on the right. Turn right onto the paved Aldridge Creek Greenway and head south.

To the left, a narrow strip of dense woods lines the path. To the right is a wide, grassy field, and Aldridge Creek flows on the opposite side of the field. You might see prickly sweet gum balls scattered across the trail, and in the spring the sweet smell of honeysuckle fills the air. The woods to the left broaden as the level path makes a long arc to the southwest. Here you have long views of the narrow greenway. At 0.29 mi., you reach the end of the wooded area. To the left you can see houses and Atwood Drive, which runs parallel to the path.

62-1 (34.66432, -86.55358) (0.58 mi.) Cross Sherwood Drive and continue to walk south.

62-2 (34.66075, -86.55392) (0.83 mi.) The greenway path ends at the junction with Mira Vista Road.

Map 1
Aldridge Creek Greenway South

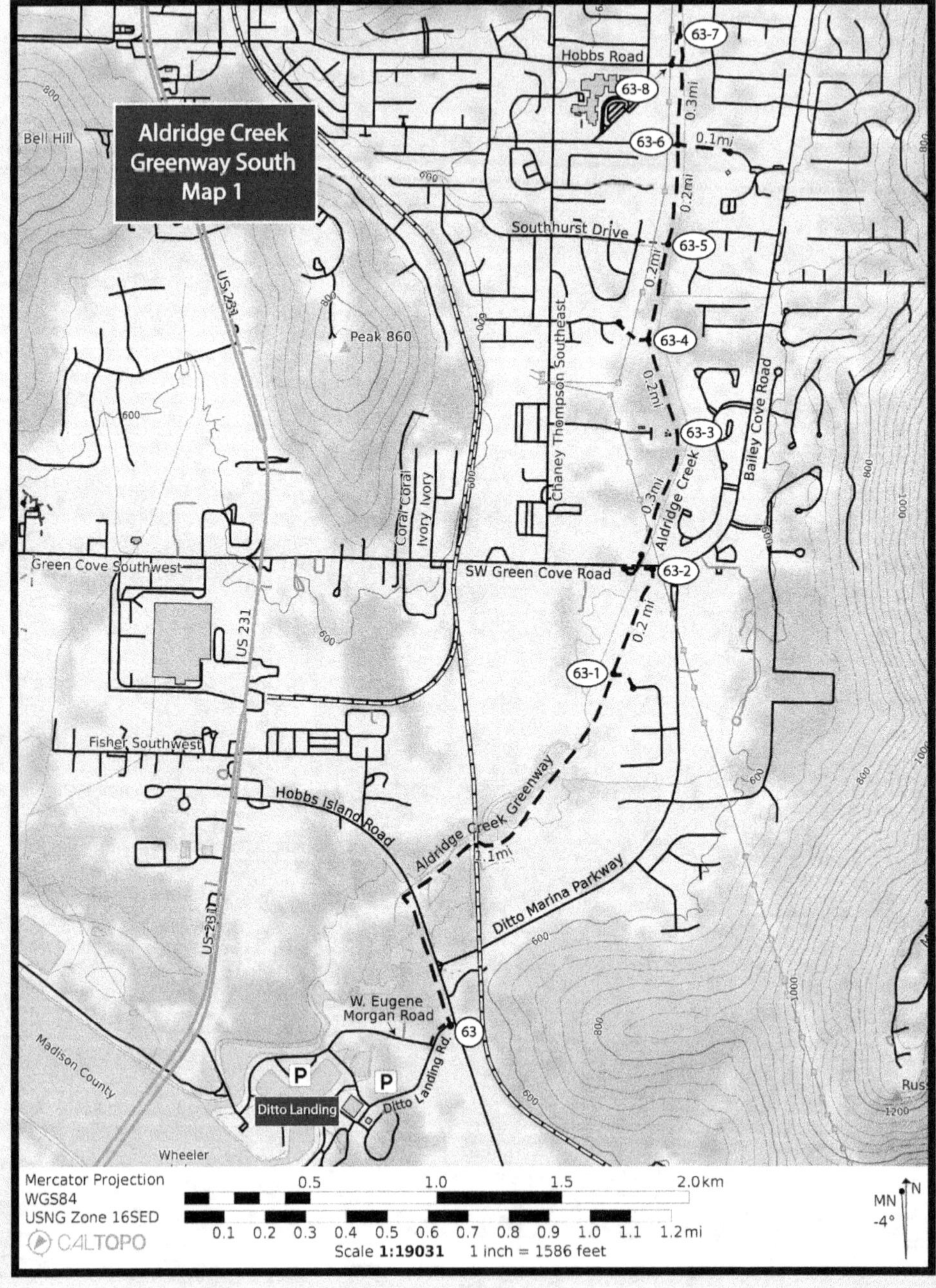

Map 2
Aldridge Creek Greenway South

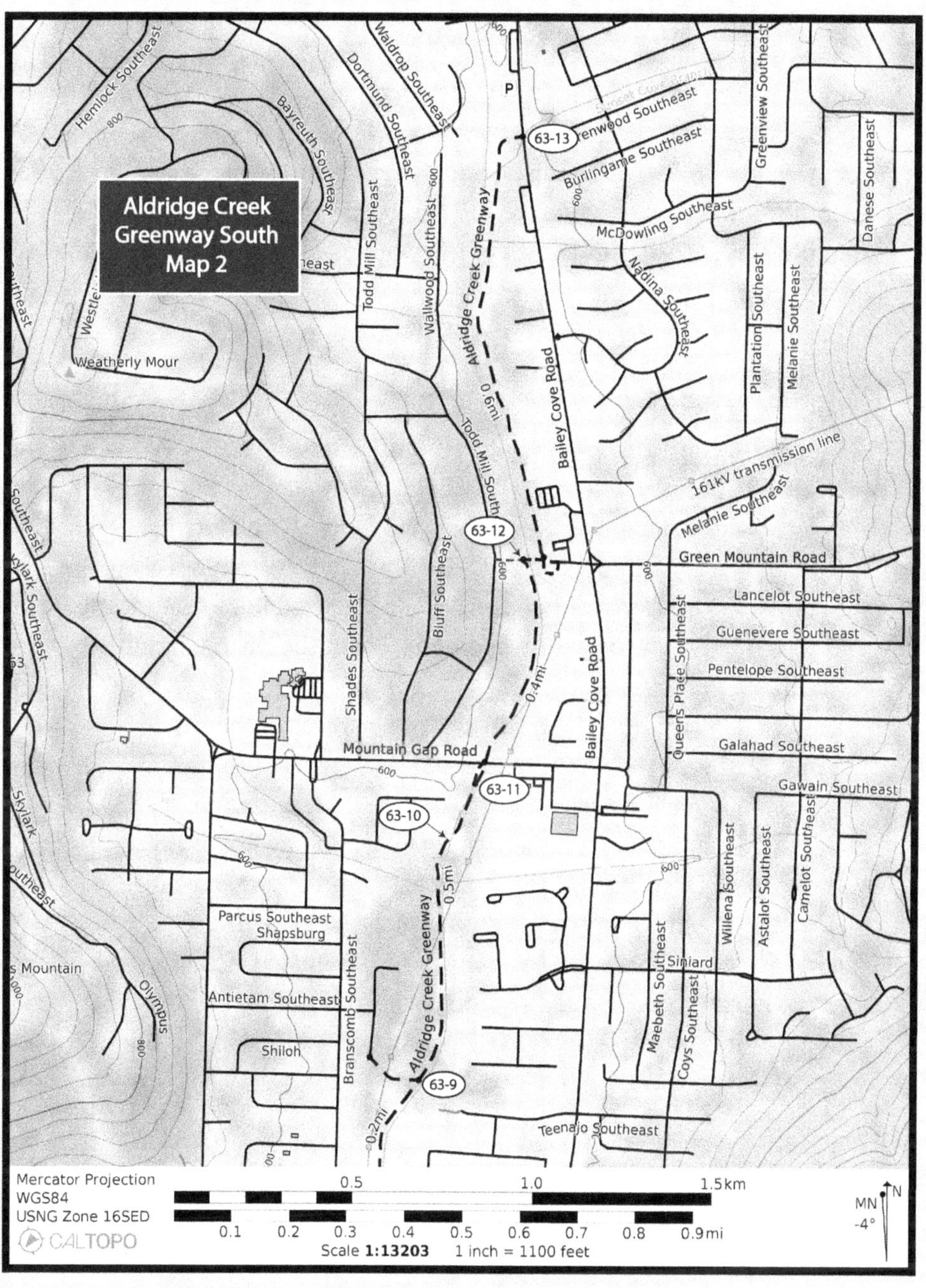

63. Aldridge Creek Greenway South
(Ditto Landing to Bailey Cove Rd.)

Stretching nearly 5 mi., this section of the Aldridge Creek Greenway is one of the longest and most attractive paved paths in the area. One minute you're walking through a secluded hallway of woods, and the next, you're taking concrete passageways beneath city streets. Along the way, the wide waters of Aldridge Creek and the slopes of Green Mountain add a wild, rugged quality to your walk. The diverse surroundings and the sheer length of the walk make this a top choice for an extended outing.

Distance: 4.8 mi.

Hiking Time: 2 hours

Elevation Gain/Loss: +51 ft., -24 ft.

Hiking Difficulty: Easy

Location: Ditto Landing Rd. (about 90 ft. west of the intersection with Hobbs Island Rd.), Huntsville, AL 35803

Facilities: There are no facilities and no sources of potable water at the trailhead. The nearest restrooms are at the Ditto Landing Marina.

Driving Directions: The nearest parking area is at the Ditto Landing Marina. From the junction of U.S. 231/431 (Memorial Parkway) and Hobbs Island Road, travel east on Hobbs Island Rd. Go 1.2 mi., and then turn right onto Ditto Landing Road. Go 404 ft. to where Ditto Landing Rd. turns right and becomes Younger Road. Go 328 ft. and turn left onto Harbor Road to enter the parking area. **Be aware that there is no designated parking area at the northern end of this section of the greenway on Bailey Cove Road. Some people do park in the lot for the senior center, which is 477 ft. north of Waypoint 63-13.

Highlights

Woods, Water and Mountains: The Aldridge Creek Greenway explores a wide variety of terrain, from the bottomland forests of Ditto Landing to the banks of Aldridge Creek. As the trail moves north, it passes parks, homes and open fields, while Green Mountain forms a rugged wall to the east. On this trek, nature has a strong presence, even though civilization is never far away.

Aldridge Creek: For an urban stream, Aldridge Creek can be a delightful distraction. In the south, the creek is a calming companion as it crawls silently among green fields. Farther north, it sings to you as water riffles across rocky shoals. In many areas, lush trees line the banks of the stream, and the emerald curtain and rust-colored water create a rich palette of colors. For most of the journey, the stream is also quite wide, giving Aldridge Creek a surprisingly strong presence.

Map 1

(See map on page 180 for Waypoints 63 through 63-8)

Waypoint/Mile

Trailhead (Waypoint 63) (34.57922, -86.55413) The Aldridge Creek Greenway begins on the north side of Ditto Landing Road, about 80 ft. from the junction of Ditto Landing Rd. and Hobbs Island Road. At the Aldridge Creek Greenway sign, walk north, following the paved path that parallels Hobbs Island Rd.

As you begin, an earthy aroma rises from a large wetland area on the left. At 0.3 mi., the path takes a sharp right turn to parallel Aldridge Creek, which is surrounded by dense woods. The next 0.2 mi. feels especially secluded. At 0.5 mi., the trail runs beneath a railroad trestle and continues to hug the stream, which makes a big bend to the north. The scenery here is particularly attractive, with a broad farm field to the right and the ridges of Green Mountain rising high in the east.

At 0.8 mi., listen for the sound of rushing water, as the creek flows through a shallow, rocky section. While houses are visible to the right, the scene is still inspiring as you get a long, unobstructed view of the creek.

63-1 (34.59132, -86.54698) (1.1 mi.) On the left, a greenway access path stretches 310 ft. and ends at the Shropshire Drive cul-de-sac. Continue straight to stay on the greenway and skirt pastureland.

63-2 (34.59494, -86.54532) (1.3 mi.) Turn left and travel west to parallel Green Cove Road and take the concrete bridge over Aldridge Creek. After you cross the bridge, walk 130 ft. and turn left to curl back to the east. The path soon turns north to carry you beneath Green Cove Rd.

For the next 0.2 mi., you'll enjoy a nice stretch of trail where woods surround the path and the creek flows on the right.

63-3 (34.59952, -86.54419) (1.8 mi.) To the left is Southside Park playground.

63-4 (34.60287, -86.54546) (2 mi.) On the left, a greenway access path stretches 0.1 mi. and leads to the Brisbane Lane cul-de-sac. Continue straight to stay on the greenway.

Near the 2.3-mi. point, you'll see a gate to a dog park on the left. Soon you'll enter an especially quiet corridor with dense woods shielding the path from nearby neighborhoods.

63-5 (34.60618, -86.54464) (2.29 mi.) On the left, a walkway goes left to intersect with Camden Circle. Continue straight to stay on the greenway.

63-6 (34.60966, -86.54420) (2.5 mi.) You reach another access point for the greenway. To the left is a large Aldridge Creek Greenway sign, and beyond that a 0.1-mi. path leads to Wynterhall Road. To the right, a concrete bridge will carry you over Aldridge Creek to McGucken Park. At this junction, go straight to continue down the greenway. In 0.2 mi., the trail runs beneath Hobbs Road.

63-7 (34.61342, -86.54411) (2.8 mi.) On the left, an access path heads back south for 366 ft. to meet Hobbs Road at **Waypoint 63-8** (34.61246, -86.54442) (2.87 mi.).

Map 2

(See map on page 181 for Waypoints 63-9 through 63-13)

Waypoint/Mile

At 2.9 mi., the sound of rushing water rises as the creek flows over a spillway. This can be one of the most relaxing spots on the greenway, especially if you happen by while the area birds are chirping.

63-9 (34.61654, -86.54294) (3 mi.) A greenway access path on the left leads to Greenway Park Circle in 0.1 mi. Go straight to stay on the main greenway path.

At 3.3 mi., you cross a powerline and soon enter another appealing stretch where thick woods envelop the path.

63-10 (34.62240, -86.54196) (3.4 mi.) The perfect rest spot lies on the left, where benches arranged in a semicircle face a small, round table made of stone. When you walk another 60 ft., you'll see a path on the right that descends to the bank of Aldridge Creek and dead-ends after about 250 ft.

63-11 (34.62372, -86.54124) (3.5 mi.) On the left, a greenway access path rises to end at Mountain Gap Road, where there is a large Aldridge Creek Greenway sign. Continue straight on the greenway to pass beneath Mountain Gap Rd.

63-12 (34.62917, -86.53977) (3.9 mi.) Turn right and travel east to take a concrete bridge across Aldridge Creek.

Over the next 1.6 mi., you'll enjoy extended views down the creek, which is really pretty in this area. On each side of the stream, mature trees create a veil between you and the nearby houses.

63-13 (34.63949, -86.53994) (4.8 mi.) The Aldridge Creek Greenway ends at Bailey Cove Road.

A shady spot to sit and relax along the Aldridge Creek Greenway

Aldridge Creek Greenway North

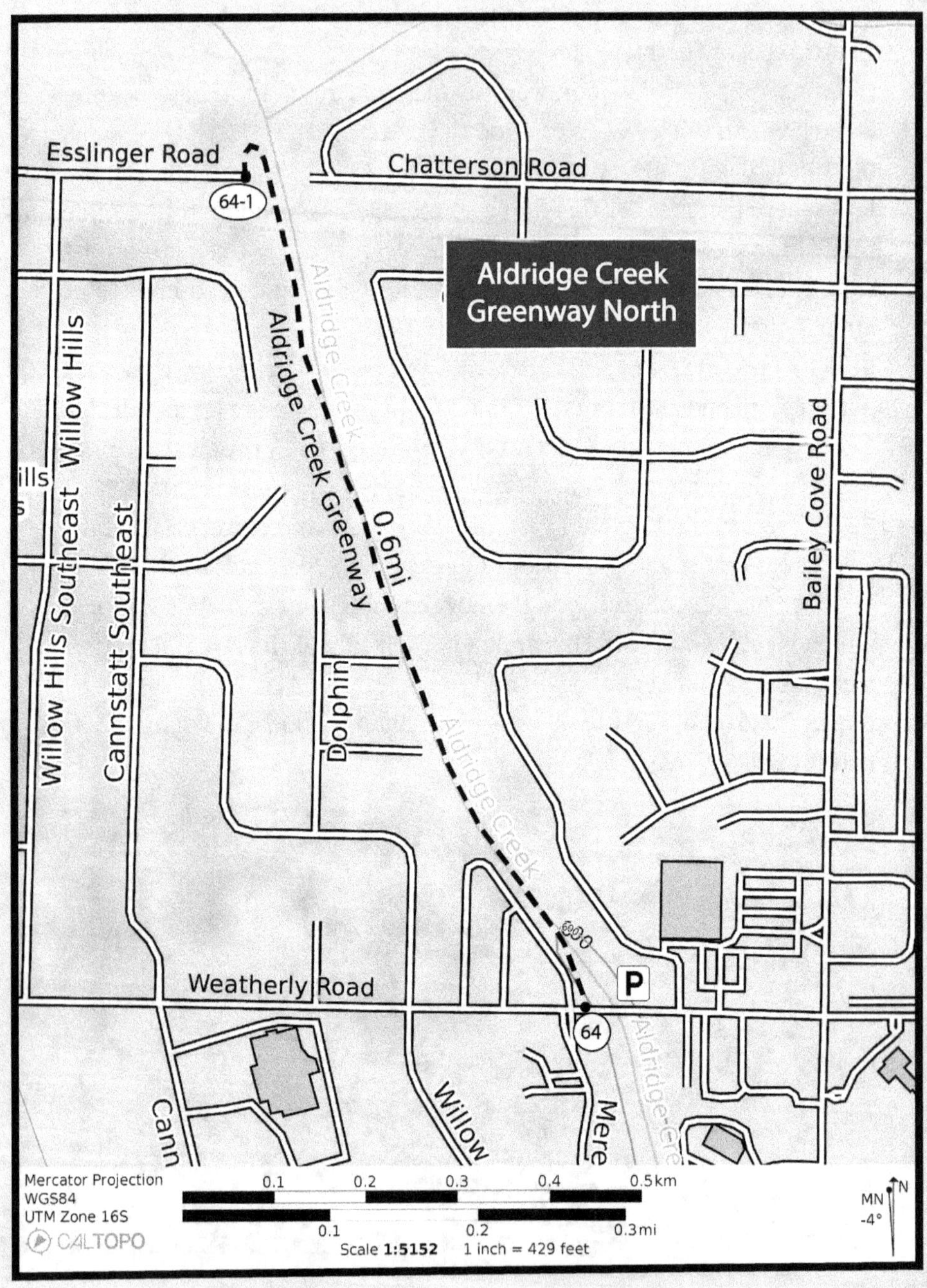

64. Aldridge Creek Greenway North
(Weatherly Rd. to Esslinger Rd.)

This northern section of the Aldridge Creek Greenway is much more of an urban walk than the southern section. Houses and apartments flanking the path are visible and nearby most of the way. But the trail is practically level, and this can be a quiet area, so this is a good destination for a brief, easy stroll or a short run. Take note that parking is available only at the southern end, so it's a 1.2-mi. out-and-back trip if you travel the entire distance.

Distance: 0.6 mi.
Hiking Time: 15 minutes
Elevation Gain/Loss: +7 ft., -0 ft.
Hiking Difficulty: Easy
Location: Weatherly Rd. (52 ft. east of the intersection with Meredith Ln., and 0.16 mi. west of the intersection with Bailey Cove Rd.), Huntsville, AL 35802
Facilities: There are no facilities and no sources of potable water at the trailhead.
Driving Directions: The nearest parking area is an open lot immediately west of the junction of Weatherly Road and a small road called Mahogany Row, near the southwest corner of the Walmart building. To reach the parking area, begin at the junction of U.S. 231/431 (Memorial Parkway) and Weatherly Rd. Travel east on Weatherly Rd. for 1.4 mi., and then turn left into the open lot on the north side of Weatherly Rd., immediately before you reach Mahogany Row. **Note that parking is not allowed at the north end of the greenway path on Esslinger Road.

Highlights

A Quiet Walk: As you walk this path, you'll pass between visible rows of houses and see metal pipes running across the creek. So this isn't the most attractive greenway. However, this can be a fairly quiet area, so you'll enjoy a peaceful walk.

Waypoint/Mile

Trailhead (Waypoint 64) (34.64634, -86.54281) To reach the trailhead, begin at the parking area south of Walmart and immediately west of Mahogany Row, near the junction of Mahogany Row and Weatherly Road. Walk west for `along Weatherly Rd. to the spot where the paved Aldridge Creek Greenway path intersects on the right. Turn right onto Aldridge Creek Greenway and head northwest. After 40 ft., the pathway includes lanes for hikers and bikers.

At the start of the trail, the shallow creek runs to the right of the path, and an apartment complex lies just beyond the creek. At 0.3 mi., a strip of trees runs between the path and houses on the right. On the left, the backyards of houses sit higher than the greenway trail.

Near 0.6 mi., look to the north to see a short bridge that crosses the water. This allows golfers to cross Aldridge Creek, which cuts through the Valley Hill Country Club. Soon, the greenway path makes a hairpin turn to the left. To the right, water from Esslinger Cove Branch, a neighboring creek, passes through a wide gap in a concrete wall, rushes over rocks and flows into Aldridge Creek.

64-1 (34.65430, -86.54685) (0.6 mi.) The Aldridge Creek Greenway path ends at Esslinger Road.

Tennessee River Greenway

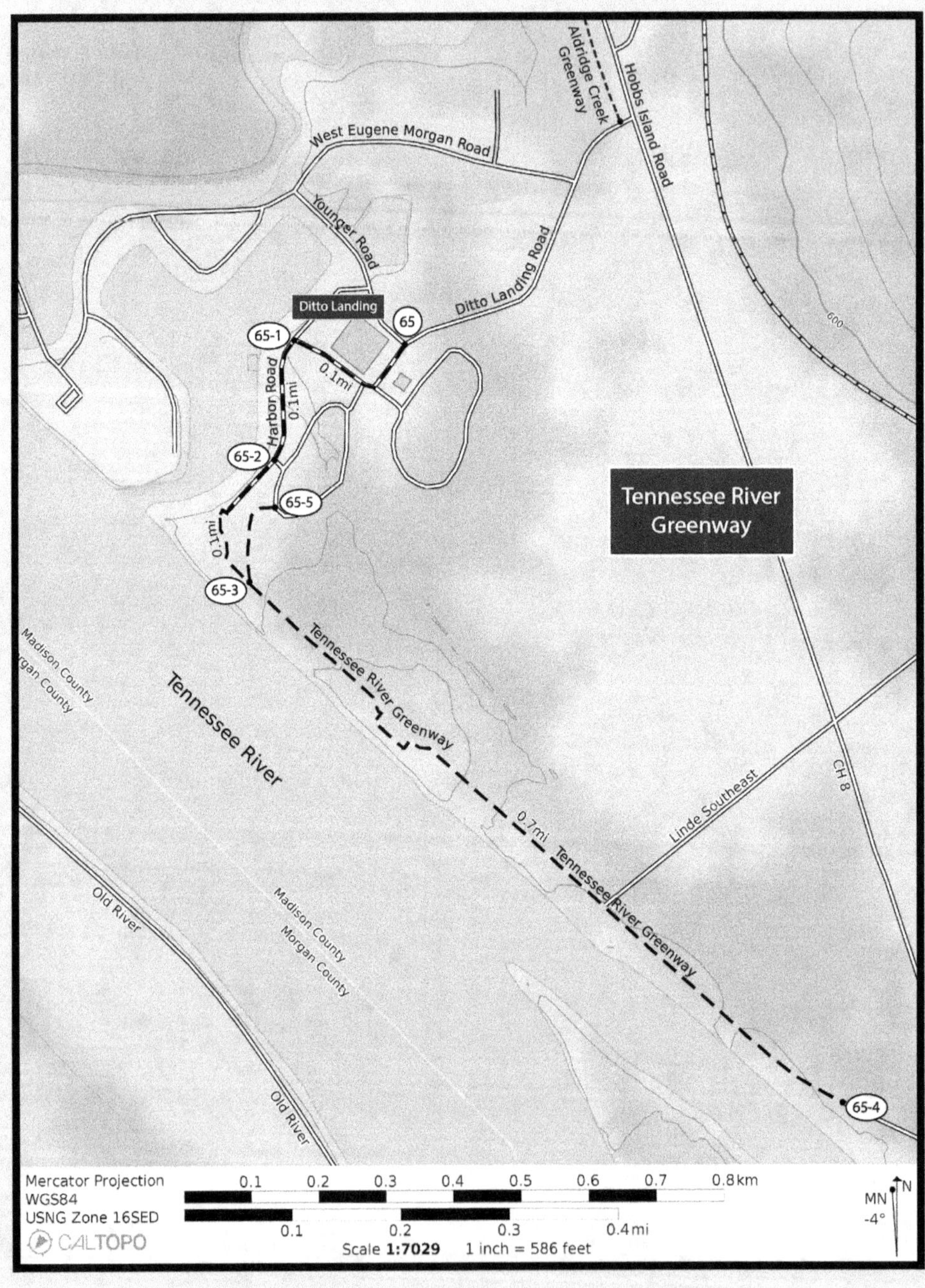

65. Tennessee River Greenway

Enjoy an impressive view of the Tennessee River while you stroll this level, paved path. Along the way, pause to sit at a riverside bench with an unobstructed view of the wide river channel.

Distance: 1.2 mi.

Hiking Time: 20 to 30 minutes

Elevation Gain/Loss: +17 ft., -17 ft.

Hiking Difficulty: Easy

Location: Ditto Landing Marina, 293 Ditto Landing Rd. SE, Huntsville, AL 35803

Facilities: There are restrooms at the Ditto Landing Marina.

Driving Directions: The nearest parking area is at the Ditto Landing Marina. From the junction of U.S. 231 (Memorial Parkway) and Hobbs Island Road, travel east on Hobbs Island Rd. Go 1.2 mi., and then turn right onto Ditto Landing Road. Go 404 ft. to where Ditto Landing Rd. turns right and becomes Younger Road. Go 328 ft. and turn left onto Harbor Road to enter the parking area.

Highlights

Tennessee River: As the largest tributary of the Ohio River, the Tennessee River stretches some 650 mi., and flows for about 200 mi. of that length through North Alabama. Where the river slides by Ditto Landing, it's about 0.25 mi. wide, providing an impressive backdrop for a greenway walk, or a day of boating or fishing. While the river plays a starring role in recreation in Alabama, it's also a central figure in our everyday lives. Hydroelectric dams along the river produce power for more than 10 million people in seven states. The river also serves as a transportation corridor for a wide range of goods. "More than 28,000 barges carry 45 to 50 million tons of goods up and down the Tennessee River annually," according to the Tennessee Valley Authority.

Waypoint/Mile

Trailhead (Waypoint 65) (34.57647, -86.55756) At the junction of Ditto Landing Road and Younger Road, head southwest on the paved road that runs between two buildings. Beyond the buildings, the road turns right and heads northeast toward the harbor.

65-1 (34.57644, -86.55935) (0.13 mi.) At the junction with Harbor Road, turn left to head southwest on Harbor Rd.

65-2 (34.57490, -86.55969) (0.25 mi.) A wide paved path intersects on the left. If you turn left onto this path and walk about 250 ft., you'll reach another access point for the greenway at **Waypoint 65-5** (34.57429, -86.55960). At Waypoint 65-2, you can also go straight and continue walking southwest toward the river. If you choose this route, go to the southwest end of the parking area and take the path that bears left toward a line of trees. At 0.36 mi. the greenway path goes left and begins to parallel the river.

65-3 (34.57332, -86.56001) (0.39 mi.) A greenway path intersects on the left. It stretches about 400 ft. and ends at **Waypoint 65-5** (34.57429, -86.55960). To continue on the main greenway path, go straight and walk along the river.

This begins the best part of this greenway walk. A few trees dot the landscape between the trail and the Tennessee River, but for the most part you have an unobstructed view of the water and forested ridges in the distance. Along this stretch, you get a good sense of the river's massive size. While this greenway isn't exceptionally long, it is definitely one of the most impressive and peaceful walks in the Huntsville area.

As you walk, you'll encounter several benches where you can enjoy a riverside picnic. You could also rest in the shade of massive oaks towering over the riverbank. When you've walked about 0.5 mi., you'll enter a fenced area and walk the perimeter of a parking lot for a building.

When you've walked nearly 1 mi., you'll lose the full view of the river, and a forested ridge dominates the scene before you. The path soon moves into a more developed area, and a chain-link fence with barbed wire borders the path.

65-4 (34.56659, -86.55051) (1.1 mi.) The greenway path ends at a metal gate and a section of Harbor Road.

Trail Facts

Ditto Landing History: Ditto Landing is named for pioneer James Ditto. In 1807, Ditto began operating a ferry with landings on both sides of the Tennessee River. In 1824, James White, an industrialist from Virginia, established a port and the town of Whitesburg at the location now known as Ditto Landing. Throughout the 1800s, the port was an important center for the shipment of cotton. However, in the early 1900s, railroads replaced boats as the primary way to transport goods, and the town of Whitesburg faded away.

The Tennessee River Greenway offers beautiful views of the broad waterway.

Elgie's Walk Greenway

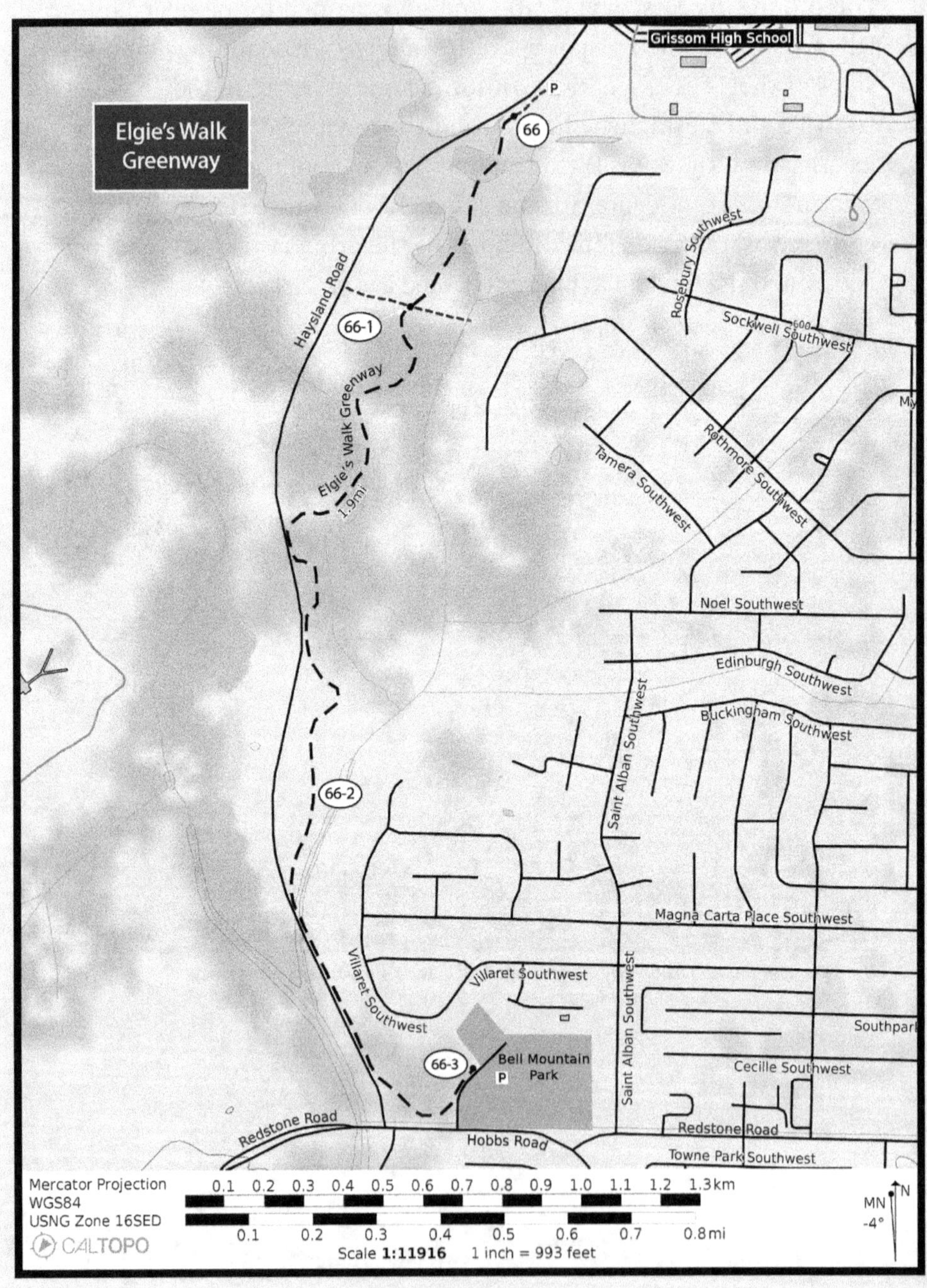

66. Elgie's Walk Greenway

Stretching from Grissom High School to Bell Mountain Park, this paved trail explores a stretch of old farmland with attractive woods, wetlands, ponds and open fields. During midday and weekends, traffic along nearby Haysland Road can be light, making this a fairly peaceful place to walk, run or bike.

Distance: 1.98 mi.
Hiking Time: 45 minutes
Elevation Gain/Loss: +35 ft., -31 ft.
Hiking Difficulty: Easy
Location
Northern Trailhead: Haysland Rd. (1 mi. southwest of the intersection with U.S. 231 (Memorial Parkway), Huntsville, AL 35803.
Bell Mountain Park: 2560 Redstone Rd., Huntsville, AL 35803
Facilities: There are no facilities and no sources of potable water at the trailhead.

Driving Directions

Trailhead Parking: From the junction of U.S. 231 (Memorial Parkway) and Haysland Road, travel west on Haysland Rd. 1 mi., and then turn left into the small parking area.

Bell Mountain Park: From the junction of U.S. 231 (Memorial Parkway) and Redstone Road, travel west on Redstone Rd. for 0.7 mi. Then turn right onto Hobbs Road, go 0.2 mi., and turn right to enter Bell Mountain Park. Continue 0.1 mi. to the parking lot.

Highlights

A Sunny Walk: If you walk on a clear day, consider wearing sunscreen, as this trail will expose you to more sun than other greenways in the area. Over the first 0.8 mi., ponds along the trail create wide breaks in the tree canopy. Plus, the path crosses wide fields for about 0.5 mi. If you find yourself in need of vitamin D, this is the perfect place to get some rays.

Thiokol History: In the 1950s, more than 2,200 Huntsvillians worked for Thiokol, making it the city's largest employer. The company pioneered rocket components for the U.S. Army and NASA and helped develop Huntsville's reputation as the Rocket City. Thiokol was founded in 1929 by scientists who had recently invented synthetic rubber. The name Thiokol is a combination of the Greek words "thio," for sulfur, and "kol," for glue. In 1982, Thiokol merged with Morton-Norwich Products (known for Morton Salt) to become Morton Thiokol.

Waypoint/Mile

Trailhead (Waypoint 66) (34.63989, -86.58153) From the parking area beside Haysland Road, walk 385 ft. to the beginning of the greenway, and head southwest on the paved, 12-ft.-wide path.

The trail winds through a beautiful wetland forest with tupelo trees and other mature hardwoods.

66-1 (34.63565, -86.58449) (351 ft.) At a four-way trail junction, a dirt and gravel path on the right heads west for about 550 ft. and ends at Haysland Road. On the left, a dirt path goes southeast for 0.1 mi. to meet a narrow, paved path that goes northeast to circle around a housing development. From Waypoint 66-1, continue straight to stay on the Elgie's Walk path.

At 0.25 mi., the path begins to wind among a group of ponds. These bodies of water create breaks in the forest, and the path is bathed in sunlight on clear days. At some points, the forest thins, and houses are visible in the distance.

Near 0.5 mi., the trail edges around the north end of a long pond. To the west, a wide patch of woods blocks much of the vehicle noise from Haysland Road, making this stretch of trail relatively quiet.

At 0.64 mi., the trail bends away from the water and soon passes a smaller pond near Haysland Road. The greenway trail parallels the road until you've walked about 1 mi. It then cuts over to the middle of a vast field bordered by a wetland area to the east. At 1.2 mi., look to your right, across Haysland Rd., to see high pines lining the border of Redstone Arsenal.

66-2 (34.62479, -86.58718) (1.3 mi.) On the right is a "Thiokol History" interpretive sign. In the 1950s, Thiokol built rocket components for the U.S. Army and NASA. During its 47 years on the Arsenal, Thiokol became a leader in solid rocket propulsion. As the sign explains, "As you face west looking across Haysland Road, the Thiokol facilities were just beyond the trees inside the Arsenal boundary."

At 1.47 mi., the path runs right next to Haysland Road and passes over a narrow, still creek. Nearby on the left is the western edge of a neighborhood. At 1.73 mi., another wetland shoulders the greenway path, while Redstone Road is directly ahead. The trail bends to the left briefly to parallel Redstone Rd., but soon takes a hard left where Bell Mountain Park is visible.

66-3 (34.61896, -86.58275) (1.98 mi.) The greenway path ends at the parking lot for Bell Mountain Park.

Trail Facts

Elgie Hays: Established in 2020, the greenway trail is named for Elgie Hays, a grandparent of local developer John Hays. In 1906, Elgie purchased the land that the greenway now occupies, and for more than a century the property was a working farm.

Gateway Greenway, Patriots Walkway and Battlefield Memorial Walkway

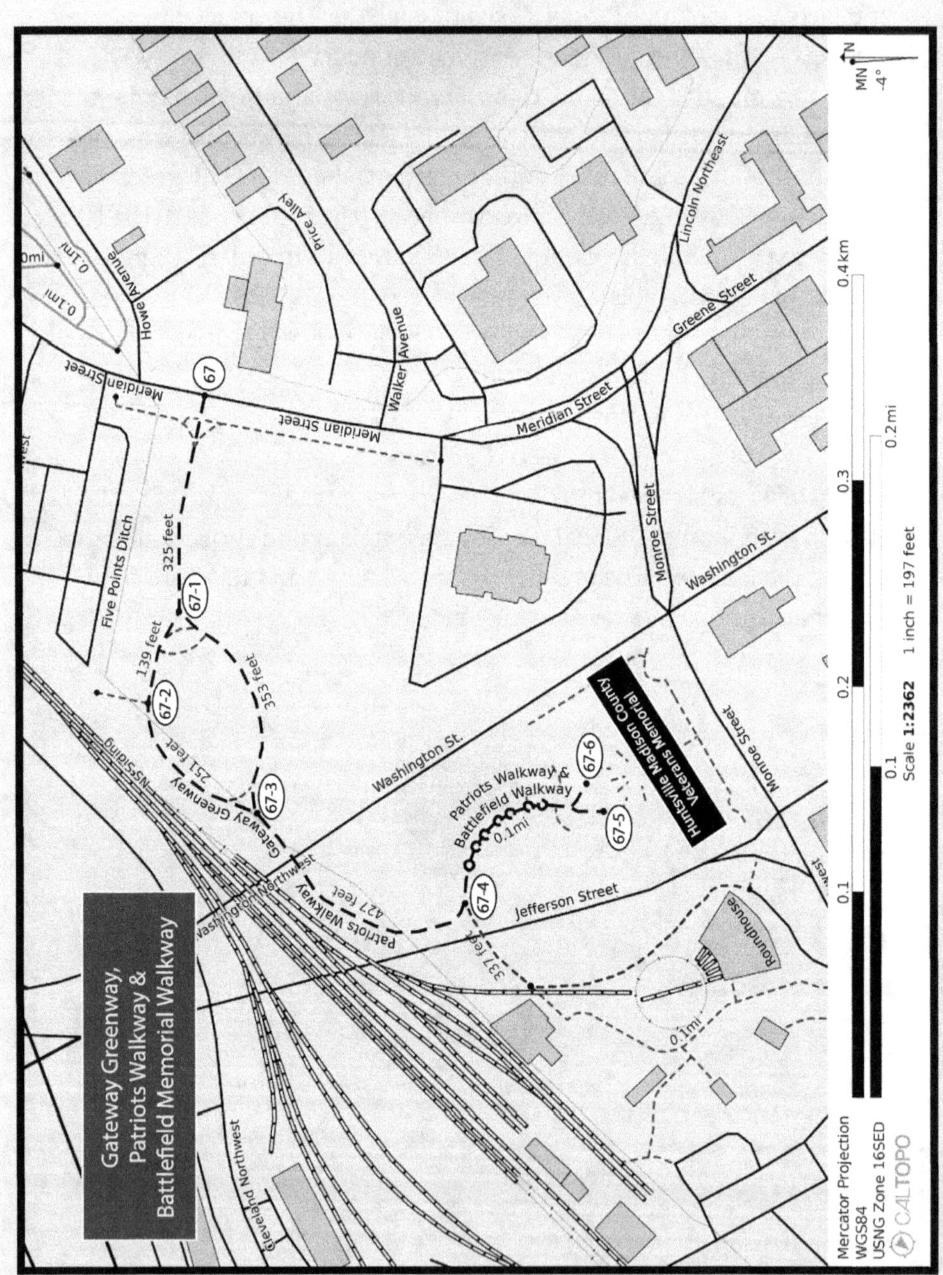

67. Gateway Greenway, Patriots Walkway and Battlefield Memorial Walkway

Looking for a good picnic spot? Make your way to the Gateway Greenway near downtown Huntsville. More a park than a hiking path, this greenway features a small creek and large lawns dotted with trees. Throughout the greenway there are metal benches where you can relax and enjoy the fresh air. When it's time for your picnic, settle in at a creekside bench, or the stone steps by the water. If you want to stretch your legs, follow the Patriots Walkway and Battlefield Memorial Walkway, walking paths that loop through the greenway and link to the Huntsville Madison County Veterans Memorial. Be sure to allow extra time for your walk through the Veterans Memorial, because the walkways are lined with a variety of interesting monuments, memorials and information kiosks.

Distance: Gateway Greenway, 0.15 mi.; Patriots Walkway and Battlefield Memorial Walkway, 0.11 mi.

Hiking Time: 10 minutes

Elevation Gain/Loss: +6 ft., -7 ft.

Hiking Difficulty: Easy

Location: Meridian St. (0.13 mi. north of the intersection with Monroe St.), Huntsville, AL 35801

Facilities: There are no facilities and no sources of potable water at the trailhead.

Driving Directions: The closest parking area is the large parking lot at the junction of Meridian Street and Cleveland Avenue. From the junction of U.S. 231/431 (Memorial Parkway) and University Drive, head east on University Dr. Go 0.3 mi. and cross Church Street where the road becomes Pratt Avenue. Travel 0.5 mi. on Pratt Ave., and then turn right onto Meridian St. Go 0.2 mi. and turn right into the parking lot that's immediately after Cleveland Ave.

Highlights

Veterans Memorial: The Huntsville Madison County Veterans Memorial honors all veterans for their courage, sacrifice and call to duty. A focal point of the memorial is a fountain that flows over black granite into the Sacrifice Pool. Markers located at the fountain and statues positioned throughout the memorial grounds detail the wars fought by the United States and highlight military members who made the ultimate sacrifice. On the north side of the fountain, memorials along the Battlefield Memorial Walkway honor fallen warriors. That path leads into the Patriots Walkway, where a series of kiosks highlight the experiences of military members in each of the country's wars.

Waypoint/Mile

Trailhead (Waypoint 67) (34.73646, -86.58654) To reach the beginning of the Gateway Greenway, exit the parking lot and turn right to walk southwest on the walkway beside Meridian Street. Go about 175 ft. to reach the beginning of the greenway, which is on the right. (There's a signpost with a blue and white Gateway Greenway sign as well as signs for other landmarks.) Walk west on the concrete walkway and begin crossing the open lawn.

Immediately to the right is the creek known as the Five Points Ditch. You'd be hard-pressed to find a waterway with a less appealing name, but it's more attractive than it sounds. Many years ago, this drainage received some TLC, and its banks are now adorned with trees, patches of grass, stones and boulders.

67-1 (34.73656, -86.58755) (325 ft.) The path splits to go northwest and southwest. (The description below heads right to go northwest.) It really doesn't matter which way you go, because the diverging walkways meet again within a few hundred feet. If you're seeking a shady place to sit, this junction is perfect, as a few benches sit in the shade of a huddle of trees.

67-2 (34.73666, -86.58797) (464 ft.) On the right, a bridge crosses Five Points Ditch and leads to the parking area. Go straight to continue on the Gateway Greenway path and walk parallel to the railroad tracks.

67-3 (34.73623, -86.58853) (0.13 mi.) At the junction, you can turn left to return to the trailhead or veer to the right to complete the greenway path and pass beneath Washington Street. Once you pass beneath Washington St., you begin the Patriots Walkway and the Battlefield Memorial Walkway.

67-4 (34.73525, -86.58907) (0.21 mi.) Bear left at the junction to continue on the Patriots Walkway. (A path on the right leaves the greenway and continues a little more than 330 ft. to the east side of a depot building.) This bend in the walkway is an especially attractive, well-landscaped area. As you emerge from the shadows of the road overpass, a stand of trees casts more shade over the walkway. Standing in the center of the walkway junction is a rough-hewn stone monument that honors the 84 Revolutionary War soldiers who are buried in Madison County. Beyond the monument is a gentle green slope with tall pines as well as hardwoods that display brilliant colors in the fall. To the left, the path arcs away from the shadows to enter a sunny section of the Patriots Walkway.

The Five Points Ditch creek is more attractive than the name implies.

As you continue, you'll enter the section known as the Battlefield Memorial Walkway. This area includes the Battlefield Memorial, which offers a symbolic representation of a fallen soldier. This part of the Veterans Memorial is intended to be a solemn place to mourn those we've lost. After you leave the pathway junction, you'll soon reach the first of seven kiosks with information panels highlighting details about the country's wars and citizens who fought in them.

Just beyond 0.25 mi., you can go left or right to complete the Patriots Walkway at **Waypoint 67-5** (34.73466, -86.58854) (0.26 mi.) or **Waypoint 67-6** (34.73471, -86.58845) (0.26 mi.).

Beyond these waypoints, you can continue to circle around to the front of the Veterans Memorial to see the fountain.

Trail Facts

Granite Markers: Eight polished granite markers at the memorial fountain contain the names of more than 365 Madison County servicemen who died in military conflicts around the world.

Indian Creek Greenway North

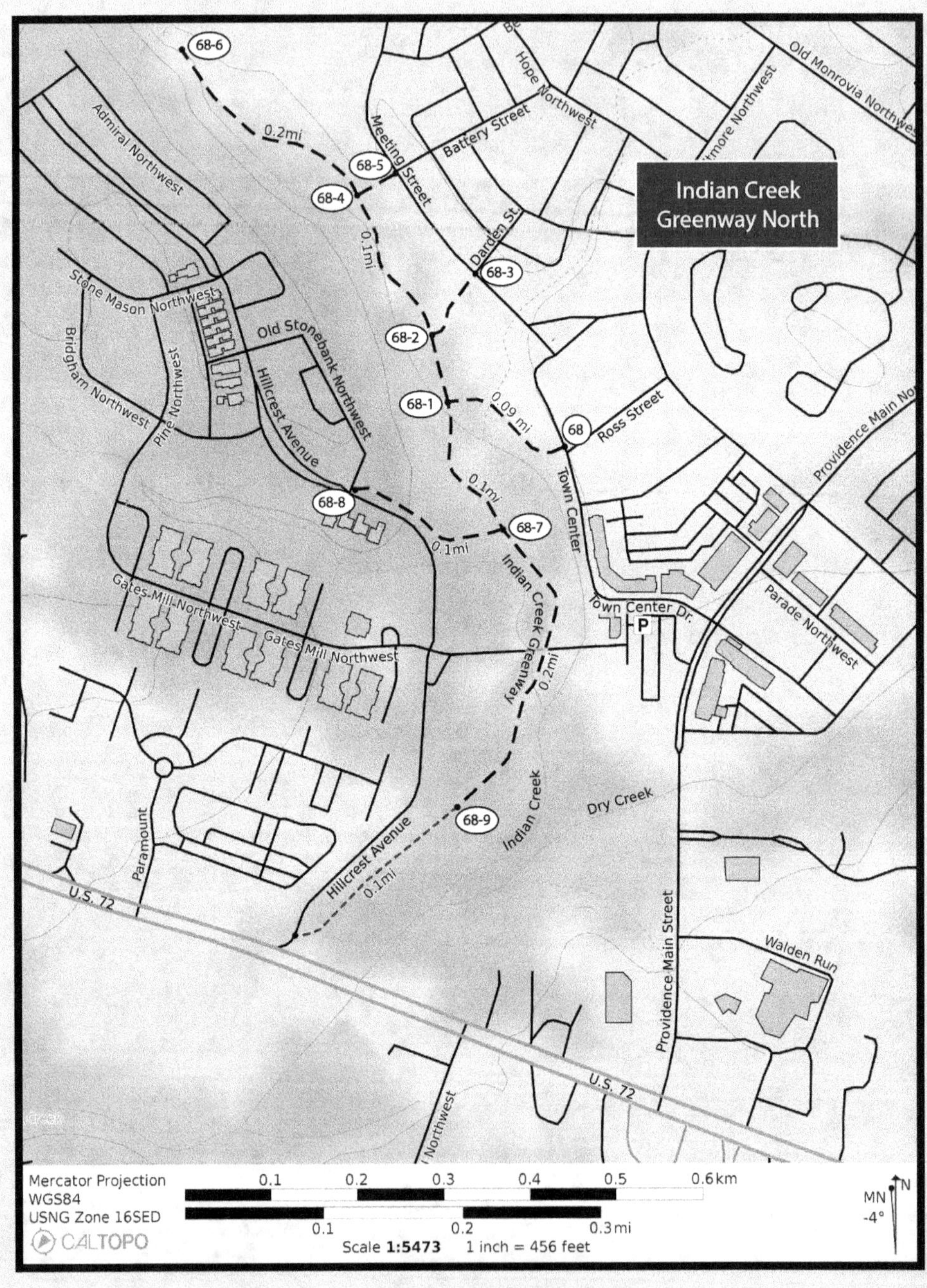

68. Indian Creek Greenway North

This section of the Indian Creek Greenway primarily serves as a recreation area for residents of the Providence community. When you enter the trail, you can turn north to walk along a peaceful stretch of Indian Creek, or turn south to enter a corridor of dense forest.

Distance: 0.96 mi.

Hiking Time: 20 to 30 minutes

Elevation Gain/Loss: +57 ft., -22 ft. (main trail plus side trails)

Hiking Difficulty: Easy

Location: Immediately southwest of the intersection of Meeting St. and Darden St., Huntsville, AL 35806

Facilities: There are no facilities and no sources of potable water at the trailhead.

Driving Directions: The nearest parking area is the large lot near the junction of Providence Main Street and Town Center Drive. To reach the parking area, take U.S. Highway 72/University Drive to the junction with Providence Main St. (This is the entrance to the planned community of Providence.) From the junction, travel north on Providence Main St. for 0.3 mi., and then turn left onto Town Center Dr. Go 351 ft. and then turn left onto Broadway Drive. Go 85 ft. and turn left into the parking lot.

Highlights

Indian Creek: Indian Creek provides a soothing soundtrack for your walk as you head north. While the waterway runs through a residential area, certain spots are especially serene as trees create a green veil between the creek and nearby houses. At 0.2 mi., there's an attractive stretch where you get a good long-distance view down the creek. After another 370 ft., a bench near a bend in the stream makes a good spot to relax and listen to the rushing water.

Waypoint/Mile

Trailhead (Waypoint 68) (34.75550, -86.69476) To reach the trailhead, begin at the parking lot near the junction of Providence Main

Street and Town Center Drive. Head west on Town Center Dr., which soon bends to the northwest. Walk a little more than 0.1 mi., pass the junction with Ross Street, and look left for the access path for the Indian Creek Greenway. Turn left onto the paved path, which heads west and soon bends to the northwest.

68-1 (34.75597, -86.69624) (498 ft.) At the T junction, the greenway heads north and south. Turn right and head north with Indian Creek rushing by on your left.

68-2 (34.75672, -86.69636) (750 ft.) On the right, an access path goes northeast 265 ft. and ends at the junction of Meeting Street and Darden Street at **Waypoint 68-3** (34.75721, -86.69581). From Waypoint 68-2, continue on the main greenway path by going straight and heading north.

68-4 (34.75811, -86.69729) (0.2 mi.) On the right, an access path goes northeast 150 ft. to the junction of Meeting Street and Battery Street at **Waypoint 68-5** (34.75828, -86.69682). From Waypoint 68-4, continue on the main greenway path by going straight and traveling northwest.

In this northern section of the greenway, woods on your left shroud the creek. As you approach 0.3 mi., you enter one of the wildest sections of the greenway. Underbrush and a line of trees on the right block your view of houses to the east. On the left, dense woods form a natural wall between the path and Indian Creek. At 0.35 mi., you can peer through the trees on the left to see houses perched on a bluff that overlooks the creek.

68-6 (34.75955, -86.69953) (0.4 mi.) The greenway ends at dense woods.

From Waypoint 68-1, you can also turn left to head south.

This part of the greenway is more removed from the surrounding residential areas. After a little more than 100 ft., a bridge carries you across Indian Creek in an area of the greenway that feels secluded. The path bends to the southeast and continues to run through the heart of the greenway woods.

68-7 (34.75471, -86.69549) (0.1 mi. from Waypoint 68-1) An access path on the right goes west for 623 ft. to the junction of Stonebank Street and Hillcrest Avenue at **Waypoint 68-8** (34.75511, -86.69735) (0.2 mi. from Waypoint 68-1).

After another 400 ft., the path leaves the forested corridor and enters a clearing to pass beneath an elevated section of Gates Mill Street. After you pass beneath the street, you'll soon enter another wooded corridor.

68-9 (34.75193, -86.69607) (0.2 mi. from Waypoint 68-1) The paved greenway path ends at a forested corridor. A gravel and dirt path continues on for a little more than 0.1 mi. and ends near the junction of Hillcrest Avenue and University Drive.

The Indian Creek Greenway provides a quiet place to walk or run near the Providence community.

Indian Creek Greenway South

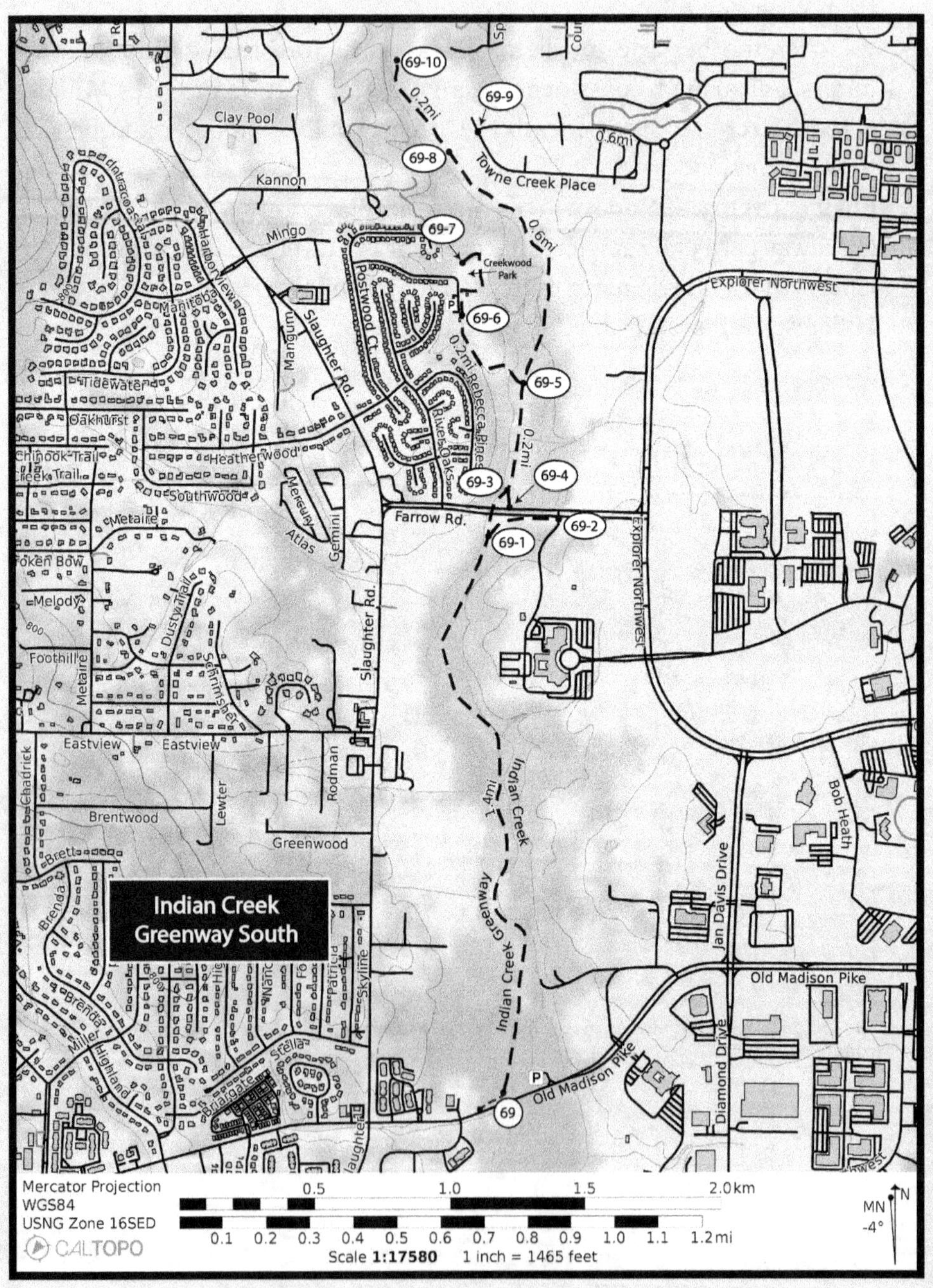

69. Indian Creek Greenway South

With 3 mi. of paved pathways, this is one of the most extensive greenways in the Huntsville area, and it's a popular destination to enjoy a long walk, run or bike ride. Bordered by woods and the rushing waters of Indian Creek, this path provides a pleasing natural escape. Plus, it's a great place to take kids, as the path is mostly level, and nearby Creekwood Park provides a playground and restroom facilities.

Distance: 2.6 to 3 mi.

Hiking Time: 1.25 to 1.5 hours

Elevation Gain/Loss: +67 ft., -29 ft.

Hiking Difficulty: Easy

Location: 7488 Old Madison Pike, Huntsville, AL 35806

Facilities: There are no facilities at the trailhead on Old Madison Pike. At the Creekwood Park trailhead you'll find restrooms with potable water, a playground, a dog park, pavilions and benches.

Driving Directions

Old Madison Pike Trailhead

Traveling West on I-565: From I-565, take Exit 14B toward AL 255 North. Go 0.3 mi. and merge onto AL 255 N. Go 0.3 mi. and take the Madison Pike exit. Go 0.1 mi. and keep right at the fork to merge onto Old Madison Pike. Go 1.8 mi. and turn right into the parking area for the Indian Creek Greenway.

Traveling East on I-565: From I-565, take Exit 14. Go 0.1 mi., keep left and follow signs for AL 255 N/Research Park Boulevard. Merge onto AL 255 N/Research Park Blvd. NW, go 0.1 mi., and then take the Madison Pike exit. Go 0.1 mi. and keep right at the fork to merge onto Old Madison Pike. Go 1.8 mi. and turn right into the parking area for the Indian Creek Greenway.

Creekwood Park Trailhead:

From the junction of U.S. 72 and Slaughter Road, travel south on Slaughter Rd. for 1.8 mi. Then turn left onto Maple Valley Drive, go 476 ft., and turn left onto Postwood Court. Travel 0.3 mi. on Postwood Ct., and then turn right onto Harvestwood Court. Go 0.2 mi. and turn left into the parking area for Creekwood Park.

Highlights

Lengthy Forested Corridors: This southern section of the greenway includes long stretches where woods surround the path and shroud neighboring residential areas. In these extended wild areas, it's easy to achieve "zen mode" and ease your mind as you walk, run or bike.

Migrant Birds: During spring, neotropical migratory birds leave Central and South America to fly to the northern United States and Canada. Along the way, many species pass through Alabama, and the Indian Creek Greenway provides quiet and easily accessible places to seek out these world travelers. "This can be a good location to find mourning warblers. This species is a secretive late spring migrant through this area that is rarely seen," reports the North Alabama Birdwatchers Society (northalbirding.com). "Wilson's, magnolia and Canada warblers, warbling vireo, yellow-crowned night heron, and a variety of other species have been encountered here in recent years."

Waypoint/Mile

***There are two access points: one at Creekwood Park on Harvestwood Court (Waypoint 69-6) and one on Old Madison Pike (Waypoint 69). The following hike description begins at Old Madison Pike.*

Trailhead (Waypoint 69) (34.70892, -86.70194) To reach the trailhead, walk to the entrance of the parking area on Old Madison Pike. Turn right and walk west on the paved path that skirts the road. After walking a little more than 0.1 mi., take the sharp right turn to head northeast and descend the paved path. The greenway begins at metal posts and an Adopt-a-Mile sign.

The paved path drops briefly but soon levels off and turns away from Old Madison Pike, heading north. This begins a long, level stretch of trail that winds through a wide and airy natural corridor. On the left, a grassy easement lies between the trail and the tree line, creating plenty of open sky. On the right, dense brush and woods border the path, but breaks in the foliage allow you to glimpse the broad

Indian Creek channel. At 0.6 mi., there's a nice spot where a gap in the woods reveals a swift section of Indian Creek. At 1 mi., a 60-ft.-long concrete bridge carries you over the creek.

From this point, you will occasionally encounter access paths that allow people from nearby neighborhoods to reach the greenway path.

69-1 (34.72725, -86.70177) (1.4 mi.) At a Y junction, an access path to the right goes northeast for about 0.2 mi. to meet Farrow Road. To stay on the main trail, go straight and pass beneath Farrow Rd.

69-2 (34.72782, -86.69901) The access path ends at Farrow Road.

69-3 (34.72875, -86.70097) (1.5 mi.) On the right, another access path leads to Farrow Road and ends after 180 ft. at **Waypoint 69-4.** To stay on the main trail, continue straight and head northeast.

69-5 (34.73224, -86.70033) (1.77 mi.) At this point the greenway path splits, and you have two options:

Option 1: Turn left and take the greenway path that goes 0.24 mi. to the parking area for Creekwood Park.

Option 2: Go straight and head north on the greenway path for another 0.9 mi.

If you take Option 1:

After walking 0.24 mi., you reach the parking lot for Creekwood Park at **Waypoint 69-6** (34.73446, -86.70282) (2.0 mi.). From Waypoint 69-6, the greenway path circles around the park for 0.2 mi. to end at **Waypoint 69**-7 (34.73605, -86.70281) (2.2 mi.).

If you take Option 2:

Go straight and head north on the greenway path to enjoy a nice, long stretch where woods surround the path and houses aren't visible.

As you continue north, you'll see on the left a break in the dense foliage that reveals a narrow, swift section of Indian Creek. Not far ahead, a large field stands between the path and a neighborhood, and a narrow island of trees bisects the ocean of grass and brush.

69-8 (34.73964, -86.70345) (2.4 mi.) An access path intersects on the right and heads northeast for 0.1 mi. to end at Towne Creek Place at **Waypoint 69-9.**

When you move past the subdivision, look left to enjoy an impressive stretch of woods with towering trees.

69-10 (34.74218, -86.70542) (2.6 mi.) The greenway path ends abruptly where woods surround three sides of a wide field.

Wade Mountain Greenway

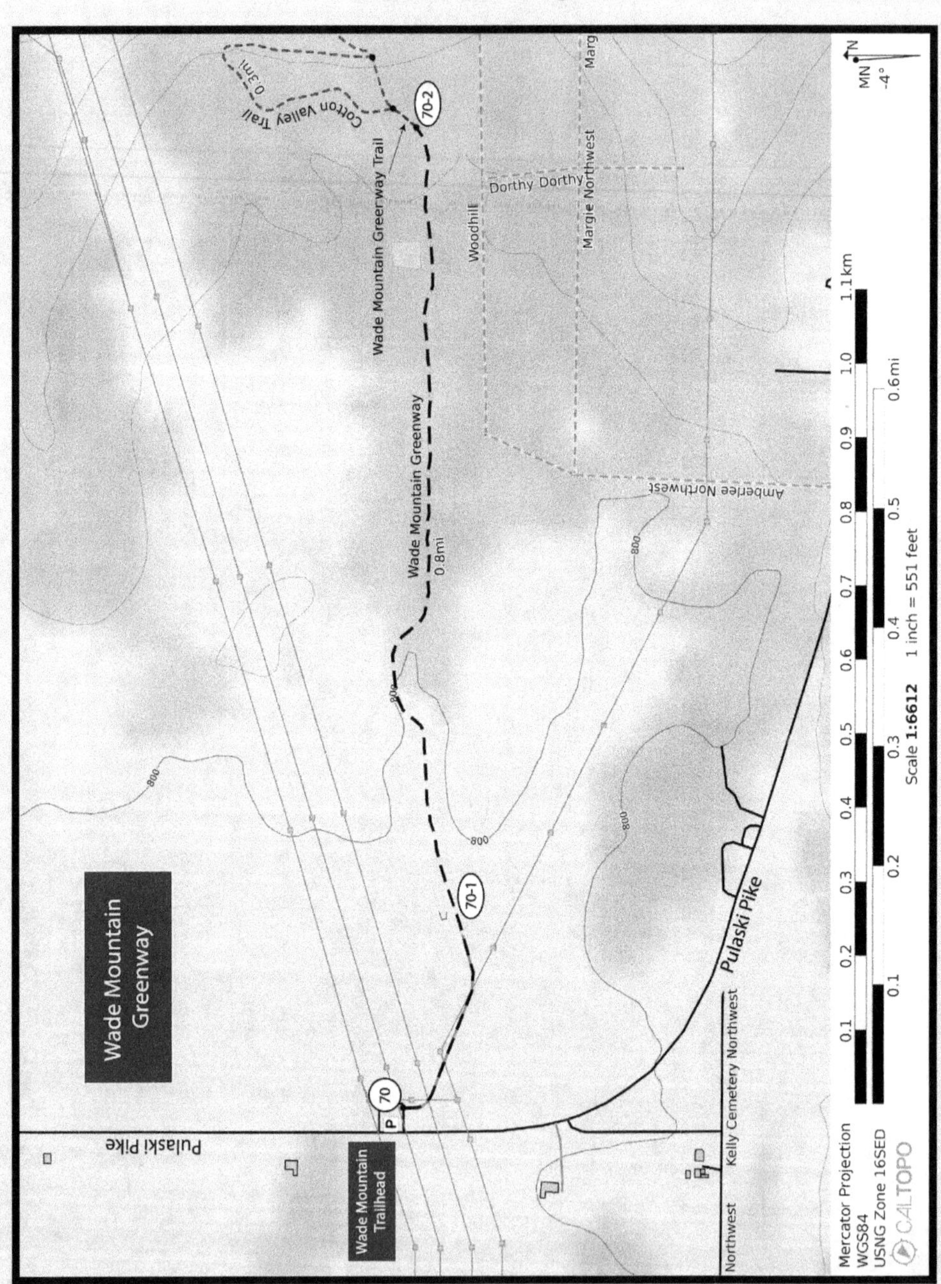

70. Wade Mountain Greenway

As it moves east, the paved Wade Mountain Greenway path rises ever so slightly, providing easy terrain for walking, running or biking. This is a popular spot for people to get exercise during lunch or enjoy a casual family outing during the weekend. The path also gives hikers access to more than 10 mi. of unpaved dirt and rock trails that explore Wade Mountain.

Distance: 0.8 mi.
Hiking Time: 20 minutes
Elevation Gain/Loss: +73 ft., -6 ft.
Hiking Difficulty: Easy
Location: 6998 Pulaski Pike, Huntsville, AL 35810
Facilities: There are no facilities and no sources of potable water at the trailhead.
Driving Directions: From the junction of U.S. 231/431 (Memorial Parkway) and University Drive, head southwest on University Dr. Go 0.1 mi. and turn right onto Pulaski Pike. Travel 6.3 mi. on Pulaski Pike and turn right into the parking area for the Wade Mountain Preserve.

Highlights

Access to Wade Mountain Trails: The greenway path is not only a great place to get some exercise, but it also provides access to miles of unpaved trails on Wade Mountain. (These unpaved Wade Mountain trails are covered in Chapter 4.) From the eastern end of the greenway, you can take the rugged Wade Mountain Greenway Trail to hike the lower slopes of Wade Mountain. If you want to explore further, combine the Fossil Bench and Bostick trails for a long loop hike, and then return to the paved greenway. For those seeking an even longer trek, follow the Bostick Trail to the 2.1-mi. Wade Mountain Trail, which crosses the mountain and connects to trails on the eastern slopes.

Waypoint/Mile

Trailhead (Waypoint 70) (34.81547, -86.64239) At the southeast corner of the Wade Mountain Trailhead parking area, follow the paved Wade Mountain Greenway path, traveling southeast.

The trail passes between two cotton fields and crosses a powerline corridor, while Wade Mountain rises prominently in the east. At 0.1 mi., the path shifts away from the powerline break and bends to the east. While the beginning of the trail is fully exposed to the sun, you'll soon enjoy shade from trees bordering the path.

70-1 (34.81484, -86.63948) (0.18 mi.) To the left is the Toyota Community Pavilion for Environmental Education. To the right are benches and a trail information kiosk.

At 0.4 mi., the path bears right to move away from the fields and pass through a pine forest. The trail is quiet and tranquil now that you're far from Pulaski Pike and close to the base of Wade Mountain. Dense forest surrounds the trail, and there are few distinguishing landmarks, except for a small pond on the left at 0.76 mi.

70-2 (34.81531, -86.62788) (0.87 mi.) The paved path ends, and the dirt Wade Mountain Greenway Trail begins.

Trailhead Greenway

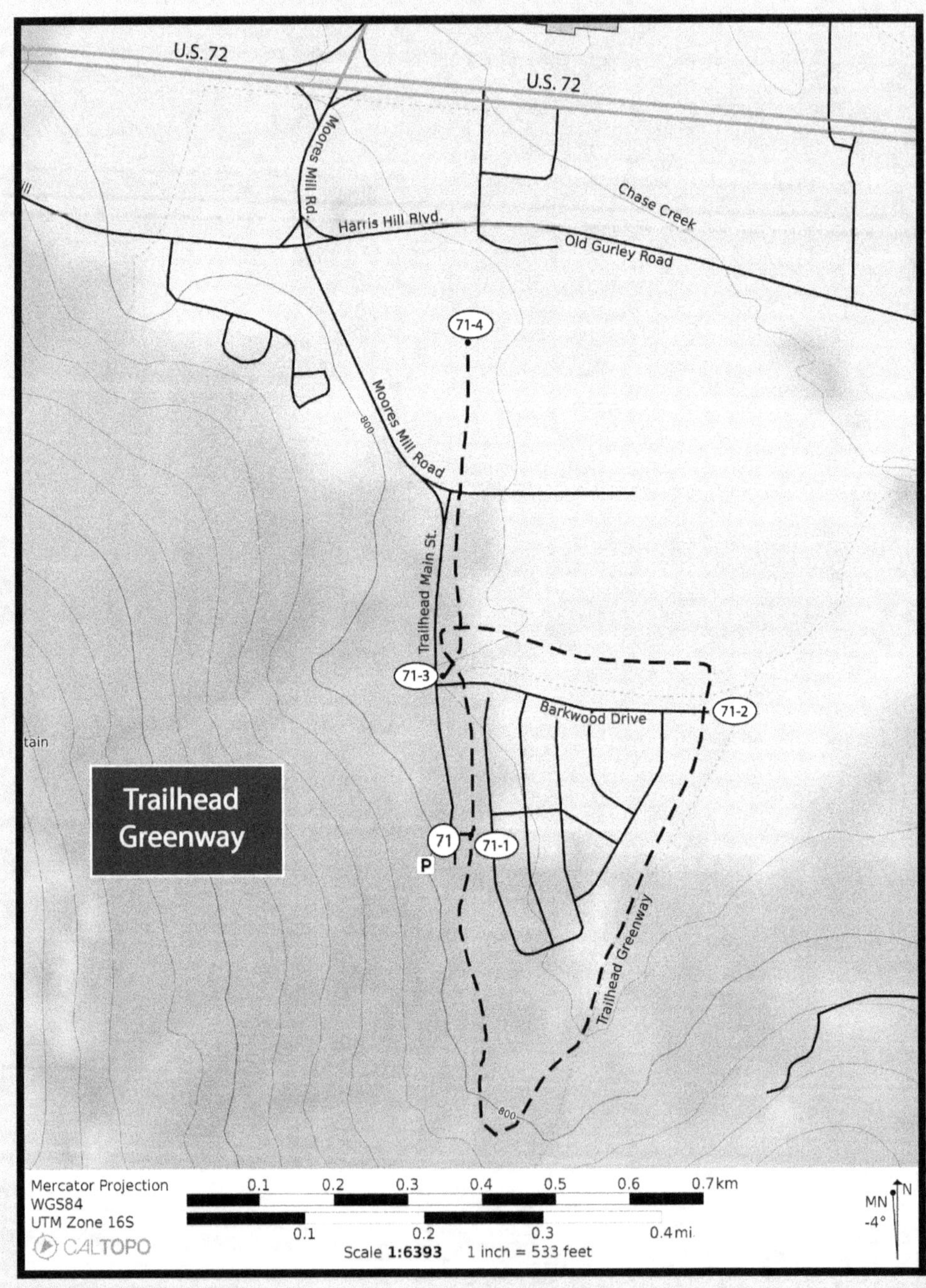

71. Trailhead Greenway

This paved path circles around the relatively new Trailhead housing development in east Huntsville. The clutch of homes is tucked into a cove at the base of Chapman Mountain. At the south and north ends of the greenway, short sections of the trail go through attractive, shady areas where trees surround the trail, and there are views of nearby mountains. However, for the most part this is an urban walk along the edge of a neighborhood. It's a good place to get exercise if you're not seeking a wild, remote trail.

Distance: 1.2 mi.
Hiking Time: 30 minutes
Elevation Gain/Loss: +82 ft., -88 ft.
Hiking Difficulty: Easy
Location: 1534 Trek St. NE, Huntsville, AL 35811
Facilities: There are no facilities and no sources of potable water at the trailhead.
Driving Directions: From the junction of U.S. 431 (Memorial Parkway) and I-565, take I-565 East/U.S. 72 East for 3 mi. and continue on U.S. 72 E for 1.4 mi. Then turn right onto Moores Mill Road. Go 0.1 mi., cross Harris Hill Boulevard, and continue straight on Moores Mill Rd. for 0.2 mi. Then turn right onto Trailhead Main Street. Go 0.3 mi. to the Trailhead Greenway parking area.

Waypoint/Mile

Trailhead (Waypoint 71) (34.76482, -86.53691) Walk to the northeast corner of the parking area and enter the paved Trailhead Greenway path, heading east. You'll be facing the rooftops of houses.

71-1 (34.76483, -86.53679) (42 ft.) At the T junction, you can go right or left on the Trailhead Greenway. The following hike description goes right and heads south toward the slopes of Chapman Mountain.

The path begins with a small hill to the right. Houses are visible below and to the left. A slope covered with high brush separates the greenway path from the neighborhood. Directly ahead, a nearby ridge on Chapman Mountain looms large.

At 0.1 mi., you reach the end of the houses and enter a shady stretch of trail surrounded by a succession forest of hardwoods and cedars. This is the most attractive and quietest portion of the greenway. At 0.2 mi., the path takes a big horseshoe bend to the northeast, and neighborhood houses come back into view. From here on, it's mostly an urban walk.

The greenway path approaches the neighborhood and passes a pond that's about 300 ft. long. To the right, through breaks in the trees, you can see a clearing and rough ground leading to a slope. Immediately to the left are the garages of homes.

71-2 (34.76634, -86.53322) (0.58 mi.) Cross Barkwood Drive, turn left and head west on the greenway path. As you skirt the road, you'll get a good look at the homes in the Trailhead community. Plus, you'll pass a couple of bike-themed streets—Shimano Street and Trek Street.

71-3 (34.76679, -86.53714) (0.8 mi.) At the junction of Barkwood Drive and Trailhead Main Street, you can go left or right on the greenway path.

If you go right at Waypoint 71-3: You'll head north and follow an attractive, shady stretch of trail lined with trees. To the right, you'll have a nice view of broad, open fields and mountain ridges. At 0.96 mi., the greenway path ends near a health club parking lot at **Waypoint 71-4** (34.76893, -86.53690).

If you go left at Waypoint 71-3: You'll head south and walk along the edge of a hill overlooking the neighborhood. After walking another 748 ft., you'll return to Waypoint 71-1 near the parking area.

Madison Greenways:
Mill Creek Greenway and Bradford Creek Greenway

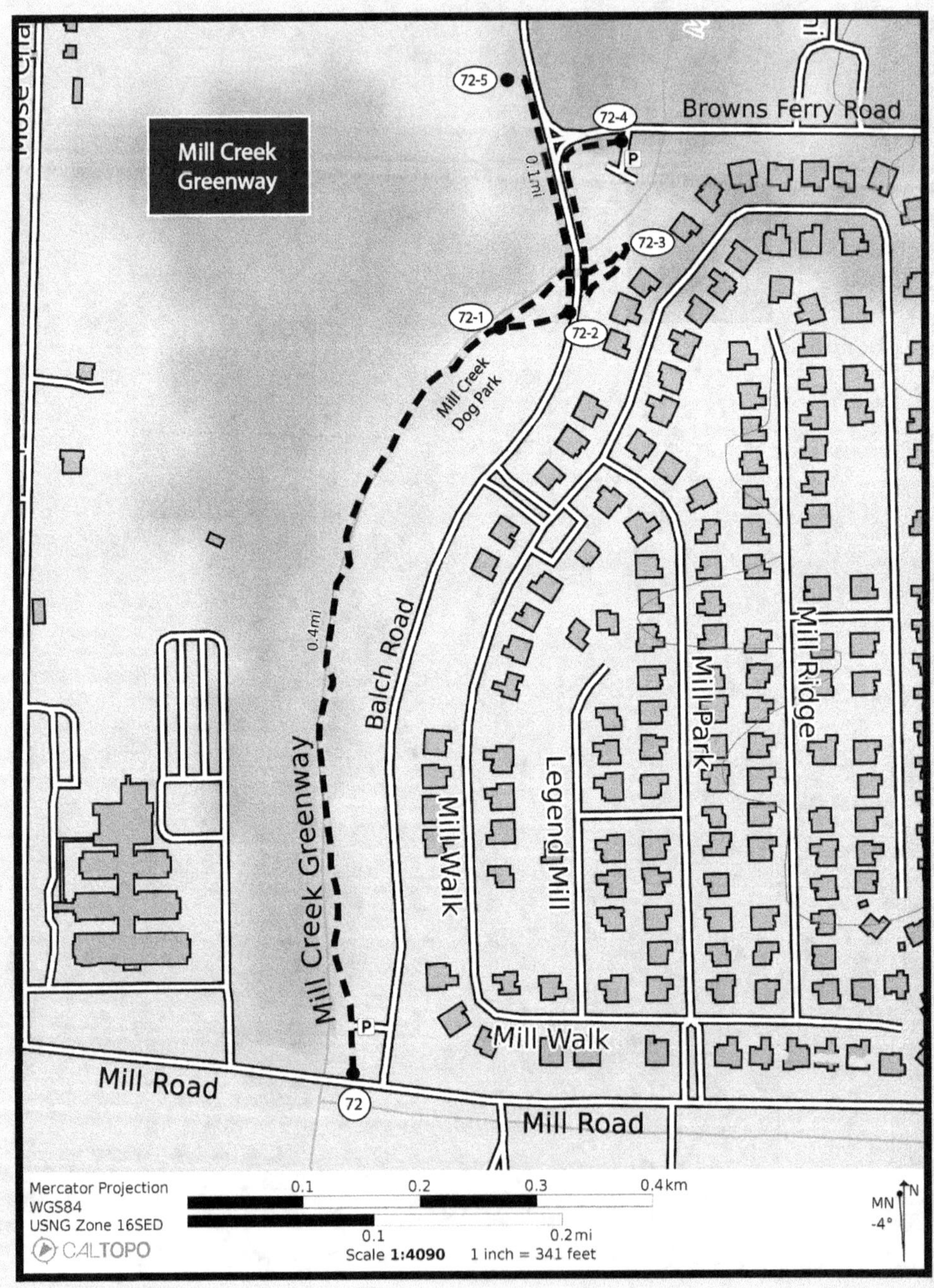

72. Mill Creek Greenway

If you want to introduce a child to the wonders of the outdoors, this greenway is a great place to start. Situated along this level, paved path are educational signs designed to stoke a child's interest in the natural world. The signs suggest activities to do and things to observe while walking the path, which hugs the shallow, slow-flowing Mill Creek. This path is also used by people heading to the Mill Creek Dog Park.

Distance: 0.5 mi. to 0.6 mi.

Hiking Time: 15 minutes

Elevation Gain/Loss: +18 ft., -3 ft. or +28 ft., -3 ft. depending on route

Hiking Difficulty: Easy

Location: Mill Rd. (90 ft. west of the intersection with Balch Rd.), Madison, AL 35758

Facilities: There are no facilities and no sources of potable water at the trailhead.

Driving Directions

Parking Area on Mill Road

I-565 Traveling West: On I-565, take Exit 7, go 0.7 mi., and then use the left two lanes to turn left onto County Line Road. Travel 2.6 mi. on County Line Rd. and then turn right onto Mill Road. Go 1 mi., and then turn left onto Balch Road. Go about another 160 ft. and turn left into the parking area for the Mill Creek Greenway.

I-565 Traveling East: On I-565, take Exit 7 and head east for 1.2 mi. Then use the left two lanes to turn left onto County Line Road. Go 2.6 mi. on County Line Rd., and then turn right onto Mill Road. Go 1 mi., and then turn left onto Balch Road. Go about another 160 ft. and turn left into the parking area for the Mill Creek Greenway.

Parking Area on Browns Ferry Road

I-565 Traveling West: On I-565, take Exit 7, go 0.7 mi., and then use the left two lanes to turn left onto County Line Road. Travel 2.6 mi. on County Line Rd. and then turn right onto Mill Road. Go 1 mi., and then turn left onto Balch Road. Go 0.5 mi., and then turn right onto Browns

Ferry Road. Go 210 ft., and then turn right into the parking area for the Mill Creek Greenway.

I-565 Traveling East: On I-565, take Exit 7 and head east for 1.2 mi. Then use the left two lanes to turn left onto County Line Road. Go 2.6 mi. on County Line Rd., and then turn right onto Mill Road. Go 1 mi., and then turn left onto Balch Road. Travel 0.5 mi. and then turn right onto Browns Ferry Road. Go 210 ft., and then turn right into the parking area for the Mill Creek Greenway.

Highlights

Wonder Walk: How do kids develop an appreciation for the outdoors? The key is to teach them to use their senses and imagination to interact with their environment. The informational signs along this greenway

The Mill Creek Greenway encourages kids to explore the outdoors.

can jump-start that process. They encourage kids to engage with their surroundings, whether it's by finding leaves, naming bugs, or looking for shapes in the clouds. Also, kids are introduced to the idea of limiting their impact on the environment, as one sign encourages kids to throw away trash and leave only footprints.

***There are two access points for the greenway: one on Mill Road and one on Browns Ferry Road. The following hike description begins at the Mill Rd. parking area, as it is closest to the Wonder Walk area.*

Waypoint/Mile

Trailhead (Waypoint 72) (34.69991, -86.76987) The Mill Creek Greenway path begins on the north side of Mill Road, just west of the junction of Mill Rd. and Balch Road. The greenway path begins about 100 ft. south of the parking area. From the trailhead, go north toward the parking area.

When you've walked 148 ft., you'll reach the Mill Creek Greenway sign. On the left, a narrow strip of grass separates the greenway trail and Mill Creek. In spring and summer, thick foliage from the trees drapes over the creek to partially obscure the waterway.

At 380 ft., you reach the "Look" sign, which directs visitors to use their eyes, nose and ears to observe the surrounding environment. Over the next 0.3 mi., there are more educational signs with titles like "Imagine," "Learn" and "Watch."

72-1 (34.70544, -86.76848) (0.4 mi.) A greenway access path intersects on the right and rises gradually for 217 ft. to meet Balch Road at **Waypoint 72-2** (34.70561, -86.76786).

At Waypoint 72-1, you have two options:

Option 1: Go straight to continue on the main greenway and pass beneath Balch Road, eventually reaching the parking area on Browns Ferry Road.

Option 2: Turn right and proceed to Waypoint 72-2. From this point you can travel north for a little more than 0.1 mi. to an alternate, unofficial trailhead on the west side of Balch Road at **Waypoint 72-5** (34.70732, -86.76840).

If you take Option 1:

72-3 (34.70607, -86.76728) (0.5 mi.) The path makes a hairpin turn to the right to go back toward Balch Road. When you reach Balch Rd., turn right and walk north to cross over Mill Creek. Follow the greenway path as it turns right and goes east parallel to Browns Ferry Road.

72-4 (34.70685, -86.76732) (0.6 mi.) The greenway path ends at the entrance to the Browns Ferry Road parking lot.

Mill Creek flows beside the paved Mill Creek Greenway path.

Bradford Creek Greenway

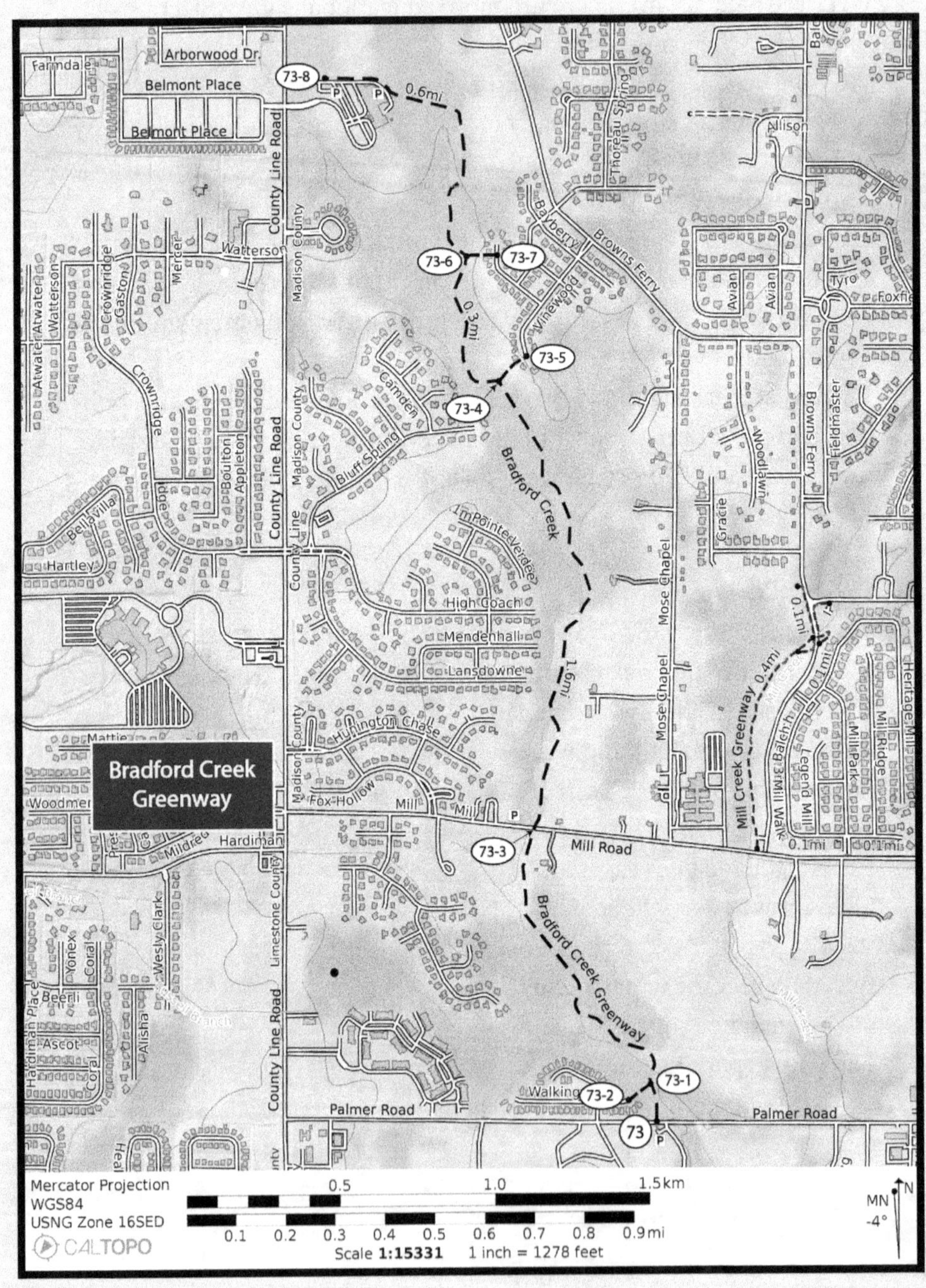

73. Bradford Creek Greenway

Stretching more than 2.5 mi. through the heart of Madison, Bradford Creek is one of the most extensive greenways in the area. Compared with other local greenways, it also boasts especially long stretches of uninterrupted forest. While Bradford Creek is ideal for a multihour trek, its multiple entry points allow hikers to enjoy shorter outings as well.

Distance: 2.58 mi.
Hiking Time: 1 to 1.25 hours
Elevation Gain/Loss: +75 ft., -25 ft.
Hiking Difficulty: Easy
Location: 556 Palmer Rd., Madison, AL 35758
Facilities: There are no facilities and no sources of potable water at the trailhead.

Driving Directions

Palmer Road Trailhead

I-565 Traveling West: From I-565, take Exit 7, go 0.6 mi., and then use the left two lanes to turn left onto County Line Road. Travel 2 mi., and then turn right onto Palmer Road. Go 0.8 mi. and turn right into the parking area for the Bradford Creek Greenway.

I-565 Traveling East: From I-565, take Exit 7, go 1.2 mi., and then use the left two lanes to turn left onto County Line Road. Travel 2 mi., and then turn right onto Palmer Road. Go 0.8 mi. and turn right into the parking area for the Bradford Creek Greenway.

Mill Road Trailhead

I-565 Traveling West: From I-565, take Exit 7, go 0.6 mi., and then use the left two lanes to turn left onto County Line Road. Travel 2.6 mi., and then turn right onto Mill Road. Go 0.4 mi. and turn left into the parking area for the Bradford Creek Greenway.

I-565 Traveling East: From I-565, take Exit 7, go 1.2 mi., and then use the left two lanes to turn left onto County Line Road. Travel 2.6 mi., and then turn right onto Mill Road. Go 0.4 mi. and turn left into the parking area for the Bradford Creek Greenway.

Highlights

Long Trek in Continuous Forest: Much of this hike visits quiet woods and farm fields, but the wildest section begins at about 1.2 mi. This is where you enter a corridor of dense forest that avoids civilization for more than 1 mi. That's pretty impressive for a path that moves through the center of a city. While other greenways can match Bradford Creek's length, few offer such an extended walk through peaceful, secluded woods.

***The following hike description begins at the southernmost trailhead on Palmer Road.*

Waypoint/Mile

Trailhead (Waypoint 73) (34.69230, -86.77345) From the parking lot, cross Palmer Road, heading north, and follow the paved greenway path into a corridor of hardwoods. You'll pass a trail information kiosk as well as a public library box where you can pick up something to read as you rest during your walk.

73-1 (34.69335, -86.77372) (371 ft.) A greenway access path intersects on the left and heads southwest for 240 ft., ending at Walking Trail Way in a neighborhood at **Waypoint 73-2** (34.69292, -86.77437).

At 0.1 mi., a 55-ft.-long concrete bridge crosses Bradford Creek, and a farm field spreads far and wide to the east. After another 200 ft., the path runs through continuous forest for about 0.3 mi. Towering hardwood trees surround the trail, and the shaded creek on the left moves in and out of sight. When you've walked nearly 0.5 mi., you'll see a large house and corral to the right. At 0.56 mi., a bench sits beneath a pavilion, providing a quiet, shady spot to rest.

73-3 (34.70056, -86.77776) (0.7 mi.) The greenway path crosses Mill Road. To the left is the Mill Road Trailhead parking area for the Bradford Creek Greenway. To continue on the greenway, go straight and cross the road. Immediately to the right, tall pines border a large farm field. I recommend that you hike this path during the spring, when marigolds blanket the green field in brilliant yellow.

At 0.9 mi., the trail bends away from the field and passes through a forest of tall pines, cedars, hickories and poplars. Not far beyond 1 mi., the path breaks out of the wooded corridor to skirt another field with golden wildflowers. At 1.2 mi., a massive pine stands sentinel on the right side of the trail, and you begin a 1.2-mi. walk through contiguous forest.

73-4 (34.71316, -86.77890) (1.6 mi.) An access path intersects on the right and heads northeast for 352 ft., ending in a cul-de-sac on Vinewood Lane at **Waypoint 73-5** (34.71385, -86.77802) (1.66 mi.).

73-6 (34.71670, -86.78006) (1.9 mi.) An access path intersects on the right and goes east for 310 ft., ending at Thornberry Lane at **Waypoint 73-7** (34.71671, -86.77905) (1.95 mi.).

At 2.4 mi., the trail leaves the dense forest and curls around the north end of Heritage Elementary School.

73-8 (34.72170, -86.78498) (2.58 mi.) The greenway path ends at the northwest corner of the Heritage Elementary School parking lot.

Long stretches of forest surround the Bradford Creek Greenway.

Hikes By Theme

Birding

Hays Nature Preserve
Chapman Mountain Nature
  Preserve
Flint River Greenway
Tennessee River Greenway
Indian Creek Greenway

History

Bethel Spring Preserve Mill Trail
Gateway Greenway
Elgie's Walk Greenway
Fire Tower Trail
Devil's Racetrack Trail
Rock Wall Trail
Moonshine Trail
Elgie's Walk
Gateway Greenway
Veterans Park & Battlefield
  Walkway

Hikes for Kids

Bethel Creek Loop
Animal Tral ID Trail
Moonshine Trail
Terry Trail
Cockpit Trail
Sherwood Forest Trail
Nottingham Trail
Narnia Trail
Beaver Dam (Harvest Square)
Eagle Trail
Stoneridge Trail

Jake's Trail
Balance Rock Trail
Ch.10 Greenways

Streams, Ponds and Lakes

Bethel Creek Loop
Carpenter Trail
Flint Trail
Beaver Dam Run/Tupelo Tree
  Path
Moonshine Trail
Beaver Dam (Harvest Square)
Senators Trail
Eagle Trail
Spring Trail
Big Cove Creek Greenway
Flint River Greenway
Aldridge Creek Greenway
Tennessee River Greenway
Elgie's Walk
Indian Creek Greenway North
Indiain Creek Greenway South
Mill Creek Greenway
Bradford Creek Greenway

Running Trails

Driskell Trail
Chasco Trail
Bulldog Trail
Field Trail
Aviation Pond Trail
Cockpit Trail
Sherwood Forest Trail

Hikes By Theme *continued*

Nottingham Trail
Narnia Trail
Fowler Trail
Ch.10 Greenways

Views
Devil's Racetrack Trail
Balance Rock Trail
High Pass Trail

Waterfalls
Falling Sink Trail
Lost Sink Falls Trail

Wildflowers
Terry Trail
Bulldog Trail
Fowler Trail
Bradford Creek Greenway

Index

About the Author

Marcus Woolf has worked as an editor and writer for outdoor adventure magazines and other media for more than 25 years. His writing has appeared in publications such as *Outside* magazine and *Backpacker*. As a native of Huntsville, Marcus grew up on Monte Sano Mountain, where he discovered his love for hiking. After living in California for eight years, he returned to Huntsville to be closer to family and Alabama football. In 2009, Wilderness Press published his first hiking guidebook, *Afoot & Afield: Atlanta*. When he isn't mapping trails for books, Marcus enjoys backpacking, canoeing and kayaking with his wife, Wendy.